MARXISM:
THE SCIENCE
OF SOCIETY

MARXISM:

THE SCIENCE OF SOCIETY

An Introduction

Kenneth Neill Cameron

Bergin & Garvey Publishers, Inc.
Massachusetts

Frontispiece photo of Marx by Mayall's Photographic Studio, London; from the original in the possession of Sidney J. Gluck.

Library of Congress Cataloging in Publication Data

Cameron, Kenneth Neill.
  Marxism the science of society, an introduction.

  Bibliography: p. 194.
  Includes index.
  1. Communism.   I. Title.
HX73.C36   1985   335.4   84-405
ISBN 0-89789-051-5
ISBN 0-89789-086-8 (pbk.)

Copyright © 1985 by Kenneth Neill Cameron

All rights reserved
Bergin & Garvey Publishers, Inc.
670 Amherst Road
South Hadley, Massachusetts 01075

56789   056   987654321

Printed in the United States of America.

Contents

Preface   viii

A Personal Statement   xiii

1. The Roots of Marxism   1

    From Godwin to Owen   5
    The Chartists   10

2. The Dynamics of History   17

    The Class Struggle   18
    The Socioeconomic Foundation   20
    The Superstructure and Stalin   26
    Critics of Marx   28
    Production and Reproduction   32

3. Patterns of the Past   35

    The Evolution of Farming Societies   36
    Feudalism in Asia   42
    The Pattern of Europe   48
    World Feudalism and Social Evolution   52

4. Capitalism   66

    Industrial Capitalism   66
    Monopoly Capitalism   83

5. Communism — 90

The Revolutionary Prelude   90
The Two Phases of Communism   97
The Socialist World   108
Projection and Reality   112

6. Women and Society — 122

The Origin of the Family   124
The Historical Record   127
The Two Faces of Oppression   133

7. Class, Ideas, and Art — 137

The Realm of Ideas   137
Marx and Engels on Literature   149

8. Nature and Society — 162

Dialectical Materialism   162
Modern Science and Nature   169
Animal and Human Society   179

Notes — 194

Index — 213

About the Author — 222

To the Memory of Julius and Ethel Rosenberg

they were very gentle, beautiful people,
lovers and young,
theirs was a courage and beauty few in the world could bear.

Now they have burned their sweet lovers' nerves to ashes, alone
with the rasp of the fire and the dark.

a strange and terrible mating this.

the long dying now is over,
the tortured bodies rest
cold in the earth,
turning as the earth turns
wheeling across the silent face of the sun,
void through the void,
a still journey.

you cannot touch them now,
you can torture them no more,
the earth has triumphed in its own,
gathered its own,
the curtain of time has fallen.

you think you have ended this
with a little sheathing of earth?
you think the tramping of the feet will stop?
you think the winds grinding your today into the dust of yesterday

will cease tomorrow?

(K.N.C.)

Preface

As Marx and Engels indicated in several places, they considered Marxism a science, for instance, in Engels' title, *Socialism: Utopian and Scientific*. "Utopian" socialism is the earlier socialism, of Robert Owen and others, which although perceiving society as evolutionary believed the cause of this evolution lay in "reason". "Scientific" socialism is the socialism of Marx and Engels, who also saw society as evolutionary but attributed this evolution not primarily to ideas but to social processes. In his speech at Marx's grave Engels said that this concept—"historical materialism"—was primarily Marx's; and he went on to say that Marx's other great contribution was to unravel the nature of capitalism. It seems likely also that they considered their views on the political aspects of society, with its unique analysis of class struggle and the State, as constituting a specific science also—political science. These particular sciences of economics and politics were not viewed as insulated either from each other or from historical materialism. The general mechanisms of social evolution were also present in the economic and political spheres, intertwined with their specific mechanisms; and so too, with the theories reflecting these phenomena.

Marx and Engels do not seem to have pursued the question further. How, for instance, would a social science differ from a natural science? In what respects would it be essentially the same? Clearly there would be differences. For one thing the mechanisms and units of society are not the same as those of nature. For another, a social scientist is part of his material in a way that a natural scientist is not. Yet a social science would have to use the same general method as natural science and its results and theories would have to be subjected to similar check. Marx and Engels were doubtless aware of these matters but they seem to have assumed the essential oneness of all science just as they saw all reality, natural and social, as a developing whole.

Were they right? Is Marxism a science, a general science containing within it special sciences of the various aspects of society? The question is basic. If Marxism is not a science then it is simply another "interesting" view of society which we can eclectically combine with other views, including those of Freud. If, on the other hand, it is a science, its views have to be considered as reflections of the segment of reality it investigates, reflections not to be found in any other body of thought except fragmentarily.

Numerous objections have been raised, directly or indirectly, to the claim that Marxism is a science. The most obvious is that although the natural sciences do have main theorists, such as Newton and Einstein, they are primarily the result of work by thousands of scientists and are constantly developing. Marxism, on the other hand, although having roots in previous thought, is almost entirely the work of two people, Marx and Engels, with the only major development in the present century coming from but one person, Lenin. The primary answer to this objection is that nature is much more complex than society. The basic mechanisms of societal functioning are comparatively few in number and once discovered there is no need to discover them again.

It might be objected also that there is no general science of nature as Marxism would be for society. What there is commonly recognized as being are two general sciences, one of which deals with matter—from the universe, to the Earth, to elementary particles—, the other with biological life. And both are subdivided into particular areas. Moreover, there are more elements in common between these two major divisions of natural science than is generally recognized. Both are subject to certain general laws of change and development, necessarily so because living matter evolved from matter. There is, then, in a fundamental sense a general science of nature. And there is a field of science also between that of nature and society, namely that concerned mainly with people, who are a blend of natural and social elements.

It might also be argued that if Marxism is the science of society why is it not recognized as such—as the natural sciences are? The answer is partly because its findings run counter to the interest of those who control the society and whose influence penetrates the intellectual community that would give it such recognition. But it is also because it does not at first appear to be a science. Its units are not atoms or molecules or cells but social classes and economic and political structures. It cannot predict or make specific change as can the natural sciences. This is because social processes, unlike natural ones, are not entirely objective but are affected by unpredictable human actions. They are, however, as Marx contended, basically objective. And because they are Marxism is able both to predict and make basic social change. The denial that it can do so relies, as I shall try to illustrate, on a selection of secondary factors and a neglect of basic ones.

The fact that a science reflects a segment of reality does not signify that it reflects it perfectly; only that it has a basic correspondence to it. A basic correspondence is of course, open to development. In fact unless a science develops it will stagnate. So, too, with Marxism. And it is this development that I am mainly interested in in this book. The detractors of Marxism depict it as a complex dogmatic system unrelated to reality. It is, indeed, complex, but this complexity is not an imposed construct but arises from the fact that Marxism attempts to reflect social reality. In short, even though the sphere of Marxism—society—is more limited than that of natural science it is still complex, and Marxism, as a reflection of it, is necessarily also complex. In fact, Marxism is far more difficult to grasp and its method of thought more intricate than is generally realized. It is partly for this reason that some attempt is made to simplify Marxist analysis—and so open Marxism to general attack. It is also because of the complexities of social phenomena that Marxism sometimes presents views that seem patently wrong. This is true also of the natural sciences. On the other hand what might be called the effective basics of Marxism are easily grasped, and in a proletarian revolution rapidly spread to provide the essential ingredients for the transformation of society.

Today, we hear much of dogmatism and revisionism; and indeed there is plenty of both, the dogmatists trying to freeze Marxism, the revisionists to water it down. Neither are new. There were both in Marx's day, and revisionism was early noted by Lenin in an essay on the subject as a serious danger—an attack on Marxism not from its avowed enemies but from professed Marxists. Today both have grown to monstrous proportions, and, although apparently at the extremes of the cultural spectrum often meet and blend.

It is time to set our sights high, to return to the scientific spirit of inquiry of Marx, Engels and Lenin, the spirit which enabled Lenin to say boldly and simply of the concept that the highly industrialized nations would be the first to become socialist: "Things have turned out differently from what Marx and Engels thought." Lenin's was not, of course, an eclectic spirit of enquiry but one acting within the peripheries of a social science. Marx and Engels may have been wrong on the particulars of the emergence of socialism but they were not wrong about its emergence. Their basic analysis of the social mechanisms in general and those of capitalism in particular were still correct. The time has now come to develop Marxism further. Unless this happens Marxism cannot grow, and if it fails to grow, it becomes subject to attacks which can discredit it. The danger in attempting such development is, of course, that advantage will be taken of it to riddle Marxism with intellectual anarchism, an anarchism that can weaken socialism and spread confusion in Marxist circles. But the chance has to be taken. The plain truth is that Marxism does need to be revised—in an ordinary sense and in certain respects; for developments have taken place which are not properly reflected in some of its classics, for instance, Engels' *Origin of the Family, Private Property and the State.* And it needs to be expanded to incorporate the social and scientific developments of recent decades, for instance, on the origins and nature of people and society.

It might appear to some that to discuss Marxist theory is not very important in an age when humanity is threatened by nuclear destruction and dangerous weather changes; and racked by capitalist crisis. But there is a connection between these things and Marxism, and it is a vital one. Marxism, as Marx early indicated is not just a theory but intertwined theory and "practice," and if Marxist theory is diluted the efforts of those struggling to save our planet and build a sane society will be hindered.

This book falls into three parts. In the first, I discuss the origins of Marxism and the basic theories of historical materialism. In the second, I examine first the views of Marx and Engels on past history and then their projections into the future. In the third, I discuss three topics which seem to need special development, the Marxist view of women and society, the problems inherent in the relations of thinking and art to society, and finally, the relations of nature and society, which encompasses a brief exposition of dialectical materialism and a compressed view of recent science. I have long had a special interest in science and two of my closest friends are scientists. One of them, Dr. Rachmiel Levine, Emeritus Medical Director of the City of Hope Medical Center in Duarte, CA, has gone over some of my material on the physical and biological sciences—with annotations and spidery drawings supplemented by insightful discussion. There is, in spite of rumor to the contrary, nothing mysterious about dialectical materialism. It is basically materialism, with roots in Lucretius, Diderot and others, which takes proper account of the clashing interconnections inherent in nature and society. Its development was due more to Engels than to Marx. Unlike Marxism, it is not a science but a philosophy and a method of thought. It is not a part of Marxism but a separate entity allied to Marxism.

My procedure is first to examine the views of Marx and Engels and then evaluate them. In examining them, I give the words of Marx and Engels themselves, making little use of synopsis or paraphrase. In doing so, I do not mean to imply Gospel but, as in my Shelley and other studies, I prefer to provide the actual text under discussion so that the reader can judge for himself. In regard to Marxism, this is especially important because distortions often hide behind paraphrase—as Marx is refuted by attributing to him views he never held.

Kenneth Neill Cameron

A Personal Statement

I first became interested in Marxism in the 1930's at Oxford University which I was attending courtesy of the imperialistic enterprise of Cecil Rhodes. The Great Depression had made apparent what had not been apparent to me before, namely that the establishment politicians, political scientists and economists, did not know what was happening and had no solution for it. Seeking other answers, I joined the Oxford Labour Club and was accepted into a "socialist" study group run by G.D.H. Cole. Soon the Labour Club was host to the unemployed army of the Hunger Marchers as they passed through Oxford on their way to London, and a group of us went on to join their London demonstrations. There, in the contrast between the humanitarianism of the Marchers and the brutality of the police, I received my first practical lessons in the Marxist primer. And I soon began to feel that Cole's Marxism was more radical reformism than Marxism.

In 1934, I used the last of Cecil Rhodes' bounty to make a trip to the U.S.S.R. The vitality of Leningrad, with its busy port and smoking factory chimneys, presented an immediate and dramatic contrast to the desolation of crisis-ridden Britain, especially the Liverpool-Birkenhead area, where I had stayed on vacations with my uncle, John R. Cameron, a shipyard worker, trade union official and active Marxist. The U.S.S.R., in spite of all I had heard—some of it from "socialists"—appeared to me to be a genuine worker's state, run by workers for workers, the first such state in history; and I began to grasp the historical vision of Marx. Incidentally, I went by ship and in passing through the Kiel Canal, we were glared at by a regimented band of stolid, Swastiked Brown Shirts, for whose benefit we sang the International, with the red flag flying from the masthead. A group of dockworkers discretely in the background gave us a clenched fist salute.

In those early days what a growing Marxist view did for me was to reverse traditional values. Instead of looking at society from the top down— which to some degree I had been doing although I was not aware of it—I began to see it from the bottom up, which essentially meant rejecting the tacit assumption that the mass of humanity is fuel to be burned for the maintainence of upper class power and comfort. I also felt like a Dante emerging from a vision of heaven and hell which was vivid to me but invisible to others. And in trying to explain things which seemed self-evident, I first encountered that defamatory scepticism which views Marxist intellectual vision as dogma. However, I was even then Marxist enough to know that change does not come about only or even mainly by proclaiming truths but by organizing, turning individuals, whether workers or intellectuals, into an effective political force.

When I returned to a Canada still deep in the depression, I worked first at organizing the unemployed in Montreal and then became a full-time organizer for The League Against War and Fascism in Toronto. If there was, as John Reed wrote, "war in Patterson" in 1912, there was war in Toronto in 1935. I organized innumerable demonstrations, meetings, and picket lines, and visited unions, church, ethnic and other organizations to try to persuade them to join in the struggle to prevent World War II and stem the tide of fascism. Concurrently I was giving a class to steel workers on Marxist economics and to university students on historical materialism. I became impressed by the width of Marxism—not only intellectually as a world-view but as interlocking vision and action. It also occurred to me that others could do this work better than I could and that there were things I could do which these others could not.

In 1936 I went to the University of Wisconsin as a Graduate Assistant in the English Department, to teach part time and to work for a Ph.D. There I began my Shelley studies with William Ellery Leonard, humanist, scholar—editor of Lucretius—author—*The Locomotive God*—poet—*Two Lives*—and defender of Tom Mooney, then the most famed United States political prisoner:

> *Tom Mooney thinks behind a grating,*
> *Beside a corridor. (He's waiting.)*
> *The Gold-men from ten cities hear in sleep*
> *Tom Mooney breathing—for he breathes so deep.*

At Wisconsin I also came to know Alban Dewes Winspear author of the Marxist study, *The Genesis of Plato's Thought* (New York, 1940).

In 1950—then at Indiana University—I published *The Young Shelley: Genesis of a Radical,* and later *Shelley: The Golden Years.* As I have noted in an essay, *Shelley and Marx,* I regard Shelley as a precursor of Marx, and I have always considered my work on Shelley as a contribution to the Marxist movement, the kind of contribution which I was best qualified to make, namely a Marxist study—although not so designated in the interests of securing publication—of the most advanced revolutionary poet of the pre-Marxist era. While in Indiana, I was the delegate from the University teacher's union to the Bloomington Federation of Labor for some five or six years. There I joined the carpenters, plumbers, furniture workers and common laborer's unions on picket lines and in other actions, always in a warm, comradely atmosphere. I felt more at home with the workers than on the campus. Through these and other contacts, I conducted in 1946 a Marxist school for steelworkers in Gary, Indiana, to which, as I later discovered—courtesy of the Freedom of Information Act—the F.B.I. had sent a stool pigeon, whose labored transcripts include detailed notes on my examinations of Marx's *Value, Price and Profit* (which, as I reread them, were not at all bad). I was assisted in the school by my wife, Mary Owen Cameron, a Marxist sociologist and ever a fountain of good facts and good sense.

In 1952, aided by McCarthyite doings in Indiana, I came to New York to edit the Shelley manuscripts at The Carl H. Pforzheimer Library, which resulted in four massive volumes, *Shelley and his Circle* (two volumes in 1961, two in 1970). At the same time, I worked with the Committee for a Sane Nuclear Policy and wrote a two volume Marxist history of the world, the first volume of which appeared in 1973 as *Humanity and Society: A World History*—also not designated as Marxist in the interest of publication, the explicitly Marxist version being systematically turned down by publishers over a ten year period. My studies in world history showed me, among other things, that the world had been a massive slaughterhouse run by the rich since the beginnings of civilization and that this basic fact was ignored by bourgeois historians. In 1976, I published (at my own expense) a little book—part of a larger work—called *Marx and Engels Today: A Modern Dialogue on Philosophy and History,* which although inadequate in some respects, makes some good points. I halted work on volume two of the history because it seemed to me that general theoretical evaluations of Marxism were needed more, and the present work is one of these studies. In 1961, I visited the U.S.S.R. again, this time accompanied by my wife and daughter; my path in hunting down Shelley and Byron manuscripts aided by the leading Russian English romantics scholar, Michel Alexeev, director of the Pushkin Institute in Leningrad. The U.S.S.R. had clearly made great strides between 1934 and 1961, in spite of the devastations of the war, but it seemed to me that, as the result of the Khrushchev "thaw", something of the old proletarian atmosphere—of workers, looking like workers, everywhere—had dissipated. (The Khruschev era and its evaluation of Stalin still needs to be examined, and I have attempted this in another work.)

In 1963 I became Professor of English at New York University. In the sixties and seventies I worked in the anti-war and other progressive movements on the campus and am at present a member of the NYU anti-nuclear organization. In the spring of 1983 I gave a paper—*Engels on Women and Society*—at a Marxist Scholars Conference at Cincinnati and am at present working to establish a similar organization on the East Coast. But my main work as a Marxist in recent years has been writing. I am at present working on a study of dialectical materialism in which I attempt to integrate its views with modern scientific advances.

K.N.C.

1

The Roots of Marxism

Marxism is sometimes presented as a doctrine that grew up in the mind of Marx, and, it is sometimes implied, has to be studied as a sacred text. Or it is seen as just one view among many—all arising in a kind of intellectual greenhouse—whose concepts can be picked or rejected as one wishes. When roots are mentioned they are almost always seen as cultural (e.g., Hegel). The roots of Marxism, however, like those of any body of thought, are primarily social; and these roots had produced some of the views that were later incorporated into Marxism before Marx and Engels set pen to paper. And if Marx and Engels had never set pen to paper Marxism would have arisen anyway—albeit more slowly and painfully.

The movement in history from which Marxism emerged was that of the Industrial Revolution, an economic development that was heralded politically by the French Revolution and was distinguished socially by the rise of a new class, the proletariat, a mass working class which operated the new factories, mines, steel mills, and railways. It was, as I shall try to show, basically out of the struggles, social and ideological, of the young proletariat, particularly in Britain, that Marxism arose.

At the outbreak of the French Revolution in 1789 France had a population of about 26 million, 24 million of whom lived in the country and 2 million in cities. Of the 24 million who lived in the country, 23.6 million were peasants; 400,000 were nobles, about 40,000 of whom owned most of the land—in short, a feudal society similar to that which had existed from the beginnings of civilization. The situation in the cities, however, was

1

different from that of earlier feudal societies—European or Asian—in which industry and transport were owned by the great landowners and, along with manufacturing, run by slave labor. Paris with a population of 500,000; Lyons, 160,000; and Marseilles and Bordeaux, about 100,000 each, were all manufacturing and trading centers, their businesses owned by businessmen and run by paid labor. The great landowners (the aristocrats) controlled the national State; the "bourgeoisie" (the businessmen and wealthier professionals) ran the city governments. And the landowners, as in all feudal societies, harassed their business rivals by excessive taxation and other means.

What happened as the revolution developed was that the bourgeoisie extended its power from the cities to the national center—at first rather shakily. The working class—largely based on cottage industry—and the middle class (petit bourgeoisie) achieved little. And as in the British revolution in the preceding century the bourgeoisie in time had to share political power with the landed aristocrats, who still had large economic holdings (in banking as well as in agriculture and trade).

The historically unprecedented increase in manufacturing in the eighteenth century in Europe continued into the nineteenth and moved from a central base in manufacturing (cloth, leather, wood) to one of heavy industry (coal, iron, steel). The horse and wagon were supplanted by the railways, the wooden sailing ship by the steam-engined iron ship.

As agriculture did not develop at the same pace as industry, the capitalist class soon outdistanced the aristocracy and mounted a further challenge to its power, this time not in France only but throughout western Europe. As a result of the British Reform Act of 1832; revolutions in France, Germany and other western European countries in 1848; and the struggle for the bourgeois unification of Italy in the 1860s, the feudal political power in western Europe was finally broken. Parliaments were everywhere established on the basis of suffrage by adult males who possessed a certain minimum of property.

The same industrial developments which so increased the strength of the capitalist class transformed the comparatively weak and often scattered—"cottage industry"—manufacturing working class into a concentrated industrial working class. These phenomena were also unprecedented.

Never before in the history of humanity had there been a civilization based economically on metal, coal, and steam power and socially on an industrial capitalist class and an industrial working class. The political and ideological consequences of these developments were also, and necessarily, unprecedented.

The new industrial working class (proletariat) soon began to push for a share of political power, first in the massive Chartist movement in Britain in the 1830s and 1840s and in the 1848 and other bourgeois revolutions on the Continent. Among those representing this Continental workers' movement was The Communist League, and it was for the League that two of its members, Karl Marx (1818–1883) and Frederick Engels (1820–1895), wrote the *Manifesto of the Communist Party,* popularly known as *The Communist Manifesto* (1848). Previously Engels—in Manchester and aligned with the Chartists—had written *The Condition of the Working Class in England* (1845). Marx had edited the *Rheinische Zeitung,* a bourgeois-revolutionary journal that was suppressed by the German government in 1843, and published *The Holy Family* (1845) and *The Poverty of Philosophy* (1847). Marx, driven into exile, moved from city to city, finally settling in London. As his wife, Jenny, wrote some years later of their stay in Brussels:

In the meantime the storm-clouds of the revolution had been piling higher and higher. The Belgian horizon too was dark. What was feared above all was the workers, the social element of the popular masses. The police, the military, the civil guard, all were called out against them, all were kept ready for action. Then the German workers decided that it was time to arm themselves too. Daggers, revolvers, etc. were procured. Karl willingly provided money, for he had just come into an inheritance. In all this the government saw conspiracy and criminal plans: Marx receives money and buys weapons, he must therefore be got rid of. Late at night two men broke into our house. They asked for Karl: when he appeared they said they were police sergeants and had a warrant to arrest him and take him to be questioned. They took him away. I hurried after him in terrible anxiety and went to influential men to find out what the matter was. I rushed from house to house in the dark. Suddenly I was seized by a guard, arrested and thrown into a dark prison. It was where beggars without a home, vagabonds and wretched fallen women were detained. I was thrust into a dark cell. As I entered sobbing, an unhappy companion in misery offered to share her place with me: it was a hard plank bed. I lay down on it. When morning broke I saw at the window opposite mine, behind iron bars, a cadaverous, mournful face. I went to the window and recognized our good old friend Gigot. When he saw me he beckoned to me, pointing downwards. I looked in that direction and saw Karl being led away under military escort. An hour later I was taken to the interrogating magistrate. After a two hours' questioning, during which they got little out of me, I was led to a carriage by gendarmes and towards evening I got back to my three poor little children. The affair caused a great sensation, all the papers reported on it. After a short while Karl too was released and ordered to leave Brussels immediately.[1]

In the meantime Engels was concluding his *Condition of the Working Class in England:*

If these conclusions have not been sufficiently established in the course of the present work, there may be other opportunities for demonstrating that they are necessary consequences of the historical development of England. But this I maintain, the war of the poor against the rich now carried on in detail and indirectly will become direct and universal. It is too late for a peaceful solution. The classes are divided more and more sharply, the spirit of resistance penetrates the workers, the bitterness intensifies, the guerilla skirmishes become concentrated in more important battles, and soon a slight impulse will suffice to set the avalanche in motion. Then, indeed, will the war-cry resound through the land: "War to the palaces, peace to the cottages!"—but then it will be too late for the rich to beware.

As the working class increased in strength it established trade and political organizations, including the International Workingmen's Association—with some five million affiliated members—which had its center in the British trade unions and was, as its name implies, aimed at uniting the working class across national boundaries.

Marx was one of the founders and became the directing force of the International, delivering its Inaugural Address in 1864 (before a group of delegates from Britain, France, Germany, Italy, and Poland):

To conquer political power has therefore become the great duty of the working classes. They seem to have comprehended this, for in England, Germany, Italy, and France there have taken place simultaneous revivals, and simultaneous efforts are being made at the political reorganisation of the working men's party.

One element of success they possess—numbers; but numbers weigh only in the balance if united by combination and led by knowledge. Past experience has shown how disregard of that bond of brotherhood which ought to exist between the workmen of different countries and incite them to stand firmly by each other in all their struggle for emancipation will be chastised by the common discomfiture of their incoherent efforts.

When the working class seized power in Paris, following the Franco-Prussian War in 1870, the International provided its most advanced leadership. When the workers' Commune was destroyed Marx reported in an Address to the International:

> Our Association is, in fact, nothing but the international bond between the most advanced working men in the various countries of the civilised world. Wherever, in whatever shape, and under whatever conditions the class struggle obtains any consistency, it is but natural that members of our association should stand in the foreground. The soil out of which it grows is Modern society itself. It cannot be stamped out by any amount of carnage. To stamp it out, the Government would have to stamp out the despotism of capital over labor—the condition of their own parasitical existence.
>
> Workingmen's Paris, with its Commune, will be forever celebrated as the glorious harbinger of a new society. Its martyrs are enshrined in the great heart of the working class. Its exterminators' history has already nailed to that eternal pillory from which all the prayers of their priests will not avail to redeem them.[2]

The uniqueness of Marx and Engels as intellectuals, then, was that they became, in effect, part of a laboring class, specifically the proletariat. They set out to become the champions of this class, to synthesize its world-view and to forward its economic and political interests. As we shall see, the Chartists and others had already made considerable headway in these matters, and it is in them that we find the immediate roots of Marxism. Some of its earlier roots, however, go back into the bourgeois intellectual turmoil of the eighteenth century as it was building towards industrialization and revolution.

From Godwin to Owen

Unlike all previous centuries, the eighteenth—as the end of feudalism and the feudal Church began at last to seem possible—spawned evolutionary theories, on both society and nature. These assumed an extraordinary variety. Immanuel Kant broke with the age-old view of celestial serenity and envisaged an active and evolving universe. Erasmus Darwin, the grandfather of Charles (who rather ignored him as a predecessor), argued that "all vegetables and animals now existing were originally derived from the smallest microscopic ones" that by "innumerable reproductions, during innumerable centuries of time, gradually acquired the size, strength and excellence of

form and faculties, which they now possess." The concept that there was
social evolution and that it was similarly subject to inherent "laws" was put
forward almost simultaneously by Antoine Nicolas Condorcet in France and
William Godwin in England (1793—some twenty-five years before Marx
was born). The universe, Godwin argued, was ruled by "Necessity
. . . connected and cemented in all its parts, nothing in the boundless
progress of things being capable of happening otherwise than it has actually
happened." The same necessitarian forces operated in society and were,
moreover, moving society forward in a progressive direction. After considering European history since the fall of Constantinople in 1453 Godwin
concluded: "And, as improvements have long continued to be incessant, so
there is no chance but they will go on." They would go on until humanity
reached a state of equality, with economic and social factors determining
psychological and cultural ones:

> The spirit of oppression, the spirit of servility, and the spirit of fraud,
> these are the immediate growth of the established administration of prop-
> erty. They are alike hostile to intellectual and moral improvement. The
> other vices of envy, malice and revenge are their inseparable companions.
> In a state of society where men lived in the midst of plenty, and where
> all shared alike the bounties of nature, these sentiments would inevitably
> expire. . . . No man would be an enemy to his neighbour, for they would
> have no subject of contention.

Condorcet had a similar vision: "the perfectibility of man is absolutely
indefinite." If, he argued, we can see the laws and directions of past history
we can project the future:

> If man can predict, almost with certainty, those appearances of which he
> understands the laws; if, even when the laws are unknown to him, ex-
> perience of the past enables him to foresee, with considerable probability,
> future appearances; why should we suppose it a chimerical undertaking
> to delineate with some degree of truth, the picture of the future destiny
> of mankind from the results of its history?

But although both Condorcet and Godwin were convinced of the fact of
historical evolution, and Godwin recognized a determining role for some
economic forces in the structures of society, both felt that the main element
behind such evolution was an innate quality in the human mind ("reason")
to advance, and, as it were, pull society after it. "The inherent tendency
of intellect," Godwin argued, "is to improvement. If therefore this inherent

tendency be suffered to operate, and no concussion of nature or inundation of barbarism arrest its course, the state of society we have been describing, must, at some time, arrive." Thus, although it is true, as Engels wrote, that some of "Godwin's ideas almost border on communism," his philosophy was basically idealist (the word breaks at idea, not at ideal, and implies in relation to history the primacy of mind over social forces).[3]

In Germany, a similar idealist evolutionary view of history was developed somewhat later by Georg Wilhelm Friedrich Hegel but put in mystical terms: behind the ideas which caused historical development lay the Absolute or God, so that history became an unfolding of the nature of God. The end of this process was to be a Plato-like union of the human and divine "minds":

> The individual as such has an infinite value as the object and aim of divine love, destined as mind to live in absolute relationship with God himself, and have God's mind dwelling in him: i.e., man in himself is destined to supreme freedom.

The unfolding of the divine spirit motivating human history Hegel saw as taking place by means of the "dialectic" and its three "laws": the interpenetration of "opposites;" qualitative change—the new—arising from quantitative change; the "negation of the negation" (the reemergence of the old within the new in a "higher" form).

As Marx early pointed out, "no credit is due to me for discovering the existence of classes in modern society nor yet the struggle between them." (This is true enough, but as we shall see, Marx and Engels developed the theory far beyond what had previously existed.) Many thinkers, including Aristotle, had been aware of a class struggle in society but it was not until the eighteenth century, as the aristocratic-bourgeois conflict increased, that class struggle views became prominent, as witness the following by James Madison in 1788, some twenty years before he became President of the United States:

> But the most common and durable source of factions has been the various and unequal distribution of property. Those who hold and those who are without property have ever formed distinct interests in society. . . . A landed interest, a manufacturing interest, a mercantile interest, a moneyed interest, with many lesser interests, grow up of necessity in civilized nations, and divide them into different classes, actuated by different sentiments and views. The regulation of these various and interfering interests forms the principal task of modern legislation, and involves the spirit of

party and faction in the necessary and ordinary operations of the government.

Godwin, who was rather timid about social turmoil, put less emphasis on class conflict, but he and other middle class thinkers, who were both anticapitalist and antifeudal, began to examine the sources of economic exploitation:

> There is no wealth in the world except this, the labour of man. What is misnamed wealth, is merely a power vested in certain individuals by the institutions of society, to compel others to labour for their benefit. . . . They [the poor] are scarcely ever benefited by this. It adds a certain portion to the mass of their labour; but it adds nothing to their conveniences. Their wages are not changed. They are paid no more for the work of ten hours, than before for the work of eight. They support the burden but they come in for no share of the fruit.

Following Godwin (in the 1790s) the evolving industrial revolution led to increased social turmoil (in, for instance, "Luddite" strikes and riots), political struggle, and war—as the Napoleonic wars devasted the Continent. As a consequence wider concepts of the historical import of class struggles began to emerge, as, for instance, in Shelley's Preface to *Hellas* (1821), his "lyrical drama" on the Greek revolutionary war against Turkish oppression, which gives a fervid revolutionary vista:

> This is the age of the war of the oppressed against the oppressors, and every one of those ringleaders of the privileged gangs of murderers and swindlers, called Sovereigns, look to each other for aid against the common enemy, and suspend their mutual jealousies in the presence of a mightier fear. Of this holy alliance all the despots of the earth are virtual members. But a new race has risen throughout Europe, nursed in the abhorrence of the opinions which are its chains, and she will continue to produce fresh generations to accomplish that destiny which tyrants foresee and dread. . . . Well do these destroyers of mankind know their enemy, when they impute the insurrection in Greece to the same spirit before which they tremble throughout the rest of Europe, and that enemy well knows the power and cunning of its opponents, and watches the moment of their approaching weakness and inevitable division to wrest the bloody sceptres from their grasp.

The "mightier fear" was mass revolution, as Shelley affirmed in addressing the fledgling proletariat in *The Masque of Anarchy:*

Rise like Lions after slumber
In unvanquishable number—
Shake your chains to earth like dew
Which in sleep had fallen on you—
Ye are many—they are few.

In France, as the bourgeois revolution developed towards 1848, new radical social theories arose. Charles Fourier and Henri St. Simon put forward cooperative schemes that implied an antifeudal union of working class and capitalists. Fourier suggested that society be split into communes of 1600 people; St. Simon, although willing to retain an industrial state, urged that it be run cooperatively with the aid of science. Both of them assumed, as did other radicals then and later, that their function was to produce a vision of the new society that people would then follow—without considering that society might have inherent evolutionary processes that had to be uncovered.

The main advance in radical thought in this period took place in Britain where the industrial revolution, already well under way, produced an unprecedented problem—the first cyclical crisis of industrial capitalism: "The deficiencies of employment for the working classes cannot proceed from a want of wealth or capital, or of the means of greatly adding to what now exists, but from some defect in the mode of distributing this extraordinary addition of new capital throughout society." Thus Robert Owen, himself a manufacturer, viewing the economic collapse that followed the Napoleonic Wars in 1815. Owen was the first to realize the immense productivity of the new machines and felt that the core of the problem was that production had been allowed to run ahead of consumption. He argued that the two should be balanced in a "socialist state." This state Owen first tried naively to achieve by converting the upper classes, and he then turned to the growing trade union movement. In the same years William Cobbett and other radical parliamentary "reformers" were leading demonstrations of 100,000 to secure male voting rights without property qualifications (in a population of 13 million 13,000 had the vote). Cobbett's *Political Register,* which championed both small farmers and the working class, had a circulation of 50,000 at a time when the London *Times* had 10,000. And Thomas Hodgkins began to analyse the new economic system (1825), going beyond Owen:

> Betwixt him who produces food and him who produces clothing, betwixt
> him who makes instruments and him who uses them, in steps the capitalist,
> who neither makes nor uses them and appropriates to himself the produce
> of both.

In the 1830's these streams of reformist mass action, socialist views and economic radicalism were blended into the "Chartist" movement.[4]

The Chartists

When the young Engels (born in 1820) went from Germany to England in 1842, he encountered, he tells us, two groups of radicals. The first were the members of the Communist League, mostly tailors and also mostly exiles from Germany:

> The members, in so far as they were workers at all, were almost exclusively artisans. Even in the big metropolises, the man who exploited them was usually only a small master. The exploitation of tailoring on a large scale, what is now called the manufacture of ready-made clothes, by the conversion of handicraft tailoring into a domestic industry working for a big capitalist, was at that time even in London only just making its appearance. On the one hand, the exploiter of these artisans was a small master; on the other hand, they all hoped ultimately to become small masters themselves.

Their outlook was that of a "narrow-minded equalitarian communism," by which Engels meant, as he explained in a note, "a communism which bases itself exclusively or predominantly on the demand for equality," that is to say on human desires rather than on the analysis of historical development.[5]

Then in Manchester, the heartland of the industrial revolution, Engels encountered the Chartists. The Chartists, he found, were "disregarded as not revolutionary" by the Communist League Members; but Engels was of a different opinion:

> In the Unions and turnouts opposition always remained isolated: it was single working-men or sections who fought a single bourgeois. . . . But in Chartism it is the whole working-class which arises against the bourgeoisie, and attacks, first of all, the political power, the legislative rampart with which the bourgeoisie has surrounded itself. . . . In 1835 a committee of the General Workingmen's Association of London, with William Lovett at its head, drew up the People's Charter, whose six points are as follows: (1)Universal suffrage for every man who is of age, sane and unconvicted of crime; (2)Annual Parliaments: (3)Payment of members of

Parliament, to enable poor men to stand for election; (4)Voting by ballot to prevent bribery and intimidation by the bourgeoisie; (5)Equal electoral districts to secure equal representation; and (6)Abolition of the even now merely nominal property qualification of £300 in land for candidates in order to make every voter eligible. These six points, which are all limited to the reconstitution of the House of Commons, harmless as they seem, are sufficient to overthrow the whole English Constitution, Queen and Lords included.

"In every factory town," Engels noted, "the Chartists have shown more activity than all the German political, socialist and religious parties taken together." "The Chartist leaders, are," he stated flatly, "already Communists."

Engels lost no time in making the acquaintance of these leaders, as one of them, George Harney, later remembered:

It was in 1843 that he [Engels] came over from Bradford to Leeds and enquired for me at *The Northern Star* office. A tall, handsome young man, with a countenance of almost boyish youthfulness, whose English, in spite of his German birth and education, was even then remarkable for its accuracy. He told me he was a constant reader of *The Northern Star* and took a keen interest in the Chartist movement. Thus began our friendship over fifty years ago.[6]

In the meantime Marx in Paris in 1844 was reading accounts of the revolt of the Silesian weavers (which inspired Heine's *Song of the Weavers* and later in the century Gerhart Hauptmann's proletarian drama, *The Weavers*). The revolt of the weavers, working not, as in industrialized Britain, in factories but in the "cottage industry" system then dominant in the still largely commercial capitalism on the Continent had, Marx felt, in some ways moved further than had earlier British and French movements:

The Silesian revolt began where the French and English insurrections ended, with the consciousness of the proletariat as a class. The whole action was of this character. Not only did it destroy machinery, the rival of the workers, but also the merchants' records, their property titles. In the beginning at least, all other movements were directed exclusively against the industrialists, against the visible enemy, but this movement was also directed against the banker, the invisible enemy.

When Marx and Engels met for ten days in the summer of 1844 in Paris, Engels found that they had been thinking along similar lines:

> While I was in Manchester, it was tangibly brought home to me that the economic facts, which have so far played no role or only a contemptible one in the writing of history, are at least in the modern world, a decisive historical force: that they form the basis of the origination of the present-day class antagonisms; that these class antagonisms, in the countries where they have become fully developed, thanks to large-scale industry, hence especially in England, are in their turn the basis of the formation of political parties and of party struggles, and thus of all political history. Marx had not only arrived at the same view, but had already, in the *German-French Annuals* (1844), generalised it to the effect that, speaking generally, it is not the state which conditions and regulates civil society, but civil society which conditions and regulates the state, and, consequently, that policy and its history are to be explained from the economic relations and their development, and not *vice versa*. When I visited Marx in Paris in the summer of 1844, our complete agreement in all theoretical fields became evident and our joint work dates from that time. When, in the spring [April] of 1845, we met again in Brussels, Marx had already fully developed his materialist theory of history in its main features from the above mentioned basis and we now applied ourselves to the detailed elaboration of the newly won mode of outlook in the most varied directions.

When we read Engels' *Condition of the Working Class in England* (completed in March 1845), it becomes apparent that the mass of material which he had accumulated on the industrial working class far surpassed anything of the kind that Marx had then encountered. Furthermore, many of the general social insights which Engels stresses in the above passage had—as we shall see—been arrived at by the Chartists even though they had not put them together into so integrated a view of capitalist society as he did.

That Marx had by the summer of 1844 really "arrived at the same view" as Engels is not borne out by his writings. He had, as Engels notes, discovered the economic base for historical evolution and the State structure but he had not really grasped the significance of the class struggle, especially that of the proletariat. It was not until their second meeting in 1845, as Engels notes, that Marx had "fully developed his materialist theory of history." The ingredient missing in 1844 must have been that of the role of the proletariat in the destruction of capitalism and the advance of humanity to socialism. And the basis for this concept must have come from the material Engels had gathered for his *Condition of the Working Class in England*. In short, Marx could not have formulated the basic tenets of Marxism without Engels conveying to him the experiences and views of the British proletariat. On the other hand, it is clear that Engels believed that he himself could not have done so, that the material needed the wider vision of Marx to form it into a rounded scientific theory.

Marx's interest in this material is shown in the fact that following their meeting in Brussels he accompanied Engels to England for a six-week visit. There he met George Julian Harney and other Chartist leaders and attended a joint conference of Chartists and continental workers living in England.[7]

The leader of the German artisan communists was a tailor, Wilhelm Weitling, whose utopian *Guarantees of Harmony and Liberty* (1842) at first impressed the young Marx. Friedrich Lessner, a member of the Communist League and later on of the Council of the International, remembered the reverence with which Weitling was held: "The respect he enjoyed in our circles was boundless. He was the idol of his followers." But in early 1848 Lessner met Marx, fresh from writing the *Communist Manifesto:*

> Marx was then still a young man, about twenty-eight years old, but he greatly impressed us all. He was of medium height, broad-shouldered, powerful in build and energetic in his deportment. His brow was high and finely shaped, his hair thick and pitch-black, his gaze piercing. His mouth already had the sarcastic line that his opponents feared so much. Marx was a born leader of the people. His speech was brief, convincing and compelling in its logic. He never said a superfluous word: every sentence was a thought and every thought was a necessary link in the chain of his demonstration. Marx had nothing of the dreamer about him. The more I realized the difference between the communism of Weitling's time and that of the *Communist Manifesto,* the more clearly I saw that Marx represented the manhood of socialist thought.

With Weitling "socialist thought" had been in its adolescence, with Marx it had attained its "manhood." The difference was not, of course, primarily personal but a reflection of a difference in class base. When we read *The Communist Manifesto* we can see what Lessner meant. The vision of the *Manifesto* is not that of radical artisans, hovering between classes, as was Weitling's, but of a massive proletarian class, feeling its power and sensing its uniqueness:

> All previous historical movements were movements of minorities, or in the interest of minorities. The proletarian movement is the self-conscious, independent movement of the immense majority, in the interest of the

immense majority. The proletariat, the lowest stratum of our present society, cannot stir, cannot raise itself up, without the whole superincumbent strata of official society being sprung into the air.

As Engels noted in writing of the Chartists: "Meanwhile a second, essentially different communism was developing alongside that of the League and of Weitling." This "second" communism was not restricted to the Chartist movement but also included radical trade unionism, which was a massive force in its own right, and other radical groupings including the Owenites. It was, as Engels also indicated, not only—in broad terms—a theoretical communism but a practical communism, one which by its actions could undermine the whole bourgeois State. Similar actions were beginning on the Continent, especially in political involvement by the newly emerging working class, including the weavers and miners. But the Chartists were the most active, the best organized, and the most advanced theoretically; and in the works of George Julian Harney and Bronterre O'Brien we can, as it were, see the social essence of Marxism in embryo.[8]

The Chartists combined the mass tactics of William Cobbett with the socialist outlook of Robert Owen and proudly gave them both a working class stamp. "The resolutions and petitions," O'Brien declared of a radical meeting in 1837, "were severally proposed and seconded by working men. The principal speakers who supported them were working men." The Chartists were well aware of the class struggle, placing the emphasis, however, unlike Madison, not on the upper but on the lower classes—the slaves of the past and the workers of the present; the connection of the two being embodied in O'Brien's characterization of the workers as "proletarian wage-slaves." They were aware of their own exploitation and knew who was exploiting them:

> You produce annually 450 millions of wealth, and the idlers [aristocrats] take 4s 6d a pound of it. They take nearly one-fourth, though they are only one in two thousand of the people. Next come the profit-mongers— those who make their fortunes by grinding the poor and cheating the rich. . . . who buy cheap and sell dear, who spoil [i.e., steal] the wholesome articles you have made and distribute them to others—they take 7s 6d a pound of what you produce. Thus 12s is gone before you have a pick. They promise you a paradise hereafter. You pay 1s to the clergy for that, on condition they preach to you to be content with your lot and to be pleased with what divine providence has done for you. . . . They take 2s 6d a pound for their military forces—to keep you down. This leaves 4s 6d. . . .

The workers felt that they were no more than tools in a vast and heartless system: "on a level with the hammers we lift, or the shuttles we throw!" Although the Chartists' immediate aim was to secure the vote for the working man—their Charter contained 4,000,000 signatures on this and other issues—their ultimate aims were militantly socialist, Harney declaring, in a spirited passage which gives the essence of the new working class outlook:

> Again I say, we are for peace, but we must have justice—we must have our rights speedily; peaceably if we can, *forcibly if we must.*
>
> *If bugs molest me as in bed I lie,*
>   *Shall I desert my bed for them? Not I,*
> *I will arise and every bug destroy,*
>   *Now make my bed, and all its sweets enjoy.*
>
> My friends, our country may be compared to a bed full of nasty, filthy, crawling, Aristocratic and Shopocratic bugs. Now in answer to our calmuniators who say that we wish to destroy property, I answer, we will not destroy the bedstead, but we will annihilate the bugs.

The Chartists did not advocate, as did some Utopians, destroying the new productive forces of capitalism but putting them under working class control, so that "instead of working to enrich a few avaricious task-masters" machinery should be "made to work for the general good." The working class should become the ruling class; or, perhaps, there should be no classes at all (1833):

> An entire change in society—a change amounting to a complete subversion of the existing "order of the world"—is contemplated by the working classes. They aspire to be at the top instead of at the bottom of society— or rather that there should be no bottom or top at all.

In spite of their class-conscious militancy, however, the Chartists lost the earlier concept of Godwin and Condorcet of historical evolutionary forces, and in their economic visions of the future they did not advance beyond the Owenite blueprint for "socialism." As O'Brien noted, they saw "the universal prevalence of a state of society not essentially different from that contrived by Owen." O'Brien advocated the nationalization of the land and argued that "Railways should not be private property: neither should canals, docks, mines, the supplying of gas, water, etc." And to this Harney added that factories should also be nationalized. But, as O'Brien's "contrived by Owen" reveals, they failed to tie up the present and the future and adhered to the simplistic idea that one should abstractly draw up a plan for socialism and then work to achieve it. How it was to be achieved they were unsure. O'Brien and others advocated a general strike—"let not an anvil be struck within the bredth [*sic*] and length of the land"—which some regarded primarily as a means of extracting reforms from Parliament. Harney, however (in 1838), advocated arming the workers—"there is no argument like the sword"—in preparation for such a strike and then turning it into a revolution: "the fact is that there is but one mode of obtaining the Charter and that is by INSURRECTION."[9]

As we read the Chartists it becomes particularly apparent that the basic roots of Marxism were social, lying not in Hegel or Feuerbach but in the working class, and, first and foremost, in the British working class. Nor could it, as Marx would have argued, have been otherwise, for cultural phenomena are the reflection of socioeconomic forces. The British working class was at the time a unique historical phenomenon: a massive, factory-based, industrial working class with a well-developed trade union structure and political organization, its own press and its own theorists, from Owen to Harney; a class which had learned social realities in decades of struggle. In addition to this base in the British working class was, as Engels noted, a secondary one in the radical Continental home-industry workers and artisans whose views had initially moved Marx beyond a bourgeois radicalism. The reason for the advanced character of the British working class was, of course, the fact that the industrial revolution began first in Britain. By 1830 Britain had an industrial capitalism whereas France, Germany and other continental countries were still at a primarily commercial capitalist stage.

2
The Dynamics of History

Although most bourgeois historians today would doubtless scorn H.G. Wells as simplistic in writing "Under the spell of Disraeli's Oriental Imagination, which made Queen Victoria [Empress of India], the Englishman turned readily enough towards the vague exaltations of modern imperialism," they themselves on the whole follow, although in more sophisticated form, his underlying assumption; namely that historical events result primarily from human thought (with its active but abstract emanations of Greed, Ambition, Evil, Injustice, Pride). This had been true also in the past, of Herodotus and Livy, and, as we saw, of Condorcet and Godwin; however, whereas Condorcet and Godwin envisaged history as evolutionary, few modern bourgeois historians do. In the main they concentrate on narration and avoid theory, seemingly implying that narrative of itself embodies explanation. And this concentration on narrative has hidden the fact that they are giving really no explanation, or but superficial explanation. Of those who have attempted to formulate a general theory in the present century, the two most prominent are Oswald Spengler and Sir Arnold Toynbee. Spengler's view of history as endless cycle in which "Each culture has its own possibilities of self-expression which rise, ripen, decay and never return" is, as Toynbee noted, more biological analogy than historical theory. Yet when Toynbee, perhaps the most widely acclaimed of modern bourgeois historians, came to proclaim his own theory, it turned out to be more theology than history:

While civilizations rise and fall and, in falling, give rise to others, some purposeful enterprise, higher than theirs, may all the time be making headway, and, in a divine plan, the learning that comes through the suffering caused by the failures of civilizations may be the sovereign means of progress.[1]

That a work, no matter how massive, based on this kind of mystical nonsense, could be hailed as a profound masterpiece indicates the level of historical theory in the capitalist world today. The plain fact is that there is little speculation on the deeper forces of history, the widely accepted and comfortably escapist rationale being that the problem is insoluble and only the intellectually naive tackle it.

The Class Struggle

The general theory of history that Marx and Engels developed when they met in Brussels in 1845 combined elements from the class struggle views of the Chartists and others, as well as from necessitarian evolutionary theories such as those of Condorcet and Godwin. Their most succinct early statement on the function of class struggles in history came in *The Communist Manifesto*.

The history of all hitherto existing society is the history of class struggles.

Freeman and slave, patrician and plebian, lord and serf, guild-master and journeyman, in a word, oppressor and oppressed, stood in constant opposition to one another, carried on an uninterrupted, now hidden, now open fight, a fight that each time ended, either in a revolutionary reconstitution of society at large, or in the common ruin of the contending classes. . . .

Our epoch, the epoch of the bourgeoisie, possesses, however, this distinctive feature: it has simplified the class antagonisms. Society as a whole is more and more splitting up into two great hostile camps, into two great classes directly facing each other—bourgeoisie and proletariat.

To this Engels later added a note explaining that earlier communal, classless forms of society were unknown at the time and that the *Manifesto* statement referred only to the period of "written history." In *Anti-Dühring* (1878) he emphasized that class conflicts existed between upper classes as well as between upper and lower classes: "But side by side with the antagonism between the feudal nobility and the bourgeoisie was the general antagonism between the exploiters and the exploited, the rich idlers and the toiling poor." Thus in recent European history there had been a kind of three-cornered class struggle: that between the rising capitalist class and the feudal aristocracy, and that between those classes and the workers and peasants.[2]

Marx and Engels, then, considered classes and class struggles in a broader historical perspective than had their predecessors. They saw them not as simply one historical phenomenon among others, but as a central directive force affecting all exploitive class societies from the beginnings of civilization. And they made constant use of class analysis in their examinations of historical events.

"After the July revolution," wrote Marx of the 1848 bourgeois revolution in France, "when the Liberal banker, Laffitte, led his godfather, the Duke of Orleans, in triumph to the Hotel de Ville, he let fall the words: 'From now on the bankers will rule.' Laffitte had betrayed the secret of the revolution." The opposition to the bankers—primarily representing the bourgeoisie—came not from the "people" but from definite classes with definite objectives. With the triumph of the bankers these other classes were defeated: "The petty bourgeoisie of all degrees, and the peasantry also, were completely excluded from political power." As for the industrial workers:

> In the National Assembly all France sat in judgment on the Paris proletariat. It broke immediately with the social illusions of the February Revolution; it roundly proclaimed the bourgeois republic, nothing but the bourgeois republic. It at once excluded the representatives of the proletariat, Louis Blanc and Albert, from the Executive Commission appointed by it; it threw out the proposal of a special Labor Ministry, and received with stormy applause the statement of the Minister Trelat: 'The question is merely one of bringing labor back to its old conditions.'[3]

History then, is not an undulating mix of good and evil, justice and ambition, decisive men and weak men; it has an underlying pattern formed by social classes and their struggles. It is, that is to say, primarily a sociological and not a psychological phenomenon. Although basically social, class struggles, particularly in bourgeois society, as Marx here indicates, often take political form. The center of the "political power" from which the workers, petty bourgeoisie and peasantry, were "excluded" was the National Assembly. The National Assembly, however, Marx and Engels did not regard as simply a governing body, but as part of a larger political organism—the State—which they viewed as containing in addition to parliamentary bodies, the armed forces, the Church, the educational system, and the press. "The bourgeoisie," they noted in *The Communist Manifesto,* "has at last, since the establishment of Modern Industry and of the world market, conquered for itself, in the modern representative State, exclusive political sway." In the class struggle, then, we have not simply classes confronting each other directly but the nondominant classes confronting the State, in which the dominant classes are fortressed and enshrined.

The Socioeconomic Foundation

The class struggle, however, although central to historical events is not the ultimate historical determinant:

> It was precisely Marx who had first discovered the great law of motion of history, the law according to which all historical struggles, whether they proceed in the political, religious, philosophical or some other ideological domain, are in fact only the more or less clear expression of struggles of social classes, and that the existence and thereby the collisions, too, between these classes are in turn conditioned by the degree of development of their economic position, by the mode of their production and of their exchange determined by it.[4]

In short, the class struggle is rooted in the relation of the classes to the economic processes of "production" and "exchange." Marx himself only attempted one succinct overall explanation of the general theory that Engels here notes, and in it he sought to outline not only the interconnections of economic factors and the class struggle, but of both with thought and culture. This famous passage, from the Preface to *A Contribution to a Critique of Political Economy* (1859), although it cannot be allowed to stand alone as an expression of the essence of Marxism—and distortions of Marxism have resulted from so viewing it—nevertheless does capture a good part of that essence:

> My investigation led to the result that legal relations as well as forms of state are to be grasped neither from themselves nor from the so-called general development of the human mind, but rather have their roots in the material conditions of life. . . . The general result at which I arrived

and which, once won, served as a guiding thread for my studies, can be briefly formulated as follows: In the social production of the means of life, human beings enter into definite and necessary relations which are independent of their will—production relations which correspond to a definite stage of the development of their productive forces. The totality of these production relations constitutes the economic structure of society, the real basis upon which a legal and political superstructure arises and to which definite forms of social consciousness correspond. The mode of production of the material means of life, determines, in general, the social, political and intellectual processes of life. It is not the consciousness of human beings that determines their existence, but, conversely, it is their social existence that determines their consciousness.

At a certain stage of their development, the material productive forces of society come into conflict with the existing production relationships, or, what is but a legal expression for the same thing, with the property relationships within which they have hitherto moved. From forms of development of the productive forces these relationships turn into their fetters. A period of social revolution then begins. With the change in the economic foundation, the whole gigantic superstructure is more or less rapidly transformed. In considering such transformations we must always distinguish between the material changes in the economic conditions of production, changes which can be determined with the precision of natural science, and the legal, political, religious, aesthetic, or philosophic, in short, ideological forms, in which human beings become conscious of this conflict and fight it out to an issue.

Just as little as we can judge an individual by what he thinks of himself, just so little can we appraise such a revolutionary epoch in accordance with its own consciousness of itself. On the contrary, we have to explain this consciousness as the outcome of the contradictions of material life, of the conflict existing between social productive forces and productive relationships.[5]

Although Marx intends this statement to portray historical development in general, it is apparent that he is thinking primarily of the era of the industrial revolution and the European bourgeois revolutions (1848) through which he had lived. Marx apparently felt that the convulsive events of this era provided a particularly dramatic example of historical process and he doubtless intended his contemporary readers to apply his generalizations to these events. Certainly, when they are viewed in this light, Marx's concepts become easier to grasp.

The political upheavals that racked Britain and the Continent in the first part of the nineteenth century were, Marx believed, stirred up by commercial and industrial advance, which involved a gigantic development of "productive forces" (iron production in Britain was 150,000 tons in 1800, 3.8 million in 1860) and consequently of the classes connected with them. In the first half of the century the old "production relationships" in Europe, namely the great landowning "property relations" of feudal society with its great estates run by peasant labor, did indeed act as "fetters" upon the new, capitalist "productive forces" and a "period of social revolution" led by the bourgeoisie began. A new "political and legal superstructure" (*Uberbau,* overstructure)—with parliamentary bodies, new or renewed—arose as the bourgeoisie began to seize control of the State (in 1832 in Britain, in 1848 in France and other continental nations). The political and other views associated with these events (part of "social consciousness") were formed by "social existence," especially by class conflicts. In these conflicts people were not free to do as they wished but had to act within the limits of the existing economic and social structures. True, the capitalists had built the new productive forces and "property relationships" that formed the ultimate determinant of these historical actions but they had not done so as part of an overall plan. Each capitalist had acted individually in the drive for profit and none had any concept of what the total effect would be or had basic control, individual or collective, of the resultant society. They built as ants build, albeit ants with consciousness. The economic structure thus created was then passed on, and others built on these foundations. These foundations although basically economic are also as Marx notes, social, the two inter-mingling to produce a general historical "basis":

> It is superfluous to add that men are not free to choose their productive forces—which are the basis of all their history—for every productive force is an acquired force, the product of former activity.
>
> The productive forces are therefore the result of practical human energy; but this energy is itself conditioned by the circumstances in which men find themselves, by the productive forces already won, by the social form which exists before they do, which they do not create, which is the product of the former generation.[6]

Behind the class struggle, then, lies economic process and "social form." The productive forces—whether the plows and windmills of feudalism or the factories and steel foundries of capitalism—determine the general character of the productive ("property") relationships, primarily those of landed

wealth in feudalism, manufacturing and commerce in capitalism; these property relationships broadly determine both the character of the class struggle—
peasant and lord in feudalism or worker and capitalist in capitalism—and
of the "political and legal superstructure"—feudal absolutism or parliaments
and courts of law. All, then, is not, as it appears at first, chaos but an
ascending series of interlinked processes—socioeconomic, political, cultural.

In a "period of social revolution" the socioeconomic complex churns
up society from its foundations, creating not only new institutions but new
ideas and art forms—the "intellectual processes of life"—which reflect, to
one or another degree of directness, the underlying complex, especially the
class struggle. This process was particularly clear in the late eighteenth and
early nineteenth centuries in Europe. The intellectuals, buffeted by conflicting feudal and bourgeois views, lined up more and more on the side of
change. Godwin and Hegel, as we have seen, developed evolutionary views
of history. Adam Smith and Ricardo provided a rationale for capitalist
enterprise, Mary Wollstonecraft championed the rights of bourgeois women,
theological disputes with social impact struck the Catholic, Protestant and
Jewish churches alike, Goya painted revolutionary antiwar pictures. Whereas
the leading poet in the mid-eighteenth century in England, Alexander Pope,
had as the theme of a major poem the playful cutting of a lock of an
aristocratic young lady's hair, Blake wrote about chimney sweeps. Blake
also depicted a future in which aristocrats and churchmen were swept away
in a revolutionary tide. Byron attacked dictatorial oppression and died in
the struggle against it, Wordsworth hailed the "budding rose" of the French
Revolution, Beethoven set Schiller's "Song to Liberty" to music, Hugo
depicted both the misery of the masses and the bourgeois revolutionary
spirit. Yet all these writers, artists, and musicians were but faintly aware
of the economic or social forces which Marx saw as ultimately arousing the
sociocultural ferment of which their creations were part. Even Shelley, the
most advanced social thinker of them all, when he envisioned a future
classless, egalitarian world republic—"Equal, unclassed, tribeless and na-
tionless"—did not realize that he was inspired to such visions by a variagated
class struggle sparked by the rising productive forces of the industrial revolution.[7]

Society, then, Marx is, in effect, saying is, like nature, not what it
appears to be. It appears to gross observation to move in accordance with
human response to various "ideological forms" just as it appears that the
earth is flat and the sun goes around it. But even superficial investigation
shows that these "forms" differ in different historical situations and that we

are not dealing with free-floating ideas but ideas shaped by social forces. When we delve deeper, we find that essentially we are not dealing primarily with people but with dynamic social structures; structures that people have, it is true, created but which once created become ultimate dominants. When Marx uses such terms as "productive forces" or "productive relationships," he is depicting phenomena which go beyond human consciousness and have an objective existence similar to those of nature as revealed by physics or biology. And when he speaks of a "conflict" between the productive forces and relationships he means an objective conflict, a conflict that, despite appearances, is not essentially between people but between social structures.

Social evolution takes place primarily because people have increased the productive forces—which produce food, clothing, shelter, transportation and so on—and this increase has carried the rest of the socioeconomic structure along with it. This has not, however, been a steady process, but has been marked by periods of rapid change, as these forces are at certain "epochs" blocked by the "existing productive relationships," which are then swept aside comparatively swiftly, thus instigating change throughout society. Marx is not, of course, saying that these things are not done by people, but that they are done by people within social frameworks which have, as it were, a life of their own. People can make new frameworks. They can destroy old productive relationships and build new ones—as they did in Europe in the nineteenth century—but once they build them, they must again operate within them and the "social forms" arising from them. Thus, when capitalist productive relations were established people lived within the capitalist system, and the kind of work they did and the kind of political actions they took were primarily determined by the nature of this system. So, too, were some aspects of their general living, thinking and creating. This did not mean that they could not in time destroy the system and set up a new system—just as they destroyed feudalism and set up capitalism—but it does mean that they can do this only within conditions set by the general processes of social evolution.

In considering this theory—Marx's "guiding thread"—we have to realize that he is not here dealing primarily with the specifics of history (even though he is reflecting them) but with the general forms of social evolution from the beginnings of civilization to his own day and beyond. He is, in short, tackling the basic, obvious problems of what society is, how it works, and how it moves: the problems, in short, that bourgeois historians generally ignore, as they concentrate on fragments of the general process, each isolated in a cell of "specialization." Even as we recognize this, however, we have also to recognize that specific processes within a general process are not, either in nature or society, quite the same as those of the general process. We cannot mechanically apply Marx's general views to particular aspects of society but have to perceive the relationship of the general process to the specific ones, as Marx himself did in examining contemporary events. We might make an analogy between Marx's general theory and the discovery that the tides are caused by the moon's gravity. Without this knowledge, the tides would be inexplicable; but on the other hand, the knowledge of their basic motive force does not enable us to understand particular tide phenomena—such as that in the Bay of Fundy, for instance. Each specific phenomenon must be examined individually, but without the knowledge of the general phenomenon of which it is part, specific analysis has no basis. This, of course, presents a difficult problem for Marxists but it is a problem arising not from a too elaborate system of thought but from the complexity of social reality.

As time went by, Marx's theory was attacked as "economic determinism," that is to say an exclusive emphasis on economic factors. This charge Engels answered in a letter in 1890 (seven years after Marx's death):

According to the materialist conception of history the determining element in history is ultimately the production and reproduction in real life. More than this neither Marx nor I have ever asserted. If therefore somebody twists this into the statement that the economic element is the only determining one, he transforms it into a meaningless, abstract and absurd phrase. The economic situation is the basis, but the various elements of the superstructure—political forms of the class struggle and its consequences, constitutions established by the victorious class after a successful battle, etc.—forms of law—and then even the reflexes of all these actual struggles in the brains of the combatants: political, legal, philosophical theories, religious ideas and their further development into systems of dogma—also exercise their influence upon the course of the historical struggles and in many cases preponderate in determining their form. There is an interaction of all these elements, in which, amid all the endless host of accidents (i.e., of things and events whose inner connection is so remote or so impossible to prove that we regard it as absent and can neglect it), the economic movement finally asserts itself as necessary. Otherwise the application of the theory to any period of history one chose would be easier than the solution of a simple equation of the first degree.

We make our own history, but in the first place under very definite presuppositions and conditions. Among these the economic ones are finally decisive. But the political, etc., ones, and indeed even the traditions which haunt human minds, also play a part, although not the decisive one.[8]

Although Engels is right in saying that Marx never asserted that "the economic element" is "the only one," Marx's general statement if taken alone—as it should not be—leaves itself open to that interpretation. Marx does not there note that the political superstructure and the "ideological forms" can affect the economic foundation but speaks only of the determining influence of this foundation upon them. That he was aware of the interaction is, of course, obvious and is exemplified in his political essays, such as *The Class Struggles in France* (1848–1850), where, as we saw, he discusses how political events can change an economic foundation even while they are ultimately dependent upon it. In a general statement in which he was trying to present the essence of his view he necessarily stresses the central (economic) factor and in doing so puts the matter more forcefully than if it had been qualified. Nevertheless, the statement presents only the basic aspect of an interactive process (and demonstrates the almost insuperable problems of formulating a succinct general statement).

"The Superstructure" and Stalin

Although Engels's letter forms an important appendage to Marx's statement, it is in some respects unsatisfactory. His division of society into an economic "basis" and "the superstructure" (overstructure, as in a building) is mechanistic and departs from Marx's fluid picture of conflicting forces. What Engels lumps together as "the various elements of the superstructure"—"constitutions," "forms of law," "philosophical theories," "religious ideas"—Marx saw as reflections of the class struggle. Furthermore, Engels depicts "the political forms of the class struggle" as part of "the superstructure," which means, in effect, subordinating the class struggle to "the superstructure." And once he does this, the element of active "conflict" which Marx saw as central to social development is lost in an abstract "structure." Engels doubtless did not perceive these implications of his statement and would have been shocked if he had lived to see the distortion of Marxism for which they laid a base.

Marx never uses the term "the superstructure" but always qualifies it to indicate that he is using it in a specific metaphorical sense. In his general statement, for instance, he speaks of "a legal and political superstructure,"

by which he means primarily the State, and "the whole gigantic superstructure" in which he includes both political-legal structures and "ideological
forms." In another passage he refers to "the superstructure of the modern
state edifice," and in still another he writes:

> Upon the different forms of property, upon the social conditions of exist-
> ence, rises an entire superstructure of distinct and peculiarly formed sen-
> timents, illusions, modes of thought and views of life. The entire class
> creates and forms them out of its material foundations and out of the
> corresponding social relations.

Here, the implied "real basis" is not just economic but social as well—
"property" and "social relations." Marx, then, evidently felt free to use both
"basis" and "superstructure" in a variety of ways to denote the general
dependence of one social phenomenon upon another or others, of social life
upon economic life, of political life upon socioeconomic life, of ideas upon
interactive economic, political, and social processes. In addition, when discussing the general aspects of his theory he ordinarily used neither "basis"
nor "superstructure," nor does Engels. Clearly Marx did not regard either
of them as scientific terms such as "value" or "surplus value," both of which
he uses consistently and exclusively in describing the phenomena they represent.[9]

In time Engels's letter was published and became known in Marxist
circles as an important supplement to Marx's statement. It was taken up
by the Russian Marxist G.V. Plekhanov, who in 1908 turned "the superstructure" into a kind of schematic category in five parts; and then by Nikolai
Bukharin, who used it to include almost everything: "We shall interpret
the word 'superstructure' as meaning any type of social phenomenon erected
on the economic base . . . including social psychology . . . as well as such
phenomena as language and thought." Marx's concept was next (1950) taken
up by Stalin who attempted to simplify it and in doing so distorted it:

> The base is the economic structure of society at a given stage of its de-
> velopment. . . . Every base has its own superstructure corresponding to
> it. The base of the feudal system has its superstructure—its political, legal,
> and other views and the corresponding institutions; the capitalist base has
> its own superstructure, and so has the socialist base. If the base changes
> or is eliminated, then following this its superstructure changes or is elim-
> inated; if a new base arises, then following this a superstructure arises
> corresponding to it.

Marx's picture reflects the interactive reality, Stalin's is dogmatic and mechanical. In a revolutionary epoch as the legal, political, religious, and educational institutions of society change, ideas swirl back and forth with the ups and downs of the class struggle, those of the new order little by little asserting themselves, but continuing in part into the new order. The concept of a monolithic weld of institutions and ideas rising and disintegrating in accordance with changes in an economic base is refuted by history. Unfortunately this simplistic "base-superstructure" mechanism of Stalin's— it is not to be found in Lenin—is still widely accepted in Marxist circles both in capitalist and socialist countries, usually without reference to Stalin, and it is assumed to reflect Marx's view. Thus Marx has been saddled with a theory which is not only manifestly false but is actually reactionary for it obscures the role of the class struggle.

In addition to the class struggle ideas in general have been devoured by Stalin's omnipresent "the superstructure." The falseness of this concept was demonstrated soon after Stalin's statement was published when a kind of "angels on the head of a pin" debate began in Marxist circles on whether science and the arts, including literature, "are part of the superstructure." In Marx's statement ideas in general are part of "social consciousness," which is the reflection of "social existence," and certain specific areas of ideas— "legal, political, religious" and so on—reflect a specific segment of "social existence," namely the class struggle. Science and the arts express the interaction of social existence and social consciousness, which in class societies are affected by class forces. The problem is contrived, not actual: the construction of a nonexistent entity and consequently nonexistent relationship.

What then, is to be done? The answer obviously is to return to Marx (and Lenin). The phrase "the superstructure" should never be used alone but only, as Marx used it, in qualified context to indicate specific relationships, and it should be made clear that Marx's general term "real basis" can be used to indicate economic, social, or socioeconomic phenomena. This does not, of course, mean that there are not basic and dependent phenomena but only interactions whose relationship to each other cannot be determined. This view, tendencies of which seem to be appearing, is a leap from dogmatism to anarchy.[10]

Critics of Marx

Since Engels' defense, various new objections have been raised to Marx's general theory, some by contemporary Marxists. For instance, two "radical historians," Michael Merrill and Michael Wallace, writing in 1982, in a compilation of Marxist essays, argue that "the older Marxist emphasis on the primacy of the economic" has been displaced by a primary emphasis on the political:

> The Bolshevik revolution seemed to prove that an economic transformation could be the effect of political power, and where Marx and Engels had insisted on the determining role of economic institutions in the process of social development, after 1917 'the primacy of politics' became the watchword.

The comment provides a good example of the needless spreading of confusion to be found in some Marxist circles—often under a cloak of sophistication— a confusion arising here from indiscriminately equating objective historical processes with political action.

The November 1917 revolution, although changing society more profoundly than did the bourgeois revolutions did not differ from them in kind.

Marx, as we saw, noted that political change in France in 1848 produced economic change as the bourgeoisie took power from the great landowners. But he was aware that this political revolution could not have taken place if it had not been for previous change in the economic foundation; change without which the bourgeoisie would not have come into being. And the Russian revolution also had its base in economic change, specifically a rapid rise of industry beginning about 1890. Without this there would have been no proletariat to exercise its "dictatorship." Both Marx and Lenin perceive an interweaving of economic and political forces, both of which are necessary for social change, but one of which—the economic—is basic and the other derivative. The Bolshevik revolution did not reverse this general process although it gave people a greater degree of control over economic forces than they had ever had before. People still, however, have to act within the general framework of the new—socialist—productive forces and relationships. These basically determine their manner of work and their social and cultural life.

A number of questions have been raised by some Marxists in recent years on a related subject, namely Marx's theory of the State, for instance, by Hal Draper, who in his two-volume *Karl Marx's Theory of Revolution* produces a theory of the "autonomized" State, a State which is "no longer the resultant of the actual class forces in society but rather stands in antagonism to all social classes." This has happened because "the political superstructure has torn loose from the social foundations."

Neither Marx nor Engels, as we have noted, saw the bourgeois State as a direct tool of the capitalist class. As Marx's comments on the French situation alone suffice to show he regarded political bodies as subject to a variety of class pressures and thus necessarily having a certain degree of autonomy, but he saw them also as ultimately responsive to the will of the class or classes that owned the means of production. Draper fails to consider this deeper dialectical interplay of class and economic forces but sees "superstructure" and bureaucracy as the basic factors at work, thus, like Stalin, in effect elevating them above class. His argument that a superstructure or culture or any other entity dependent on the socioeconomic "basis" of society could be "torn loose" and take off on its own has clearly nothing to do with Marxism. That the State is the instrument of class rule has been further revealed in the present century. The monopoly capitalist State has clearly expressed—in two world wars, for instance—the economic and other interests of monopoly capitalism. It is now apparent even to liberal observers that this was also true of the State in Nazi Germany, which seemed to them at the time to have become autonomous. As we shall note later, the ways in which the will of the monopoly bourgeoisie is expressed in the State and other aspects of rule are complex but complexity does not denote ineffectuality. Draper's theory is in its essence an extension of the old reformist-socialist view that the State runs the capitalists and not the capitalists the State.

Another objection to Marxist theory, particularly to Marx's 1859 statement, is typified by Stanley Aronowitz in his *The Crisis in Historical Materialism* (1981). "Marx's scheme," Aronowitz writes, ". . . operates at a level of abstraction so broad as to render its analytic value doubtful when faced with concrete historical developments." Marx, however, as we have noted, was not in the passage concocting an abstract "scheme" to be applied mechanically to specific situations but was describing the general process of social evolution. Nor can the passage be considered alone or as a sacred text but must be examined in the light of Marx's work as a whole. Marx himself did not try to fit events into a general process but examined them in terms of their specific processes, sometimes alluding to connections with the general process, sometimes not, as in his analyses of European nineteenth history or the U.S. Civil War. Specific events obviously must be examined individually. Yet without the knowledge of the general phenomenon involved, these events could not be properly understood and would appear fragmented. Marx, as we saw, analyzed French events in terms of the classes involved but he was aware of the roots of these classes in the productive forces and relations of emerging French capitalism and this knowledge gave his political analysis a coherence and depth it would not otherwise have had.[11]

These and similar views result from a simple failure to distinguish levels of development in interactive process. On the other hand some aspects of Marx's general statement are genuinely open to Marxist criticism.

"Just as little as we judge an individual by what he thinks of himself, just so little can we appraise such a revolutionary epoch in accordance with its own consciousness of itself." However, Marx and Engels could certainly "appraise" the bourgeois revolutionary epoch; and so, too, though to a lesser degree, could the Chartist and other working class radicals. Yet all of them were certainly part of the age's "consciousness of itself." Marx is clearly thinking primarily, indeed almost exclusively, of the "ruling" ideas of the age, not of the total class-divided social and cultural complex. There is actually no such thing as a single "consciousness of itself" in class-divided society. Before the rise of the proletariat, there was, it is true, no possibility of any real understanding of any age or of history in general.

Although the working masses of precapitalist society—slaves, peasants, artisans—often arose in revolutionary struggle and were aware of their oppression by upper classes they had little understanding of the nature of social forces. Nor, in spite of their apparent sophistication, did the ruling classes. Aristotle and Confucius, Caesar and Napoleon alike attributed movement in history—as do bourgeois historians today—ultimately to psychological causes ("greed," "ambition," "honor") because that is the way things appear to gross observation. No one before Marx and Engels knew what society really was, how it had evolved, or where it was going.

The dependence of the productive relations—the "economic structure"—on the productive forces is a more reciprocal relationship than Marx indicates: "production relations which correspond to a definite stage of their productive forces." This is true but it omits the fact that the productive forces are also the creation of the productive relations. The steel mill with its Bessemer furnaces came into being because of capitalist productive relations. It could not have emerged from feudal productive relations. The forces and the relations form an interpenetrative whole in which each has its identity, yet is dependent on the other for that identity. It is, however, true that once new productive forces arise out of this complex, it is they and not the structure that determine the general historical evolution. As in process in general, in nature as well as in society, both factors are necessary but one is basic and the other derivative. As we have noted, both basic and derivative forces have to be taken into account in any specific analysis, with the emphasis in such an analysis often necessarily on the derivative ones.

A similar objection can be raised to the statement "it is not the consciousness of human beings that determines their existence, but, conversely, their social existence that determines their consciousness." Once more, Marx, although pointing to the basic process at work fails to emphasize dialectical interaction. By consciousness he does not, as the context shows, mean consciousness as such but ideas in general. He is repeating, in summary form, his contention that these ideas are formed by and reflect society. However, as the 1848 revolution—not to mention the socialist revolutions of the present century—suffices to show, ideas affect social structures in decisive ways even though "social existence" is the basic factor. Consciousness, although derivative, is a dynamic force; and history is a process in which both basic and derivitive forces are necessary and act in unison.

In considering this overemphasis upon primary factors we have not only to recognize the problems inherent in a summary statement but to remember that Marxism was at the time (1859) an obscure theory surrounded by an ocean of bourgeois obfuscation. Interconnection as such was recognized by many Victorian social thinkers, both between economic and political factors and between consciousness and social existence, but they were presented as chaotic and incapable of solution. Marx had to challenge this debilitating scepticism if the workers were going to understand the world and "change" it. Hence, he seized upon what he believed to be the essential truth and drove it home with dramatic impact. If Marx were alive today, he would doubtless recognize the dialectical deficiencies in his general statement but doubtless also he would reply, as he and Engels did in 1872 regarding deficiencies in *The Communist Manifesto:* "But then, the *Manifesto* has become a historical document which we have no longer any right to alter." Moreover, his statement is still true in its essence.[12]

Production and Reproduction

In attempting to get a complete view of Marxist general theory, one more germinal passage must be considered: one by Engels in his Preface to the first edition (1884) of *The Origin of the Family, Private Property and the State:*

According to the materialistic conception, the determining factor in history is, in the final instance, the production and reproduction of the immediate essentials of life. This, again, is of a twofold character. On the one side, the production of the means of existence, of articles of food and clothing, dwelling, and of the tools necessary for that production; on the other side, the production of human beings themselves, the propagation of the species. The social organization under which the people of a particular historical epoch and a particular country live is determined by both kinds of production: by the stage of development of labor on the one hand and of the family on the other.[13]

As Engels was writing of the family he was particularly interested in establishing the role in society of the second aspect of its "twofold character," namely sexual reproduction. Marx was, of course, as aware as was Engels of the effects of sexual reproduction on "social organization" but it was not relevant to his statement, which was centered on historical development and not on society as such. Although sexual reproduction supplies the biological foundation without which there would be not only no history but no human society, it does not directly affect historical development. It does, however, affect society as such directly and in many ways. As Engels notes, it creates family life, and it also creates the relationships between the sexes in general, social, biological, and psychological. This is a vast area of society, an area moreover independent in its essence from economic factors, for although economic factors have both direct and indirect influence on this general social area the area itself has its own identity. It arose, as we shall see, in prehuman societies before there were human economic structures, and since their development it has existed side by side with them. Family life, for instance, has an essential and unique character of its own—from hunter-gathering societies on—which has been modified in various ways but not changed in its essence by economic factors. Thus, while Marx is clearly right in seeing economic and socioeconomic factors as basic to political and legal structures and to a certain area of ideas, these are not the only formative factors involved in society. A large area of social life rooted in sexual reproduction basically affects social structures and culture. A vast area of ideas—and the arts—revolve around family and related functions: courting, giving birth, child care, mainly or exclusively male and female social groupings (clubs, etc.), and so on. These are all part of "social consciousness" but they are not essentially political, religious, or aesthetic "idealogical forms" although the two areas overlap. And this social area includes other biologically based social factors, particularly those of death and the ceremonies and grieving arising from it. This aspect of social life also, although subject in various ways to economically determined change has a continuing individual character. It was perhaps a general awareness of all this that made Marx and Engels sometimes speak of an economic basis and sometimes of an economic and social basis. At any rate, Engels's definition of the "twofold character" of society has more implications than he seems to have realized.

On the other hand, Engels's comments can be misinterpreted, in part because of his faulty formulation: "the determining factor in history." Sexual reproduction is certainly not, as we have noted, a determining factor in history although it determines much of the nature of society. The importance of keeping this distinction clear is apparent from the mechanical equating by Wilhelm Reich and others of sexual and economic factors as historical determinants, a tendency which is expressed also in the confused equating of Freud and Marx by Herbert Marcuse and his followers.[14]

Although Engels perceived the social implications of sexual reproduction in early communal society, he did not fully see their general significance in society as a whole, particularly in civilized societies. Communal societies, he continues, were dominated by "the family system." But with the change to civilized society brought about by economic development the "old society built on groups based on ties of sex, bursts asunder" and "in its place a new society appears, constituted in a state." The development of the State we shall note in the next chapter but it is clear even to gross observation that the State did not burst asunder "the old society" but only changed certain of its aspects, particularly political ones. What we have actually are two basic aspects to society, the social aspect, which is ultimately biologically based and has its own identity, and the economic. Historical development is determined basically by the economic, which also affects the social area but does not determine its essential nature; and economic and social blend in shaping cultural life.[15]

3

Patterns of the Past

Engels, in his speech at Marx's grave, stressed two aspects of Marx, the "revolutionist" and the "man of science." "Marx," he commented, "was before all else a revolutionist. His real mission in life was to contribute, in one way or another, to the overthrow of capitalist society." Yet at the same time: "Just as Darwin discovered the law of development of organic nature, so Marx discovered the law of development of human history." Furthermore: "Marx also discovered the special law of motion governing the present-day capitalist mode of production and the bourgeois society that this mode of production has created."

Engels, then, believed Marxism included both a general social science that explained historical evolution and a specific economic science that explained capitalism. The two aspects of Marx, scientist and revolutionary, he regarded not as antithetical but as complementary. Marx arrived at his conclusions not separately from his social activism—in the pre-1848 revolutionary upheavals, in 1848, in the International—but as part of it. His laboratory was society itself.

Although Engels, here and elsewhere, attributes the main theoretical concepts of Marxism to Marx, he did note that he himself "had an independent share in laying the foundation, and more particularly in elaborating the theory." And he added: "What I contributed—at any rate with the exception of a few special studies—Marx could very well have done without me." The reference presumably is, as we have noted, mainly to Engels's work on dialectical materialism and his studies on the origins and early development of society.

The Evolution of Farming Societies

Towards the end of his general statement (1859) Marx commented briefly on the past stages of society:

A social system never perishes before all the productive forces have developed for which it is wide enough; and new, higher productive relationships never come into being before the material conditions for their existence have been brought to maturity within the womb of the old society itself. Therefore, mankind always sets itself only such problems as it can solve; for when we look closer we will always find that the problem itself only arises when the material conditions for its solution are already present or at least in process of coming into being. In broad outline, the Asiatic, the ancient, the feudal and the modern bourgeois modes of production can be indicated as progressive epochs in the economic system of society. Bourgeois productive relationships are the last antagonistic form of the social process of production.

Presumably, then, "the Asiatic, the ancient" (the slave empires of Athens and Rome) and "the [European] feudal" were all "epochs" in which the underlying economic forces determined the nature of institutions and (ultimately) of ideas, epochs, each of which represented a higher form than the one before it, and in all of which the movement of society was basically determined by the "conflict" between the productive relations and the productive forces.[1]

"Asiatic" society Marx and Engels regarded as having remained virtually unchanged from its beginning, still existing, for example, in nineteenth-century India as it had for thousands of years. But, as Engels indicates, he and Marx presumed in Europe first a transition from slave to feudal society and then from feudal to capitalist:

Slavery is the first form of exploitation, the form peculiar to the ancient world; it is succeeded by serfdom in the middle ages, and wagelabor in the more recent period. These are the three great forms of servitude, characteristic of the three epochs of civilization: open, and in recent times disguised, slavery always accompanies them.[2]

When Marx wrote his general statement (published in 1859) little was known, as we have seen, of "the prehistory of society." As anthropological and other evidence began to accumulate, Marx and Engels felt that a special study was needed, and in 1884—the year after Marx's death—Engels published *The Origin of the Family, Private Property and the State.* Following one of the most advanced anthropology texts of the time, Lewis Henry Morgan's *Ancient Society* (1877), Engels divided the past of humanity into three stages: "savagery" (hunter-gathering), "barbarism" (farming society) and "civilization."[3] Marx's Asiatic, slave, feudal and capitalist societies are all divisions of Engels's third stage, civilization. In discussing hunter-gathering (hunting, fishing, plant collecting) and early farming societies (the terms "savagery" and "barbarism" should be dropped as inexact and pejorative), Engels, again following Morgan, divides them both into three periods, lower, middle, and upper. In the first stage of food-gathering society, Engels believed, Man was still "partially at least a tree-dweller" and language was just developing. The second stage began "with the utilization of fish for food," and in it people "by following the rivers and coasts, spread over most of the earth." In this stage the "gens" or clan (a group of family units) formed the basic community. The upper stage began "with the invention of the bow and arrow" and the consequent big game hunting; "wooden vessels and utensils" existed beside stone tools; there were dugout canoes and plaited baskets.[4]

A great deal of research on these matters has, of course, been done since Morgan, and many of his conclusions have gone by the board. For instance, Engels' first stage of "savagery" belongs to biological rather than social evolution and is a confused mixture of simian and prehuman societies—even pre-humans did not live in trees—separated by several million years from the first human society; and there was no special fish-eating stage, although fishing may have played a bigger part in hunter-gathering society than is realized. Similar errors, arising from a lack of research data at the time, occur throughout both Morgan and Engels and are repeated in some Marxist works today. Nevertheless, the general approach of Engels—which is only fragmentarily present in Morgan—with his emphasis upon underlying socioeconomic factors, gives the essence of the materialist evolutionary view of precivilized societies.

In the first stage of farming society, Morgan and Engels believed, came the invention of pottery, along with plant cultivation and animal domestication. The second stage differed somewhat in the Eastern and Western hemispheres, for in the Americas there were few potential farming animals (no pigs, sheep, cattle or horses) and of the major grains only corn. There was no wheat or rice (although there were potatoes and yams). Because of these deficiencies, in the Americas "this stage was never superseded before the European conquest." The stage—in both hemispheres—was marked by the joining of a number of "gens" (groups of families) to form a tribe, by the invention of the loom and the smelting of copper. "Pastoral tribes separated themselves from the mass of barbarians," namely agriculturalists—*"the first great social division of labor"*—and this resulted in increased production. This in turn led to wars between tribes, and war resulted in the taking of slaves. Engels also believed—following Johann Jacob Bachofen's *Mother Right* (1861)—that in food-gathering society "mother right" was dominant over "father right" and women were the tribal rulers. This high position of women continued into early farming society but when animal herds became the main economic activity the position of women declined, for while plant cultivation was mostly woman's work, animal tending was mostly man's: "The 'savage' warrior and hunter had been content to take second place in the house, after the woman; the 'gentler' shepherd, in the arrogance of his wealth, pushed himself forward into the first place and the woman down into the second."[5]

In his picture of the middle stage of farming society Engels seems to be thinking primarily of Asia. For the final stage his main model is Homeric society. In this stage *"the second great division of labor* took place: handicraft separated from agriculture." Iron smelting took the place of copper, producing the iron sword and the iron plowshare. As a result came still greater economic increase and, with it, a demand for more labor:

> Slavery, which during the preceding period was still in its beginnings and sporadic, now becomes an essential constituent part of the social system; slaves no longer merely help with production—they are driven by dozens to work in the fields and the workshops.

Private property began to dominate:

> The inequalities of property among the individual heads of families break up the old communal household communities wherever they had still managed to survive, and with them the common cultivation of the soil by and for these communities. The cultivated land is allotted for use to single families, at first temporarily, later permanently. The transition to full private property is gradually accomplished, parallel with the transition of the pairing marraige into monogamy. The single family is becoming the economic unit of society.

The "greed for riches" splits "the members of the gens into rich and poor." Consequently there arises "a new cleavage of society into classes" and this has profound political as well as economic consequences. The "organs" of government "change from instruments of will of the people" into organs "for the domination and oppression of the people." These organs—military, governmental, religious, legal—form the State. Thus the political and other instruments for the directing of society change from being primarily administrative to being primarily repressive.

Although the essence of the State is repression and necessarily involves force, it also involves disguising its nature:

> [The State] is the product of society at a particular stage of development: it is the admission that this society has involved itself in insoluble self-contradiction and is cleft into irreconcilable antagonisms which it is powerless to exorcise. But in order that these antagonisms, classes with conflicting economic interests, shall not consume themselves and society in fruitless struggle, a power, apparently standing above society, has become necessary to moderate the conflict and keep it within the bounds of 'order'; and this power, arisen out of society, but placing itself above it and increasingly alienating itself from it, is the state.[6]

In Engels's day little was known of early hunter-gathering societies and many of them have been shown to be on a higher level than was then believed. Some of these societies, for instance those which remained into modern times in Tasmania and Tierra del Fuego, were indeed "primitive," with people living in rude shelters, but some of them of 30,000 and more years ago were quite wealthy—as European excavation has shown—with extensive trade routes and group hunting of large animals. Moreover, there was not the rigid division that Morgan seems to assume between these societies and early farming ones. Modern investigations have shown that in some hunter-gathering societies there was cultivation of crops or rearing of animals or both, although neither provided the main means of sustenance. There were not three distinct stages of farming society (as Morgan had argued) but only an earlier and a later stage. The earlier stage of farming society proper apparently began—as Engels did not know as these dates have only recently been established (by radio-carbon dating)—about 10,500 years ago in West Asia, and possibly at about the same time in Southeast Asia, although here the evidence is sketchy. By 7,000 B.C. there was a farming town of perhaps several thousand inhabitants at Jericho with a stone wall around it, which indicates both extensive trade and warfare. The indication is also that there were other towns and villages in the area, and interlocking farming and commercial economies. By 4,000 B.C. there were towns with large temples in Mesopotamia. Although early farming society sites indicate no great wealth or unequal division of what there was, by 4,000 B.C. there were large estates and squalid village quarters. Valuable goblets have been found in the more opulent graves. The anthropological evidence from similar societies existing into modern times supports this indication of the existence of classes and of a community run by a "council of nobles," that is to say, major landowners.[7]

In America, although the lack of farm animals perhaps held down the rate of development, some communities were on higher farming levels, and the Aztecs, Incas, Mayans, and others advanced to a feudal form of civilization—of which Engels was unaware. There is no evidence, in America, Asia, or elsewhere, of an early major "division of labor" between agricultural and pastoral peoples such as Engels describes, with pastoral people on a higher economic level—a misconception which also has continued in modern Marxist writing. Nor is there any evidence of a matriarchial society, in which women were dominant. The position of women in food-gathering communities was not particularly high, if we are to judge by such societies continuing into civilized times. In these societies the general affairs of the community are run by a council of male elders.

Women apparently did make some social gains in the early stages of farming society for they did much of the agricultural work. They were deprived of their gains not by herd-raising—most farming societies seem to have been agricultural—but apparently by the rise of the male professional potter and weaver; and also by the coming of war as the struggle for farming land (indicated by the Jericho remains) began, for war is almost entirely a male operation and raises the economic and political status of men. Part of what Engels considers the last stage of farming society was in fact a mixture of later-stage farming society with developing (feudal) civilization, such as existed in Mesopotamia from 4,000 to 3,000 B.C. The Aegean society depicted by Homer, which Engels takes as his example of the final stage of farming society was, in fact, primarily commercial (about 800 B.C.), with bustling port cities, extensive manufacture and sea trade, and a full-fledged State. The separation of handicrafts from agriculture in the area had taken place many centuries before.

Engels's concepts of two "great divisions of labor" with special socio-evolutionary significance is clearly false. The first—the separation of "pastoral" from agricultural communities—was never a "stage" of human development and may never in fact, have occurred, and the second—the separation of crafts from farming—although important, was not itself a stage but simply part of the development of farming society from its early to its later form.

No doubt some families obtained more private property than others in early farming societies but the evidence indicates that the first major change came through the acquisition of land by military, governmental, and religious rulers as institutional property. The community, to judge by Caesar's observations on the early farming society Germanic tribes and by other evidence, struggled against inequalities in property, and, according to Tacitus' later observations of the Germans, tried to hold its rulers in check:

> Then such hearing is given to the king or chief as age, rank, military distinction or eloquence can secure; but it is rather their prestige as counsellors than their authority that tells. If a proposal displeases them, the people roar out their dissent, if they approve, they clash their spears.

But in time the chiefs and kings and priests won special concessions. As George Thomson has noted of early Greek society:

> In early Greece this principle [of economic equality] had already been limited by the custom of reserving portions of land for the special benefit of priests, chiefs, and kings. In the plantation of Lesbos a tithe of the holdings was "set aside" for the gods. The settlers at Brea were granted the whole of the land with the exception of certain estates "set aside" for the priesthood. Similar estates were "set aside" at Kyrene for the king.

As farming society developed towards civilization, this institutional property of the government, the army and the church—apparently mostly seized in war—grew to large proportions, and inequalities in private property also arose. In observing such developments, we have to realize that we are dealing with general socioevolutionary phenomena that take place wherever the same basic conditions exist. For instance, G.C. Vaillant in his pioneering study of Aztec society writes:

> The tribal council divided the land among the clans, and the leaders of each, in turn, apportioned its share among the heads of families justly and equitably. Sections were also reserved for the maintenance of the chief and the temple staff, for war supplies and the payment of tribute; these were worked communally, with some amount, no doubt, of slave labor.

The motive force behind these changes was not primarily "greed"—as Engels, rather strangely, implies—but objective economic developments in a society becoming increasingly wealthy and splitting into classes.[8]

In food-gathering and early farming societies the basic labor was that of the members of the community, and although in the wealthier communities there were also some slaves (captured in warfare), slave labor—as observed in later such societies and as Engels indicates—was a minor factor.

In considering stages of social development and transitions from one form of society to another, we have to remember that they did not occur everywhere at the same time. In fact, sometimes some of them did not occur at all. In Australia, Tierra del Fuego, and other "fringe" areas society remained in a hunter-gathering stage; in North America and Samoa it remained at an early farming stage—basically the same kind of society that Tacitus had observed among the Germans. In the Canary Islands or New Zealand, it remained in a later farming stage—with a developing State run by "nobles." Nevertheless, in spite of this unevenness there were stages and there were transitions. There was, in short, as Engels contended, social evolution. Moreover, as modern discoveries have shown, Engels was right in his argument that early human societies had neither classes nor a State, and hence neither class exploitation nor oppression.

Feudalism in Asia

Engels, as the title of his book indicates, was particularly interested in the State—which with the development of civilization assumed new historical significance:

> As the state arose from the need to keep class antagonisms in check, but also arose in the thick of the fight between the classes, it is normally the state of the most powerful, economically ruling class, which by its means becomes also the politically ruling class, and so acquires new means of holding down and exploiting the oppressed class. The ancient state was, above all, the state of the slave-owners for holding down the slaves, just as the feudal state was the organ of the nobility for holding down the peasant serfs and bondsmen, and the modern representative state is the instrument for exploiting wage-labor by capital.[9]

Once the ruling class was organized in the State, the mass class struggle, as we have noted, became one of the working-mass against the State as well as against the exploiting classes as classes. With the full development of a class society—first, Engels, wrongly believed, in slave society—the State became increasingly an instrument of repression. It was the State that crucified the 6,000 defeated followers of Spartacus along the Appian Way— where the Roman elite in their chariots could watch their final agonies— and massacred 30,000 workers after the Paris Commune. It was the State that lent legal sanctity to Athenian slavery. State armed forces guarded and goaded the shackled slaves in the Roman mines. It was the State that declared war and waged war. ("The hand that signed the paper felled a city.") The State was prison and torture. It was also "the first ideological power over man," the purveyer of stultifying superstition and divisive prejudice; class, racial, and sexual. It was the State that had kept the ruling classes of the world saddled on the backs of the working mass. In effect these classes put aside part of their wealth into a kind of insurance fund against revolution. Such was the reality of the State. And that reality became apparent in the beginning—as an ancient Egyptian document testifies:

> And now the scribe lands on the river bank and is about to register the harvest tax. The janitors carry staves and the Nubians (policemen) rods of palm, and they say, "Hand over the corn," though there is none. The cultivator is beaten all over, he is bound and thrown into the well, soused, and dipped head downwards. His wife has been bound in his presence, his children are in fetters. His neighbors abandon him and are fled.[10]

Engels, however, was wrong in his projected sequence of slave, feudal, and capitalist State forms, just as he and Marx were in seeing this as a general historical sequence. The truth is that what developed from later-type farming society—on all continents—was not a slave but a feudal society; a basically slave-labor society was an aberration confined to the Mediterranean area. In fact, the whole panorama of the origin and early development of civilization was unknown in the nineteenth century. We are now able to perceive what was hidden from Marx and Engels: namely the actual patterns of the rise and spread of civilization, first in Asia, then in Europe.

Civilized societies first grew out of later-farming societies in about 3,000 B.C. in the Upper West Asia, North Africa and Eastern Mediterranean areas with their main centers in Mesopotamia (Sumer) and Egypt. Both centers were of the same general type, namely societies in which irrigated agriculture operated by peasant labor and owned by a few great landowners— more jointly than individually—provided the socioeconomic base. This society was, therefore, in essence feudal for the basis of feudal society is the exploitation of a peasant mass by a great landowning ruling class. Whether this land is owned in the main jointly by these great landowners through their State or individually is of secondary significance. To support the great landowners—in government, army or church—the peasants were taxed a quarter or more of their crops and also worked without pay at forced labor for several months each year on palaces, churches, tombs (pyramids), irrigation systems, and so on. Slave labor was employed in transportation (by ship or wagon) and in industry (mining, quarrying, lumbering), which was owned by the great landowners. There were also small workshops employing some slave labor and a great mass of domestic slaves, who were mostly women. Merchants were heavily taxed. Trade, generally controlled by the State, was extensive. Sumer, for instance, traded with the Mediterranean area and India, a vast and complex operation: "Sumerian merchants travelled from the Indus Valley to Syria exchanging grain, dates, carpets, textiles, weapons, and jewelry for raw materials lacking in Sumer—copper, lead, wood, and so on . . . . Trading houses, with branch offices and foreign connections arose."[11]

In spite of conflicts between great landowners and merchants—based on rival economic interests and resulting in revolts in some Sumerian cities—there was also obviously an area of overlapping interests. The goods that the merchant traded came largely from the great landowner's farms, mines, forests or quarries; and some, often most, trade was done directly by the great landowner, either individually or through the State (the political corporation of great landowners). In thinking of feudalism, whether in Asia, Europe, or elsewhere, we have to avoid the bourgeois historian's image of placid land cultivation as the feudal essence. Feudalism was an actively exploitive, mass-oppressive, and violently expansionist society with mixed agricultural and mercantile drives. Among the earliest of the Egyptian records are those of war, depicting the wholesale slaughter of war prisoners. One of the first wars was fought over copper mines (in the Sinai). The fact that everywhere it evolved very slowly should not blind us to the fact that feudalism was always the scene of clashing interests, internal and international, struggles between landowner and landowner, landowner and merchant, landowner and peasant, slave and slaveowner.

The classes that the productive relationships of feudalism created were great landowners, peasants, slaves, and a small middle class of merchants, craftsmen-manufacturers, and lower echelon professionals. As agriculture was by far the most extensive section of the economy (to judge from later such societies at least 90 percent) peasants—serfs, who owned no land—

constituted the great mass of the labor force. The slaves, although doubtless large in total numbers, formed but a small fraction of the whole.

The State was the State of the great landowners, with some modification in some Sumerian cities where the merchants were particularly strong. The landowners' police beat the peasants if they failed to provide their crops in taxation; the landowners constituted the officer caste in the army and the priestly hierarchy in the Church; the peasants were the foot soldiers; the legal system decreed flogging and mutilation for the lower class and fines for the upper class. The upper class males were educated; women, peasants, and slaves were not. The great mass of women began to bear the triple burden of economic exploitation, State oppression and male dominance. Yet for the first time in history a small group of women, those of the upper classes, was elevated above the mass of men.

In the succeeding centuries, societies basically the same as those in Egypt and Mesopotamia grew up throughout Asia. When we perceive this basic similarity, the center of the historical picture in these centuries begins to emerge. We are not, as Toynbee and other historians including some Marxists imply, dealing with a multitude of diverse "civilizations" but one basic social form, namely that of feudalism. The parallels, not only between these societies and the earlier ones, but between each of them are extraordinary. For instance, in India there arose in about 2,300 B.C. a state in the Indus valley, much larger than either Sumer or Egypt, with two great cities, Mohenjo-Daro and Harappa. As no written records exist we can only rely on the archaeological evidence, and this—revealing great palaces in one part of the cities and small, cramped dwellings in the rest—indicate the same kind of state as the Egyptian. When this state was overthrown in about 1,700 B.C. by "Aryan" invaders the same kind of society continued. The first written account, by a Greek visitor, Megasthenes, in about 300 B.C., could have been written in Egypt 2,700 years before. The land was nominally owned by the king but actually owned by a group of great landowners of whom the king was one. Most of the land was owned jointly, but the landowners also had private estates, sometimes running to a thousand acres. The Church was powerful and owned much land. All the land was worked by peasant labor and the peasant had to give up between a third and a quarter of his produce as state tax. He was also taxed for his cattle and for the use of water. He had to work at forced labor several months a year on the irrigation system and other public works. The great landowners also owned the mines, quarries, and forests and their products, including ships, which the merchants could rent but not own. One-tenth of the merchants' sales was taken in taxes. In addition there were road taxes and taxes at city gates. Slave labor was employed in industry and transportation as well as in household work.

The State was a great landowners' State. A hierarchy of superintendents—of forest products, shipping, irrigation, graneries, workshops—was under the control of a top governmental council of great landowners (including a Superintendent of Prostitution). The king was, as in Egypt, represented as divine. Each village had a "head man" whose main job was to collect the taxes and who was responsible to the provincial governor. In the army the officers (landowners) had armor and metal weapons, the soldiers (peasants) had no armor and fought on foot with spears. The upper classes were fined, the lower executed, tortured or imprisoned. The whole nation, Megasthenes found, was "riddled with secret agents" and spies.

About 1500 B.C. there arose in the area of what is now Turkey the kingdom of the Hittites. The king had private estates of "vast extent"; so too did other landowners, and their estates could be willed. The "majority" of the people were "peasants working on the land." The mines were owned by the State. There were merchants and craftsmen.

Of another early civilized society, that of Persia (Iran) we have a fairly full description of about 500 B.C. There was a king, and "great lords" who had large estates. The main labor was peasant and the peasant had to turn over between a third and a sixth of his yield. He had to work at forced labor on roads, canals, bridges, and fortification. The great landowners were themselves exempt from taxation but the merchants were taxed by the State. A thousand years later the picture has not changed significantly. The "greater part" of the land was "divided between State lands and great estates." The peasants, who "formed the great mass of the population," were sold along with the land.[12]

At about the same time as the Hittite kingdom was arising (1,500 B.C.) a feudal society was developing in China, first, apparently, in the area of the Yellow River, with a central city called Shang.

> In theory all land belonged to the king, who gave it to his vassals in return for service. They gave lands to still lesser vassals, who might parcel it out still further. The king had the right to take back any land from any of his vassals and give it to another . . . but just as in medieval Europe, the powerful vassals soon ceased to look upon their title to lands as provisional.

The great working mass were peasants who had to deliver part of their produce to the landlord and were subject to forced labor and unpaid army service. Although there were apparently many women household slaves, male slaves have been estimated as comprising only one percent of the population. Although the merchants were subjected to "taxes and tariffs," some of them "became very rich," and after 300 B.C., when the sale of land was legalized, were able to invest in land. The king or emperor was represented as divine (as in Egypt) holding his authority by the Decree of Heaven, but in actuality he was simply another great landowner. The legal system was class-divided. The poor were beaten, tortured, mutilated or executed; the rich paid fines.[13]

In Japan the situation was similar. The land, although nominally the king's, had early passed into the hands of great estate owners. The peasants had to give over part of their produce and were subject to forced labor. The produce tax often had to be collected by force. The king was a kind of chairman of the board of the great landowners.

Thus we have from North Africa through the vast tracts of West Asia and East Asia essentially the same form of civilized society arising at various times over a period of some 2,000 years. The only major socioeconomic difference between all these societies was the degree to which the land was owned jointly by the great landowners or privately in estates. In Egypt and India, for instance, the bulk of the land was jointly owned (State controlled), whereas in China and Japan and perhaps in Persia it seems to have been mainly in private estates. In China and Japan also we seem to find more commercial centers and great merchants.

How can all this be explained? Why these extraordinary parallels? Some historians have favored a theory of the "diffusion of culture," which means that cultural parallels—say between the Mayan temples and those of Indo-China—came about by imitation. There was certainly a great deal of cultural interconnection, more, even in food-gathering societies, than has been realized, because trade throughout the continents and later over the oceans was much more extensive than had been believed. But obviously imitation cannot be the basic factor at work. Something has to exist in order to be imitated, and the distinctive aspects of all cultures are so clearly rooted in their particular societies that they must have grown out of them. Moreover, we are not talking primarily of cultural but of social phenomena, and these are not easily imitated. A Chinese "adventurer" could not travel to India in 1500 B.C., decide that feudalism was a good thing for a then farming-society China, and simply import it. On the other hand, we would expect to find in all societies in which a great landowning class was dominant that legal forms and social customs favored that class and that the dominant culture reflected this situation. And this is what we do find. We are not, as some commentators imply, facing sociocultural chaos but—as Marx would have recognized—social structures with basic and dependent factors and cultures that reflect the whole. A system such as feudalism had to evolve from later farming society, for there was no other way it could come into existence, and later farming society had to have its roots in early farming society, and early farming society in those of later hunter-gathering society. The indication is that everywhere there were essentially independent social developments, all of which took the same form. Also, the basic processes involved are—in spite of the surface complexity—essentially simple ones. Early-type farming societies—with their spindles whorls and pots—evolved into later-type farming societies—with their temples and towns—by the process of larger land units devouring the smaller ones; and the transition from later-type farming societies into feudal ones, with their great estates and cities, took the same form. The process did not, of course, take place automatically but in response to underlying economic drives, basically the conflict between productive forces and relations, but there is no mystery about the process itself. It is, in fact, as we shall see, the same as that which Marx noted for capitalism: "one capitalist kills many." Within this general process there was, of course, "influence" between societies. Influence, however, can only occur between societies on the same or about the same socioeconomic level and it does not come about—as one would gather from some texts—by a kind of academic imitation but through war and trade.

The evidence shows, then, that there was, as Marx and Engels contended, a general socioevolutionary process at work and its basic determinant was economic. Once a food-gathering society (which existed almost universally) evolved into a farming society the potential base for further development was laid.

The Pattern of Europe

The idea that there was a special slave stage in human history arose from too exclusive an emphasis on European history and its so-called Greek and Roman "roots." True, in the Mediterranean area civilized societies arose that were based mainly not on peasant but on slave labor. But what might at first appear to be a separate socioevolutionary pattern turns out on examination to be a variation from the same basic pattern. If the Egyptian economy was 90 percent agricultural the slave work force—in industry, manufacturing and trade—would be under 10 percent, but as Athenian agriculture was secondary, most of the national wealth coming from industry (including rich silver mines), manufacturing and trade, there was more slave than peasant labor. These quantitative differences changed status of the society from a feudal one to a slave-commercial one; that is to say, a society based economically upon a commercial capitalism run by slave labor. The reason that the Athenian economy was mainly capitalist and not feudal is that Athens (Attica) had comparatively little agricultural land but good natural resources and an important seaport; and it grew up in the midst of an already wealthy sea-trading area sustained mainly by long-established feudal societies. As manufacturing and commerce develop faster than agriculture and as sea trade was more profitable than land trade, Athens pulled rapidly ahead.

With the rise of Roman Italy, a further change in the pattern took place: slave labor was introduced also into agriculture and peasant labor was for a time largely displaced. This was possible because Roman Italy was larger and wealthier than Athens and was able to capture or purchase slaves on a massive scale. The Roman landowner, Cato, reckoned that while it cost him 250 to 300 denarii a year to keep a peasant and his wife, it only cost 75 to keep a slave (a peacock cost 50 denarii). Slaves had no wives—or husbands—or families. When one died another was purchased. Slave labor in agriculture, then, was a paying proposition but could only exist in a state with great commercial wealth. Apparently only Roman Italy (and possibly Carthage) had in sufficiency such wealth to indulge in it. No other area in the world, including the East China Sea, had the concentrated wealth of the Mediterranean, and no other nation such a monopoly on area wealth. The Roman was the last of the great Mediterranean empires and had devoured its competitors. When Rome fell slave-commercial society fell with it.[14]

And the Roman leaders well knew where their wealth came from and how they had to protect it, as is evident in the following comment by Cicero:

> The whole system of credit and finance which is carried on here at Rome is inextricably bound up with the revenues of the Asiatic provinces. If these revenues are destroyed, our system of credit will crash. . . . Prosecute with all your energies the war against Mithridates, by which the glory of the Roman name, the safety of our allies, our most valuable revenues, and the fortunes of innumerable citizens will be effectively preserved.[15]

When the empire began its "decline" what declined was not Roman agriculture but Roman commercial capitalism, which had reached the limits imposed upon it by the ultimately stultifying effects of slave labor, which, among other things, blocked technological progress. And although it is true that the Roman Empire as a political unit did indeed "fall," civilization in Italy did not—as one would gather from some accounts—simply vanish. Its agriculture continued although on a feudal and not a slave-owning basis. And commerce continued also but in a feudal setting. In short, the whole slave-commercial system that had dominated the rich Mediterranean area fell back into the feudal patterns from which it had emerged and which were still—and been continuously for many centuries—dominant in Asia, West and East. The expansion of cities ceased, and contraction began. "After A.D. 275, Autun had shrunk from nearly five hundred to less than twenty-five acres." Other cities fell into ruins and were not repaired. The great estates became more and more self-sufficient units relying on their own workshops and cutting off city trade. Peasant labor began to take the place of slave labor. "The troops of slaves who had once lived on the great estates dwindled from year to year mainly because their masters were always turning them into tenants, 'hutting' them as the phrase goes, giving each his own hut (*casa*), of course with the necessary fields." (Actually they were not "given" anything but became tenants and serfs—however they were no longer slaves.)[16]

As the Roman slave-commercial economy failed, various peoples, some in early feudal societies, some in advanced farming societies, began a long series of attacks upon the declining empire, first splitting it into two, East and West, and then invading Roman Italy itself. As some of these peoples had been exploited and enslaved by the Roman rulers, the attack upon the Empire assumed an antislaveocracy aspect. "Robbery, butchery, rapine, the liars call Empire; they create a desolation and call it peace." So, Tacitus recorded, spoke one of the British (Celtic) leaders facing the Roman tide. And when the tide turned, the slave system was dealt a massive blow.

It was generally assumed by nineteenth-century historians—and is still usually assumed today—that feudalism was a uniquely European phenomenon and that it arose out of the economic impetus given European society by the Roman Empire. Marx and Engels shared this view (which was general at the time):

> In contrast to Greece and Rome, feudal development at the outset, there-
> fore, extends over a much wider territory, prepared by the Roman conquests
> and the spread of agriculture at first associated with them.[17]

However, as we have seen, feudalism had existed for more than two thousand years in Egypt and West Asia before Athens was founded and in the intervening centuries had arisen throughout Asia. Roman wealth may have provided some impetus for the later development of feudalism in the rest of Europe but this cannot have been the major factor at work. It had existed in Europe long before the decline of Rome, for instance, in Gaul and eastern Europe, and its development in Britain, Germany and other areas seems to have been the normal one, from later farming societies which we observe in Asia. And not in Asia alone, for the rise of feudalism was not confined to Asia and Europe but was virtually world-wide. We can also see it although in a less-developed stage in Middle and South America among the Aztecs, Incas and the Mayas, in the African kingdoms of Ghana, Benim, Nubia (the Sudan) and Ethiopia, and in Hawaii. Everywhere the basic economy is agricultural; the land is owned, partly jointly, partly individually, by great landowners; the State is the great landowners' State; the peasants are produce-taxed and subject to forced labor; slave labor is employed in industry, transport and manufacturing; the male slaves are foreigners and the women mainly native. Usually the king is a god and the titular owner of the land.

Historians, in their over-specialization, have consistently missed these basic common patterns and have concentrated on secondary differences. For instance their concept of the European feudal system as a unique entity rests on legal technicalities or cultural variations, none of which the exploited peasant would have found impressive. In feudal England, for example, the land was nominally owned by the king, who ruled by "divine right"—a modification of the god-king—but was actually owned by great landowners on individual estates (as in China), and although the land-labor population was divided into "freemen" and "serfs," in fact they were all peasants, as everywhere in Asia. Few if any peasants—despite legal fictions—actually owned any land but rented it from the lord of the manor, the "freeman" renting more, the serf less, payment usually being "in kind." The peasants worked part of the time on the rented land and part on the lord's land without compensation. The peasant in Europe as in Egypt or India or China was driven to "forced labor" on roads and in the forests. He dug canals, drained marshes, built dykes—all for no pay. Like the Asian peasant also, he was subject to a multitude of taxes. He paid a tax for pasturing his animals on the lord's land. He was taxed for grinding his wheat in the lord's mill and for baking his bread in the lord's oven. When he died the Church seized his farm animals. He and his family were bought and sold with the land. Their progeny were not called *familia* in legal documents but *sequela* (brood or litter). Like the slave he was not a person in the eyes of the law but a *res* (thing). Slave labor has been estimated at about 9 percent in early feudal England, which means, as there was at first comparatively little paid labor, that some 90 percent of the work force were peasants—again as in Egypt and Asia. Mines, quarries, and forests were owned either by individual great landowners or by the State (the king and other great landowners). Mines (as in India) were rented out to entrepreneurs. The merchants were taxed and exploited by the great landowners—as in all Asia. The concept of the "sturdy" independent English "yeoman" in contrast to the inferior Asian "serf" is a myth, based on racial prejudice, as is the whole conception of European feudal uniqueness.[18]

Although Marx and Engels were well acquainted with Greek and Roman history, with some aspects of feudal Europe and contemporary India, comparatively little was then known of Asian history. The uncovering of Sumer and early Egypt, the Indus valley civilization, the Hittites, Shang China, early Japan, and other areas was mostly done in the twentieth century. There were narrative histories of India and Persia available, and these Marx and Engels studied, but information on economic and social matters was fragmentary. As a result they did not perceive that Asian civilization was feudal and the basic world transition was from farming society to feudalism, the Greek and Roman slave societies being a secondary aberration from this pattern, resulting from the concentrated commercial wealth of the Mediterranean area. Their European orientation and a lack of historical knowledge at the time led them to think that the transition from farming society had been to slave society in Europe and to what they called "the Asiatic" in Asia, with the implication that the Asiatic might itself have had an earlier slave "stage." And today, we still find Marxist historians writing of a slave society preceding feudalism, not only in Europe but in Asia.

World Feudalism and Social Evolution

What Marx and Engels meant by "the Asiatic" comes out in their correspondence. "Bernier rightly considers," Marx wrote to Engels in 1853, "that the basic form of all phenomena in the East—he refers to Turkey, Persia, Hindustan—is to be found in the fact that no private property in land existed." Engels replied:

The absence of property in land is indeed the key to the whole of the East. Here lies its political and religious history. But how does it come about that the Orientals do not arrive at landed property, even in its feudal form? I think it is mainly due to the climate, together with the nature of the soil, especially with the great stretches of desert which extend from the Sahara straight across Arabia, Persia, India and Tartary up to the highest Asiatic plateau. Artificial irrigation is here the first condition of agriculture and this a matter either for communes, the provinces or the central government.[19]

Marx and Engels did not consider "the Asiatic" was a feudal system because the land was owned by the State and not, as in Europe, concentrated in private estates. But the difference between the two was actually minimal. It mattered little to a peasant whether he was exploited by one large-landowner or by joint large-landowners organized as the State. And, as we have also noted, in China and other parts of Asia the dominant feudal pattern was one of individual great landlord ownership, and in India and other west Asian countries the princes had large private estates as well as joint holdings.

Feudal landowning whether private or State would move an economy forward, if it moved it at all, at a very slow pace. Whatever progress there is in a feudal society comes primarily not from the agricultural but from the commercial (manufacturing and trading) side of the economy. True, much of the trade and manufacturing is based on agricultural products but the stimulus to development comes mainly from commerce. Commerce is perhaps held back more in a feudal society based on State ownership than in one based on large individual holdings—as the contrast between Indian and Chinese history suggests. In India State land ownership placed great power in the hands of the central governments, some of which had armies of a hundred thousand soldiers. Against such a force both peasant rebellion and individual merchant development made slow headway. In China, on the other hand, peasant rebellions were frequent, the great estates were broken up and middle-size land-owning became dominant; and large trading-manufacturing enclaves developed especially in the port cities. Individual landowners, often at odds with each other, were increasingly unable to prevent peasant revolts or to hamper commercial development.

"The ancient communes," wrote Engels in *Anti-Dühring,* "where they continued to exist, have for thousands of years formed the basis of the most barbarous form of state, oriental despotism, from India to Russia." Although both Marx and Engels realized the backwardness of these village communities they seem to have attributed it to something inherent within them, perhaps remnants of primitive communistic society—"idyllic republics," Marx wrote, that formed the "foundation for the stagnation of Asiatic despotism." "Asiatic despotism," however, was not a special entity but simply a variety of feudal rule, and the main basis for this rule was not the village commune but great land ownership, joint or private. The "stagnation" was imposed from above by the feudal great land owning system.[20]

Although Marx and Engels were wrong in thinking that there was no "landed property" in Asia, Engels's suggestion that the situation he describes—actually that of joint great landlord ownership—was the result of irrigation and topographical features seems to be at least partly true. Joint ruling class ownership in Egypt, Sumer and the Indus valley may well have been fostered by the need for central control over the irrigation system. But joint ownership doubtless arose originally from the acquisition of land in later farming society by the army, Church, and government, and then, in some areas, was further consolidated, as the society moved into feudal civilization, by natural conditions. Topographical factors may also have played a role in establishing feudal systems dominated by individually owned estates. In large unbroken areas with comparatively little seacoast, joint ownership might tend to continue but in areas such as Britain, Japan, Italy or parts of China which are broken up by mountains or rivers individual ownership would tend to arise. As these areas usually also had comparatively large sea coasts with access to large navigable bodies of water, commerce, would tend to develop. This would bring merchant and agricultural capital together, some landowners engaging in trade and some capitalists purchasing land, and this process would aid the development of private estates.

The lack of knowledge at the time about Asian history and the exaggerated concept of Roman influence, then, lay behind Marx and Engels's view that "the three great epochs of civilization" were successively slave, feudal, and capitalist. Engels was also misled by his European, specifically Greek, model and his ignorance of the historical facts involved, when he declared that "the advance to a society based on class antagonisms could only be accomplished in the form of slavery." The transition, as we have seen, was not from farming society to slave society but from farming society to feudal society, the Greek "heroic age" of which Engels was speaking being a comparatively late development. Sumer and Egypt had civilized societies by 3,000 B.C., Homer lived about 700 B.C. and the society he depicted—romantically—was that of the port cities of the eastern Mediterranean. These city states, although having roots going back to Crete (2000 B.C.), owed their existence to the rich feudal agricultural regions of Egypt, Mesopotamia, and other areas, for they were non-self-sufficient manufacturing and trading states. Like Athens also, they simply continued the old pattern of slave labor in manufacturing and transport, and as they had comparatively little agriculture this meant that their basic labor force was slave. Thus although Crete apparently did first come into being on a slave-commercial basis, this was not the general pattern and it would not have been possible for Crete to have done so if the feudal states had not existed. The fact that there was also slave labor in feudal states and in the later farming communities from which they emerged should not be allowed to confuse the issue. Engels is not speaking of societies in which slave labor was secondary but of those in which it was primary. These societies, he believed, laid the base for feudal society. The situation was, in fact, the reverse: the slave-commercial states arose on the back of feudalism.[21]

> Without slavery, no Greek state, no Greek art, and science; without slavery, no Roman Empire. But without Hellenism and the Roman Empire as a basis, also no modern Europe. We should never forget that our whole economic, political and intellectual development has as its presupposition a state of things in which slavery was as necessary as it was universally recognised. In this sense we are entitled to say: Without the slavery of antiquity, no modern socialism.[22]

Engels is here clearly still basing himself on the view that European feudalism was given its impetus by Roman slave society, which he viewed as a general "transition" in historical evolution—from a lower (slave) to a higher (feudal) form. He seems also to some degree to be confusing social and cultural matters. In order to perceive the historical movement involved, we have to consider southern Europe, especially Italy, separately from northern Europe, particularly Britain, France, and the Germanic states.

In its early centuries Roman Italy, like Tuscan Italy before it, was primarily a feudal, agricultural state, with the usual pattern of peasant labor working on the great estates and slave labor in industry and transport. It was only as the empire spread that enough wealth was accumulated to permit slave labor also to be introduced in agriculture. Then, as we have seen, when the empire began to decline, the Roman Italy which had arisen out of feudalism fell back into it (as the slaves were "hutted"). It was three centuries later when Venice and other Italian cities began to revive and in the succeeding centuries became major Mediterranean trading centers. That the previous Roman slave-commercial society had little directly to do with this revival is apparent in the time gap. The source of the revival must, in the first instance, have been the produce of Italian feudal agriculture and its later flourishing due to economic stimulation from the rest of the Mediterranean area, particularly Constantinople, a city of a million inhabitants.[23]

If commercial development in southern Europe had received some early impulse from Roman slave-commercialism this must have been of even less consequence in northern Europe. In Gaul, which had had considerable commercial development before the Roman conquest, in Germany, Britain, and Russia, advanced farming societies made their own slow way into feudalism. Within this feudal society in the North Sea and Baltic Sea areas, trade and commerce began an inexorable rise until the great merchants of the Hanseatic League had power in the port cities. By the late eleventh century Britain was exporting 7,000,000 pounds of wool, and in French Flanders manufacturing centers had grown up. Grain, wool, butter, cheese, salt, potash, furs and fish, were widely traded. This rapid growth within a still basically feudal farming economy was rooted in the fact that the nations involved had, like Italy, comparatively large port areas compared to their landmasses, and large inland or semi-inland seas for trading.[24]

Although these economic developments both in southern and northern Europe would clearly have taken place without an early Roman stimulus, in one important respect this empire might have had an effect in shaping the social structures of the emerging new nations. In all these nations manufacturing labor was not mainly slave but paid. The old Roman pattern of the small manufacturer or builder employing a few paid craftsmen and a mainly slave workforce did not continue into the new societies or did not continue long; most, and, in time, all such labor became paid. The importance of this fact can hardly be exaggerated, for without it European feudalism could not have advanced—by about 1350—in some nations into commercial-feudal society; and then on into commercial capitalism and—in the nineteenth century—into industrial capitalism. The factors behind the breaking of the old slave pattern have not yet been sufficiently investigated but they may go back to the early antislave rebellion aspects of the overthrow of the Roman Empire. People who had been enslaved by Rome and overthrew it would not be disposed to allow the system to be restored by their own rulers or by others. And later the emerging manufacturers and craftsmen—who were often the same person—must have seen that slave labor was a fetter upon capitalist production.

Although this European development was unusually rapid it was not unique. The same centuries witnessed a similar growth in the Chinese, Indonesian, and Japanese port cities. As early as the seventh century, Chinese merchants had ships of 800 tons (the Mayflower was 180 tons) and by the tenth century they were trading with Arabia. In the seventeenth century 1,500 ships sailed into Tokyo each year. The port city of Osaka became, like London or Genoa, a bourgeois, free city, free that is to say, of feudal bonds. This east Asian development obviously had nothing to do with the Greek or Roman slave-commercial societies. Both the Chinese port cities connected with the China Seas and the Japanese port cities were by the eighteenth century making progress within a commercial capitalist framework although at a slower pace than in Europe.[25]

Engels's argument, then, that capitalist Europe grew out of the Greek and Roman slave states is incorrect. Its "economic, political, and intellectual development" would have been essentially what it was whether the Athenian or Roman slave-commercial empires had existed or not. As we have noted, it grew out of feudal and then feudal-commercial society. Its "legal and political superstructure" arose from its own socioeconomic "basis." Whatever "intellectual development" was influenced by Greek or Roman culture was restricted to the upper classes and was moreover peripheral to the central stream, which was "determined" by the "social existence" of capitalist society itself. Hence, also, Engels's conclusion that "Without the slavery of antiquity, no modern socialism" is also wrong. The socialist movement's ultimate roots were the same as those of the capitalism from which it sprang.

It is, of course, in the interests of a ruling class to throw a mantle of universality over its culture and so disguise its actual social basis, and Engels seems to have been unconsciously affected by this. In doing so, he does not, of course, accept the accompanying fiction of that culture ascending in an insulated realm of mind, but his use of "Hellenism" (Greek culture) in the passage, without qualification, could lead to confusion in this regard.

Although Marx and Engels, growing up in a semifeudal Germany, were sensitive to the political evils of feudalism—"the mad, blind onrush of feudal reaction" wrote Engels of the persecution in 1851 of the Communist League—they do not seem to have realized the scope of feudal exploitation, much of the research on which has been done in the present century. And although they recognized that capitalism was, for all its evils, an advance over feudalism, at times they give a muted picture of feudalism in contrast to capitalism:

> The bourgeoisie, wherever it has got the upper hand, has put an end to all feudal, patriarchal, idyllic relations. It has pitilessly torn asunder the motley feudal ties that bound man to his "natural superiors," and has left

no other nexus between man and man than naked self-interest, than callous "cash payment." It has drowned the most heavenly ecstasies of religious fervour, of chivalrous enthusiasm, of philistine sentimentalism, in the icy water of egotistical calculation. It has resolved personal worth into exchange value, and in place of the numberless indefeasible chartered freedoms, has set up that single, unconscionable freedom—Free Trade. In one word, for exploitation, veiled by religious and political illusions, it has substituted naked, shameless, direct, brutal exploitation.[26]

It was essential at the time (1848) to develop proletarian anticapitalist class consciousness and this was no doubt why Marx and Engels here suggested that some aspects of feudalism were preferable to capitalism. Nevertheless the passage inadvertently gives a false emphasis. There were no "idyllic" relations in feudal society for peasant or worker and little recognition of "personal worth." "Feudal ties" were worse than capitalist ones. In feudal exploitation there was plenty of "naked self-interest" and even more "direct, brutal exploitation" than in capitalism. The "heavenly ecstacies of religious fervor" were coverups for feudal Church exploitation and there was—and is—as much of this religious miasma in capitalism as in feudalism. The "chivalrous enthusiasm" of the landowning class was designed to promote chauvinism both national and sexual.

Behind some of these concepts lay the belief of Marx and Engels that in European feudalism the peasant had owned land and the worker his means of production (for instance in cottage industry):

The instruments of labour—land, agricultural implements, the workshop and tools—were the instruments of labour of individuals, intended only for individual use, and therefore necessarily puny, dwarfish, restricted. But just because of this they belonged, as a rule, to the producer himself.

This "petty" mode of production was, Marx noted, destroyed by capitalist expropriation: "the transformation of the individualised and scattered means of production into socially concentrated ones, of the pigmy property of the many into the huge property of the few, the expropriation of the great mass of the people from the soil, the means of subsistence, and from the means of labor . . . ."

Engels elaborates:

In commodity production as it had developed in the Middle Ages, the question could never arise of who should be the owner of the product of labour. The individual producer had produced it, as a rule, from raw material which belonged to him and was often produced by himself, with his own instruments of labour, and by his own manual labour or that of his family. There was no need whatever for the product to be appropriated by him; it belonged to him as an absolute matter of course.

An important factor in this individual ownership, Engels believed, was the guild system: "The regulations of the guilds ensured that the journeyman of today became the master craftsman of tomorrow."[27]

The reality was very different. The mass of agricultural workers were exploited peasants who owned no land and lived in poverty. The town workers owned little or nothing and were exploited by capitalists either in the "putting-out" system or in factories or workshops. There were, it is true, a few "individual producers" who "worked in most cases on their own premises and owned capital equipment of some value, such as the weaver's loom, the fuller's troughs and tenters, the dyer's vats," but these were not the workers but small capitalists: "men of property . . . and employers of labour." It was they who ran the guilds (which were more like chambers of commerce than trade unions). The basic industrial working mass in industry, mines, quarries, forests, transport, and manufacturing was brutally exploited:

> Thus great clothing towns such as Douai, Ypres or Brussels were in effect like one vast factory. In the early morning many thousands of workers might be seen flocking to the workshops of the entrepreneurs or of the weavers, fullers, dyers or shearmen, and the streets would empty as the bell rang out and they "clocked in" to their labor.

The exploitation of labor in these manufacturing towns was even worse than in later capitalism. The weavers "had to work without stopping from dawn to dusk, taking with them their bread for the day," and "if they wished for soup their wives must bring it to the looms where they worked so that they should in no way be interrupted in their work." Strikes were forbidden, yet there appear to have been secret unions, and at times the class struggle flared up in violent rebellion:

> To gain their demands, they [the workers] could only count on force, and they did not fail to use it. Throughout the fourteenth century, we see them constantly rising, seizing power and refusing to give it up except when, starved out by a blockade or decimated by a massacre, they were compelled to yield to the coalition of their adversaries.[28]

Certainly there is nothing idyllic about any of this. The historical accounts available to Marx and Engels must have carried little material on the condition of the working mass in European feudalism. Nor did capitalism arise, as Marx and Engels thought, primarily by the confiscation of the means of production of individual workers or peasants. It arose through the elimination of the smaller capitalists by the larger ones, who owned factories or banks or other businesses, which then became bigger, a process speeded up by the industrial revolution. The new wealth behind this development came, as Marx noted, largely from the exploitation of foreign labor: "The discovery of gold and silver in America, the extirpation, enslavement and entombment in mines of the aboriginal population, the beginning of the conquest and looting of the East Indies, the turning of Africa into a warren for the commercial hunting of black-skins, signalised the rosy dawn of the era of capitalist production."[29]

The seizure of the common lands which Marx describes so vividly in *Capital* was not a primary but a secondary aspect of the general commercialization of feudal landholding, and the seizure of small farm holdings was but a minor part of it. There were, in fact, few such holdings, the agricultural work-force consisting basically of hired farm laborers or landless peasants who rented land from the great landowners. The demand for a larger urban work force was met primarily not by migration to the cities but by an increase in population, the birth rate rising, as usual, to meet economic need.

In his general statement in 1859, Marx, as we have seen, argued, as a basic premise, that human consciousness is controlled by social conditions and not, as is usually assumed, the other way round. He then argued that the basic social force behind historical evolution was an increase in productive forces—machines, tools, factories, human power—and a tendency of the existing productive relations at a certain point to hold back this increase, at which the dam burst and further progress began with a rush. As we saw, he was thinking primarily of the era of industrial capitalism in Europe with its triumph over feudalism and its internal conflicts. But what of the previous long history of humanity, first, in food-gathering societies on all continents and then in early farming societies? And in later farming societies prior to the rise of feudalism? And what of the transitions between these systems? Were the same processes at work?

In considering hunter-gathering society, we are speaking of a period of some 200,000 years, as human hunter-gathering societies emerged from prehuman hunter-gathering societies. It was apparently only in the last

30–40,000 years of this period that an increase in productive forces began, as shown in the development of new stone tools—in an extraordinary variety, from hammers and axes to chisels and spearpoints—and, then, perhaps 20,000 years ago, the bow and arrow. Certainly in this development the basic socioevolutionary directive force was that of social conditions—primarily economic—and not of human consciousness, for although it is true that human consciousness invented the new tools and weapons, once invented they began to form an economic system that shaped the society and determined its movement—as in observed hunter-gathering societies. The increased supply of food and clothing (from hides), of tools and shelter (houses have existed for 30,000 or more years) brought about extensive trade (in Europe, and elsewhere, up and down the rivers) and larger communities developed. However, the simple, communal productive relationships of a hunter-gathering—and, hence, mobile—society would begin to "fetter" the growing productive forces as farming started to supplement hunting and food-gathering (in some areas at least by 15,000 years ago). More tools, clothing, shelter, trade must have been needed to meet the needs of expanding and increasingly settled communities. These socioeconomic developments must have created ideological struggles, some of them perhaps—as in later societies—couched in religious terms. Food-gathering societies existing into the present century demonstrate considerable intellectual and artistic development, and European cave paintings alone suffice to show that this was so in the past also.

Even though some agriculture and animal raising had developed in the last stages of food-gathering societies, when farming finally emerged as a dominant system, this was both a basic change and a relatively rapid spurt forward. New productive forces, the plough, the spindle whorl, the loom, and the potter's wheel, became dominant, and the old tools were improved, especially after (malleable) copper took over from (rigid) stone. Farming enabled people to produce for the first time really large surpluses, and these—as in observed early-type farming societies—increased trade far beyond what had been possible even in prosperous food-gathering societies. Trade, in turn, stimulated further production and further acquisition of land.

These factors as a whole made possible the advance of early farming society into later farming society and then that of later farming society towards (feudal) civilization, advances which, as we have noted, laid the foundation for all that has followed. They also led to conflict over both goods and land and to the beginning of class formations in the rise of chiefs and priests. Something of these conflicts in an early-type farming community was observed by Caesar among the German tribes:

> No one possesses any definite amount of land as private property; the magistrates and tribal chiefs annually assign a holding to clans and groups of kinsmen or others living together, fixing its size and position at their discretion, and the following year make them move on somewhere else. They give many reasons for this custom . . . that they may not be anxious to acquire large estates, and the strong be tempted to disposses the weak . . . and to keep the common people contented and quiet by letting every man see that even the most powerful are no better off than himself.

Reading between the lines one can see a class struggle developing. There are already "powerful" people and "common people," and although the "chiefs" and "magistrates" no doubt were among the more powerful—on a basis of institutional property—they were clearly under popular pressure to slow down the rate of development of property inequality. That the popular effort failed was shown not only in Europe but in Asia and elsewhere as early-type farming societies developed into later-type ones and later-type ones into feudalism. As later farming society moved inexorably towards feudalism and its inherent commercial drive, the mass of farmers must have struggled to prevent the seizure of their land by the great landowners, either their "own" or foreign, and their oppression as landless peasants; in all, a vast and varied movement of rebellion, war, and growing State power. But once again the underlying objective historical process was that of the productive relationships (essentially communal) fettering the productive forces represented by the great landowners and merchants; and once again the productive forces broke through, and great agricultural and commercial civilizations (as in Egypt and Sumer) arose, a process that was repeated time out of mind in the succeeding centuries as feudal societies arose in Asia and elsewhere. In none of these massive movements can the people involved have had any perception of the underlying socioeconomic forces that were in fact controlling their lives, and the "ideological forms" in which they "became conscious" of the "conflict" and "fought it out" were doubtless seen as primary motivating forces. In the transition from later farming society to feudalism—as the Sumerian records indicate—these forms may have attained considerable sophistication (and wit): "the pork butcher slaughters the pig, saying: 'Must you squeal? This is the road which your sire and your grandsire traveled, and now you are going on it too! And yet, you are squealing!' "[30]

Thus although Marx was thinking primarily of the struggle between feudal and capitalist forces and capitalist and labor forces, his implied extension of his view to the earlier major transitions of human history is borne out by present-day research into the past. The extraordinary thing is that Marx did not really know what these transition points were. As we have seen, there was no transition from slave societies to feudal ones. And Marx knew nothing of the vast and global transition from hunter-gathering societies to farming societies or of that from later farming societies to feudalism. Yet it is clear that all these transitions took place by the general objective process that he indicated, namely by an increase in the productive forces, a "conflict" between these forces and the "productive relations," a conflict that manifested itself in social struggle. Furthermore, there is evidence that all these transition struggles moved—as Marx indicated—relatively swiftly in their final stages.

The level of information on the past available to Marx and Engels produced inaccuracies in their description of past classes and class struggles:

> Freeman and slave, patrician and plebian, lord and serf, guild-master and journeyman, in a word oppressor and oppressed, stood in constant opposition to one another, carried on an uninterrupted, now hidden, now open fight, a fight that each time ended, either in a revolutionary reconstitution of society at large, or in the common ruin of the contending classes.

Slaves did not struggle against freemen but against slave-owners (some, perhaps most, freemen did not own slaves). The term *plebian* or *Plebs* was first used in Roman Italy to designate a middle class grouping and later the nonslave lower classes in general; the term *patrician* first designated the landed aristocracy and later higher office-holders from the upper classes, landed and capitalist. The journeymen in European feudal society were part of the class of paid workers, the guildmasters part of the capitalist class. The class struggle was between the total classes. None of the struggles noted here had ended in a "revolutionary reconstitution of society"; such reconstitutions arose primarily from the struggles between the upper classes themselves, the great landowners and the capitalists, most notably in the British Revolution in the seventeenth century and the French Revolution in the eighteenth. It has been argued that in "the common ruin of the contending classes" Marx and Engels referred particularly to "the disintegration without revolution of the society of the Roman Empire." However, although in various periods of Roman history some class forces—as in the seizure of power by Julius Caesar—suffered defeat there was no "common ruin." Nor does there appear to be an example elsewhere in history of such a phenomenon. Following a revolution one class or the other assumes power or a balance of power results. Classes can be destroyed only with the destruction of their economic base, or as a general phenomenon only with the destruction of class society. Marx and Engels must be using the word "ruin" in a modified sense. The statement, however, is basically incorrect.

Although Marx and Engels were aware of the general pattern of the class struggles of the past, they were not aware of all their specific historical forms.

The class structure of feudal society as it first emerged in Egypt and Sumer was well defined: great landowners, peasants, slaves, and a small middle class of merchants, craftsmen-manufacturers, and small professionals. And this pattern was repeated endlessly in the succeeding centuries in Asia, Europe, and elsewhere. The slave-commercial states of the Mediterranean area modified it by adding a powerful slave-owning capitalist class and greater slave population (with consequence massive slave rebellions and wars—such as that of Spartacus). The first major change in it was confined at first to Europe, where over the centuries there evolved a commercial capitalist class; a middle class; and a new class of paid workers, a class which with the coming of the industrial revolution in Europe and America became an industrial working class.

In all the feudal and slave-commercial societies of the past, the class struggle pattern was, as we have noted, similar to that which Engels had observed for commercial capitalist Europe, namely a three-cornered struggle: commercial against landed interests and the working mass against both.

This struggle was obviously rooted in the ownership of the means of production, agricultural and commercial, and it helped to develop the productive forces, primarily those of commercial capitalism. Although the major force in this development was the capitalist class itself, it might again be emphasized that there could have been no modern capitalism, with its great expansive power, if there had not been a paid working class; capitalist development on a slave basis, as Greece and Rome demonstrated, had relatively small growth potential. Furthermore, the continuing class struggles of workers and peasants played an important part in capitalist development, especially after feudal society evolved into commercial-feudal society. The peasants' struggles against the great landowners weakened the feudal structure, for instance in fourteenth-century England and later—with dramatic impact—in the French Revolution. The workers in commercial-feudal and commercial capitalist structures in their struggles for better wages and working conditions increased competition between capitalists, spurred inventions (many coming from craftsmen), and helped to drive the system forward. With the success of the bourgeois revolution the struggle of the capitalists against the landowners was no longer of significance in the major capitalist countries—although it still has significance in some "third world" countries—and the central class struggle, as Marx and Engels emphasized, became that of the working class and the bourgeoisie.

As we look back over the past it is apparent that the basic patterns of historical development are few and simple. Early-type farming societies, as we saw, developed into later-type ones essentially by the larger land units—often jointly owned—devouring the smaller ones; and the continuation of this process resulted in feudal societies, first in Egypt and West Asia. The rise of the Greek and Rome slave-commercial states was, as we noted, a deviation from the feudal pattern rather than an independent one, resulting from the greater concentration of commerce and industry in an inland sea area with a rich feudal base. Nor was the development of capitalism any more complex than that of feudalism. It had its origins in the surplus of goods produced in later-type farming societies, such as those in Mesopotamia, with their temples and ports. Within feudal societies—in Asia and then in Europe—enclaves of traders, bankers and manufacturers developed, mainly in the port cities. Because commercial wealth develops at a greater rate than agricultural, capitalism tended to move ahead. In areas with inland seas and long coastlines in comparison to total land area, it moved faster than in areas (such as Russia) with large land masses and, consequently, dominant feudal power. Thus capitalism rose to dominance in certain European countries, and was doing so in Japan and other parts of Asia when imperialism intervened to speed up the process. The rise of capitalism, first with small units, and then larger ones, and the decline of feudalism brings to mind the fall of the dinosaurs and the rise of the—at first very small—mammals.

4

Capitalism

Industrial Capitalism

In November 1842, Engels, then a young man in his early twenties, went from a Germany which was a commercial capitalist state with feudal trimmings to an England which was essentially industrial capitalist. In 1845 he published a book on his experiences, *The Condition of the Working Class in England,* which is the first historical examination of industrial capitalism, a form of society which had not previously existed, although some of its aspects were present in slave-commercial and commercial-feudal societies. In this work, Engels also laid theoretical foundations on which Marx was later to build in *Capital* and other works.

Sailing into London, Engels was impressed by the "masses of buildings" and the "countless sailing ships," all so "vast" that he felt "lost in the marvel of England's greatness." But he soon encountered the slums where those whose work had produced the ships and buildings lived. In Manchester, where he settled, he began to examine the conditions of the workers, partly from personal observation, partly from parliamentary reports and other sources. Everywhere he found ruthless exploitation. The new bourgeois society, once hailed by the French revolutionaires and others as ending the shackles of feudalism had provided shackles of its own:

> The worker is, in law and in fact, the slave of the property-holding class, so effectually a slave that he is sold like a piece of goods, rises and falls in value like a commodity. If the demand for workers increases, the price

66

of workers rises; if it falls, their price falls. . . . The only difference as compared with the old outspoken slavery is this, that the worker of today seems to be free because he is not sold once for all, but piecemeal by the day, the week, the year, and because no one owner sells him to another, but he is forced to sell himself in this way instead, being the slave of no particular person, but of the whole property-holding class.

Examples of this wage-slavery and its vicious exploitation were seen everywhere, in factories and in the mines:

The coal would be too expensive if a part of the adjacent sand and clay were removed; so the mine owners permit only the seams to be worked; whereby the passages which elsewhere are four or five feet high and more are here kept so low that to stand upright in them is not to be thought of. The working-man lies on his side and loosens the coal with his pick; resting upon his elbow as a pivot, whence follow inflamations of the joint, and in cases where he is forced to kneel, of the knee also. The women and children who have to transport the coal crawl upon their hands and knees, fastened to the tub by a harness and chain (which frequently passes between the legs), while a man behind pushes with hands and head.[1]

"Operatives forty years of age" in the mills were thrown out as "old people," and many of them had no recourse but to go to workhouses, known by the workers as Poor Law Bastilles: "the paupers wear a workhouse uniform, and are handed over, helpless and without redress, to the caprice of the inspectors."

Women as well as men were exploited, and the social effects of their exploitation were even more devastating:

The employment of women at once breaks up the family; for when the wife spends twelve or thirteen hours every day in the mill, and the husband works the same length of time there or elsewhere, what becomes of the children? They grow up like wild weeds. . . . Women often return to the mill three or four days after confinement, leaving the baby, of course; in the dinner hour they must hurry home to feed the child and eat something.[2]

Tuberculosis, typhus, syphilis, scarlet fever, and other deadly diseases were rampant in the slums (57 percent of working class children died before the age of five); and to these had to be added the toll taken by accidents at work and specific diseases caused by working conditions:

By far the most unwholesome work is the grinding of knife-blades and forks, which, especially when done with a dry stone, entails certain early death because of the quantity of sharp-edged metal dust particles freed in the cutting, which fill the atmosphere, and are necessarily inhaled. The dry grinders' average life is hardly thirty-five years . . . .

Unable to afford a doctor the workers were exploited by quacks and patent medicine manufacturers:

Morrison's Pills, Parr's Life Pills, Dr. Mainwaring's Pills, and a thousand other pills, essences, and balsams, all of which have the property of curing all the ills that flesh is heir to.

Alcohol became the great narcotic. Prostitution was rife; there were 40,000 prostitutes in London alone.

This new system of exploitation and oppression was supported by the State, with its police force, laws and courts:

It is quite obvious that all legislation is calculated to protect those that possess property against those who do not. Laws are necessary only because there are persons in existence who own nothing; and although this is directly expressed in but few laws. . . . enmity to the proletariat is so emphatically the basis of the law that the judges, and especially the Justices of the Peace, who are bourgeois themselves, and with whom the proletariat comes most in contact, find this meaning in the laws without further consideration.[3]

If the bourgeoisie thought that, confronting such massive demoralizing forces, the early nineteenth-century worker would sink into passivity they soon learned better. Unions had been legalized in 1822 after decades of working class struggles; strikes, often long and violent, were common. The workers entered politics. Along with others they had battled for "parliamentary reform," especially the extension of the franchise, since the late eighteenth century and in the 1830s their efforts were consolidated when the massive Chartist movement presented a petition with four million names to parliament demanding the vote, an act, Engels felt, of special significance:

In the Unions and turnouts opposition always remained isolated: it was single workingmen or sections who fought a single bourgeois . . . . But in Chartism it is the whole working class which arises against the bourgeoi-

sie, and attacks, first of all, the political power, the legislative rampart
with which the bourgeoisie has surrounded itself.

In addition to the unions and Chartism some workers had moved on
to the "socialism" of Robert Owen. "To Owen, the new mighty productive
forces, which until then had served only for the enrichment of individuals
and the enslavement of society, offered the basis for the reconstruction of
society, and were destined, as the common property of all, to work only for
the common welfare of all." The young Engels discovered that Owen—
partly influenced by Shelley's *Queen Mab* (which Engels had begun to translate
in Germany)—considered "marriage, religion, and property the sole cause
of all unhappiness since the beginning of the world;" and he contributed
to Owen's publication *The New Moral World*.[4]

As Engels looked out over the new sea of human misery created by
industrial capitalist exploitation he asked himself, as did Owen and the
Chartists, how was it all to end? His answer—anticipating a famous passage
in Marx—was in social polarization and revolution:

> But assuming that England retained the monopoly of manufactures, that
> its factories perpetually multiply, what must be the result? The commercial
> crises would continue, and grow more violent, more terrible, with the
> extension of industry and the multiplication of the proletariat. The pro-
> letariat would increase in geometrical proportion, in consequence of the
> progressive ruin of the lower middle-class and the giant strides with which
> capital is concentrating itself in the hands of the few; and the proletariat
> would soon embrace the whole nation, with the exception of a few mil-
> lionaires. But in this development there comes a stage at which the pro-
> letariat perceives how easily the existing power may be overthrown, and
> then follows a revolution.

The young Engels, then, was not merely describing conditions but had
(by 1844) developed certain general theoretical concepts, most of which had
roots in the Chartists and Owenites: capitalism was an economic system
based upon private property in the industrial means of production; the
worker was a new kind of slave, held not by legal but economic bonds, the
slave of the whole bourgeoisie, which bought and sold him like any other
commodity in a profit-controlled market; the workers received back only a
small proportion of what they earned by their work; they made the machines
and operated the factories but the capitalists owned them; the capitalist
system was one of ruthless profit making and competition; every few years

it collapsed in an economic crisis; these crises plus the concentration of the capitalists and growth of the working class would in time lead to a workers' revolution. This would be more violent than the French and other bourgeois revolutions: "The war of the poor against the rich will be the bloodiest ever waged." When Engels arrived at these conclusions—in 1844–1845—Marx had only just begun his economic studies.[5]

In the succeeding years Marx and Engels examined the functioning of capitalism in detail, taking as a particular starting point the economic theories—on "value" and other matters—developed by David Ricardo. The problems they encountered proved to be complex, and soon Engels, busy in Manchester managing a family business, left the analysis mainly to Marx.

In capitalist countries today, there is actually little general economic theorizing, as bourgeois economics has been fragmented into a series of specializations, the experts in each compartment often knowing little of the others and showing little interest in the whole. Their function is not to determine how capitalism works but how it can be made to work most profitably. Some argue that this can best be accomplished by leaving the system to run itself; others advocate high government spending, especially military; and theoretical constructs have been erected on these pragmatic bases. There are also "Marxist" economists who seek to tell the capitalists how to reform the system "before it is too late."

Marx, on the other hand, was attempting to discover the structures and evolutionary processes of the system. In examining the structures he developed his theories of value and surplus value; in examining its evolution he developed his theories of constant and variable capital, the division between capital goods and consumption goods, capitalist accumulation and social polarization, and the tendency of the rate of profit to fall. Marx expounded these theories most completely in the three volumes of *Capital*, the last two of which were edited from his papers after his death by Engels (1885, 1894). Although the presentation is frequently vivid, as in the historical sections, and the power of the logic cumulatively impressive, the work, as Engels hinted in a letter to Marx, is overly abstract. The treatment of some aspects of the theory by Engels in *Anti-Dühring* or by Marx in *Value, Price and Profit* is more suited for popular exposition. Even so, we have to recognize that the economic system of capitalism is a complex phenomenon about some of the intricacies of which Marxist economists differ. Its analysis is not just a matter of sifting data but of grasping abstractions which reflect interactive movement, a process not unlike that of modern physics in which practical and theoretical work intertwine. In spite of these problems, however, it is possible for the noneconomist to grasp the fundamentals of Marx's theory and to see to what degree it has been borne out by the subsequent history of capitalism.[6]

In examining the structures of capitalism Marx early became interested in prices and wages, neither of which, he found, were what they seemed to be. In regard to prices he dismissed the current view that price as such was determined primarily by supply and demand: "Supply and demand regulate nothing but the temporary fluctuations of market prices." Otherwise if locomotives were in good supply and chairs in short supply a chair could cost more than a locomotive. Obviously there must be some general factor at work behind supply and demand. This general factor, Marx, following earlier economists, called the "exchange-value" of the goods exchanged. In doing so he was, in effect, pointing out that beneath the deceptive intricacies of a money economy with its bonds, banks and stocks lies as a foundation the production and exchange of goods, just as in a barter economy. Money only greases the economic machine; it does not supply the power for it. And price is the distorted reflection of the underlying exchange-value in a money economy. In such economies, the exchange-value of the goods exchanged constituted "the center of gravity around which prices fluctuate."

Goods, then, are being exchanged and they are being exchanged in a series of comparable values. But if they are thus capable of being exchanged, they must have some quality in common, otherwise it would be impossible to know whether to exchange a pair of shoes for a house or for a cooking pot (either in a barter or a money economy).

> Besides, if I say a quarter of wheat exchanges with iron in a certain proportion, or the value of a quarter of wheat is expressed in a certain amount of iron, I say that the value of wheat and its equivalent in iron are equal to some third thing, which is neither wheat nor iron, because I suppose them to express the same magnitude in two different shapes. Either of them, the wheat or the iron, must, therefore, independently of the other, be reducible to this third thing which is their common measure.[7]

In giving such examples Marx—here addressing a working class audience—is trying to present the essence of a large and complex system in which millions of transactions take place each day. Beneath all this complexity, he is, in effect, saying, the basic processes at work are simple (the same general phenomenon which scientists today are finding in physics and biology). In this system as a whole, he contends, goods over a period of time must ultimately and in general be exchanged at their values in spite of fluctuations in price. Otherwise a system of exchange would be impossible.

What, however, is the "third thing" which ultimately determines the exchange-value of the goods being sold?

> What is the common social substance of all commodities? It is labor. To produce a commodity a certain amount of labor must be bestowed upon it, or worked up in it. And I say not only labor, but social labor. . . . If we consider commodities as values, we consider them exclusively under the single aspect of realised, fixed, or, if you like, crystalized social labor. In this respect they can differ only by representing greater or smaller quantities of labor, as, for example, a greater amount of labor may be worked up in a silken handerkchief than in a brick.[8]

Again Marx is dealing with a complex phenomenon and seeking out the basic factor at work. There are, of course, many kinds of labor, and often many stages of labor go into a particular product. These stages can involve the initial industrial production of the product, such as the mining of iron ore, successive production stages, for instance, of the iron into steel and the steel into motor vehicles, with clerical labor involved in all stages. The working class includes both skilled and unskilled workers, both mechanics and typists, both men and women. Marx was perhaps less aware of the diverse spread of the working class than we are today but he was not unaware of it, as his political writings indicate. In his strictly economic works, however, he clarifies matters by considering a kind of composite worker as one of his basic units. In the above passage he is speaking of human labor in a general sense.

By *value* in this passage, Marx means *exchange-value.* Value in the general everyday sense of the word he called *use value,* and he contrasted the two: "A man who produces an article for his own immediate use, to consume it himself, creates a product, but not a commodity." An object does not become a commodity until it is put up for sale; only then does it acquire exchange value. Tables made by carpenters have *use value* if the carpenters keep them or give them away, but once they put them up for sale they enter the area of *exchange value,* and it is this *exchange-value* which determines their general price category (but not the specific price of any one table). The word value, then, is used to denote two different things—unfortunately—one social and cultural, the other economic.[9]

By the time we have advanced this far into Marx's analysis, it becomes apparent that he is examining aspects of capitalism in which the capitalists—

and their economists—understandably have little interest. But it is apparent also that these aspects of capitalism are of interest to the working class.

Although Marx does not go into this particular question historically, both use-value and exchange-value must have existed in previous societies. In the earlier stages of food-gathering societies, the goods produced—stone tools, spears, baskets, etc.—were intended only for the use of the makers, the community and its families. But in later food-gathering societies there was considerable trade, doubtless even trade fairs such as those later held by the native Australians; and once trade began, exchange-value was born. With the greater surplus accumulated by farming societies trade became extensive and in the first civilizations international in scope—Sumer to India, for instance. In both later food-gathering society and early farming society most exchange was by barter. Price, as such did not exist; exchange-values— frozen labor—were being directly exchanged for each other. With the coming of later farming society and the transition to civilization money arose; the gold shekel was worth eight silver shekels in Sumerian trade. With this development, price in money terms became the medium of exchange and its fluctuations disguised the fact that it was ultimately based on exchange-value (in the total exchange system). And this relation between exchange-value and price was further disguised in the first civilizations when credit and letters of credit arose. But, to repeat, underneath it all what was happening was the exchange of goods for each other, goods whose exchange-value Marx would have seen as determined fundamentally by the amount of labor—of slave, small workshop owner, peasant or paid craftsman—embodied in it.

In both Egypt and Sumer, a considerable manufacturing, commercial, and financial structure arose, with money and financial houses with their branch offices in other countries. Although this commercial system existed within a basically feudal society it was in itself capitalist, exchanging goods for profit. The slave-commercial societies of Greece and Rome differed economically from these earlier feudal societies mainly in having more concentrated wealth, the result of the greater exploitation allowed by slave labor, and greater emphasis on trade and manufacturing. In Athens, in fact, because of its dependence on outside agriculture for its food supply, commercial capitalism formed the heart of the economy. Commercial capitalism, as we have seen, also developed within commercial-feudal society—although on a paid-labor and not a slave basis. The phenomenon Marx is discussing, then, is not a new one, but in industrial capitalism, as the feudal remnants faded, it became dominant and developed new complexities.

According to Marx, all we are doing in a capitalist economy is exchanging one block of congealed labor for another even though the transaction takes a money form: "a particular quantity of money merely expressed a particular quantity of embodied labor." Thus, for instance, although it appears to gross observation that a worker's wages come from his employer— just as it appears that the earth is flat—actually they are created by the worker's own labor, which creates all exchange value, not, again, in any particular case but "for human labor in general."

If, however, goods are ultimately sold at their exchange values and these values are embodied labor, how can we account for profit? The answer, Marx contended, lay in the fact that some of the embodied labor is in fact unpaid—"surplus labor." What the worker sells is not his labor as such but his "Laboring Power, the temporary disposal of which he makes over to the capitalist."

> What, then, is the Value of Laboring Power? Like that of every other commodity, its value is determined by the quantity of labor necessary to produce it. The laboring power of a man exists only in his living individuality. A certain mass of necessaries must be consumed by a man to grow up and maintain his life. But the man, like the machine, will wear out, and must be replaced by another man. Beside the mass of necessaries required for his own maintenance, he wants another amount of necessaries to bring up a certain quota of children that are to replace him on the labor market and to perpetuate the race of laborers. Moreover, to develop his laboring power, and acquire a given skill, another amount of values must be spent.

In effect, then, as Engels had early contended, the worker is also a commodity on the market—like grain or iron. He offers his labor power for sale. His exchange value in this transaction is ultimately the amount of labor—provided by himself and other workers—needed to produce and maintain him and his family: the labor embodied in him, the collective worker. This exchange-value, however, is not equal to that of the goods the collective worker produces and that contain his "crystallized social labour."

> Take the example of our spinner. We have seen that, to daily reproduce his laboring power, he must daily reproduce a value of three shillings, which he will do by working six hours daily. But by paying the daily or weekly value of the spinner's laboring power the capitalist has acquired the right of using that laboring power during the whole day or week. He will, therefore, make him work daily, say twelve hours. Over and above the six hours required to replace his wages, or the value of his laboring

power, he will, therefore, have to work six other hours, which I shall call hours of surplus labor, which surplus labor will realise itself in a surplus value and a surplus produce.

Once again, although Marx takes individual examples he intends them as symbols for mass phenomena. He is, as it were, totaling up on the one hand the exchange-values of the commodities needed to maintain the mass of workers and on the other the exchange-values of the commodities produced by them. And, as Engels succinctly put it: "The value of the labor power, and the value which that labor power creates in the labor process, are two different magnitudes." In the difference between them lies the basis for profit.[10]

Profits, then, like prices (or natural phenomena) are not what they seem to be. Just as prices *in general* are not determined by supply and demand but by exchange value, profits *in general* are not the result of clever dealings by businessmen but represent the extraction of "surplus value" from the workers—the total workforce—by paying them for only part of their labor. The situation is similar to that of the relation of peasant and lord (or, as Engels had noted, of slave and master):

Take, on the other hand, the peasant serf, such as he, I might say, until yesterday existed in the whole east of Europe. This peasant worked, for example, three days for himself on his own field or the field allotted to him, and the three subsequent days he performed compulsory and gratuitous labor on the estate of his lord. Here, then, the paid and unpaid parts of labor were visibly separated, separated in time and space; and our Liberals overflowed with moral indignation at the preposterous notion of making a man work for nothing.

In point of fact, however, whether a man works three days of the week for himself on his own field and three days for nothing on the estate of his lord, or whether he works in the factory or the workshop six hours daily for himself and six for his employer, comes to the same, although in the latter case the paid and unpaid portions of labor are inseparably mixed up with each other, and the nature of the whole transaction is completely masked by the intervention of a contract and the pay received at the end of the week. The gratuitous labor appears to be voluntarily given in the one instance, and to be compulsory in the other.

Certainly no one argued that the surplus which the lord extracted from the peasant was due to the lord's business skill. It was clearly the result of his ownership of the land. The point was to see that essentially the same kind of situation with its consequent economic exploitation had continued in capitalism although in disguised form. In fact, Marx might have gone on to argue that in all societies in which the means of production are privately owned and operated for profit surplus value forms the basis for operation. After Cato paid the 78 denarii to keep his slave for a year or the 300 to keep the peasant and his wife, the rest was profit, and the profit was derived ultimately from the difference between the exchange value of slaves or peasants and the exchange value (in congealed labor) of the commodities that they produced. So, too, with paid workers in feudal and slave-commercial societies. True, in such societies there were comparatively few paid workers, but skilled craftsmen were paid, either directly or through a contractor. As feudalism developed into commercial-feudal society, surplus value must have reigned supreme in the European manufacturing towns in the centuries before capitalism became the dominant system. Goods must then as later have been exchanged at their values and the surplus value scooped out of the labor of the workers of Ghent or London in, say, the fourteenth century. The transition to industrial capitalism was not, as we have seen, a change from a bucolic cottage system with the worker owning his machines, but a development of a basically exploitive system—with the workers, either in factories or "home" industry, owning nothing—into a more extensively organized exploitive system. It was not, as Marx and Engels thought, a major break with the past but an expansion of an existing system.

In considering surplus value in capitalism as in considering exchange-value Marx intends us to take the whole system in its workings over a period of years into account. In individual cases and in different periods considerable fluctuations occur. The capitalist can increase the rate of surplus value by either increasing the working hours or the intensity of labor exploitation (through speedups, beltlines and so on). In periods of capitalist expansion and with the aid of unions the worker can reduce the rate of surplus value but in other circumstances it can increase. On the whole, Marx argues, the worker ends up with what is needed to sustain him as a working and biologically reproductive machine.

A capitalist can increase his profits by employing fewer workers and more machines—as Marx noted. Here we seem to face a paradox. If the surplus value which lies behind the profits of the total system ultimately comes from labor power, one would think that capitalists would employ more labor power and less machinery. But the capitalist is not primarily interested in the total system or "ultimately" but in his own profits and "now." And in the "now" he can get more profit from having to pay fewer workers in relation to his total output. Nevertheless, Marx argued, the "ultimately" is still there. The source of surplus value, and hence of profits, is still labor. Indeed, it can be nothing else. Machines produce neither exchange-value nor surplus value—both of which existed before there were machines. What happens, according to Marx, is that concerns with more labor in proportion to machines do actually produce more surplus value, and capitalists with fewer workers in proportion to machines produce less, but in the competitive struggle things even out and an average rate of profit is established for the system as a whole.[11]

In turning from the structure of capitalism to its future evolution, Marx and Engels at first concentrated on the periodic crises of the system. As early as 1844, Engels, in Manchester, noted the phenomenon:

> The economist comes along with his lovely theory of demand and supply, proves to you that "one can never produce too much," and practice replies with trade crises, which reappear as regularly as the comets, and of which we have now on the average one every five to seven years.

And the *Communist Manifesto* contained a classic description of such crises:

> Modern bourgeois society with its relations of production, of exchange and of property, a society that has conjured up such gigantic means of production and exchange, is like the sorcerer who is no longer able to control the powers of the nether world whom he has called up by his spells. For many a decade past the history of industry and commerce is but the history of the revolt of modern productive forces against the property relations that are the conditions for the existence of the bourgeoisie and of its rule. It is enough to mention the commercial crises that by their periodical return put the existence of the entire bourgeois society on its trial, each time more threateningly. In these crises a great part not only of existing products, but also of the previously created productive forces, are periodically destroyed. In these crises there breaks out an epidemic that, in all earlier epochs, would have seemed an absurdity—the epidemic of overproduction. Society suddenly finds itself put back into a state of momentary barbarism.[12]

Marx and Engels, then regarded cyclical crises as symptoms of the general "conflict" between productive forces and productive relations. In his 1859 statement Marx seems to be stressing the retardation of the productive forces of capitalism by the productive relationships—great landowning—of feudalism. In this statement, however, he and Engels are clearly thinking of an internal conflict within capitalism: the productive forces of capitalism were being hindered from their potential development by capitalist productive relations. This was because these relations were based on the capitalists' ownership of the means of production with the production of goods, as it were, a byproduct of profit. Hence, there was no planned balance between production and consumption, with a consequent steady development, but instead a series of feverishly fluctuating booms and busts that ultimately reflected the fact that the growing productive forces were not achieving their potential.

The immediate key to cyclical crises, however, lay in the drive for profit. And it is on profit that Marx in his later economic studies of capitalist crises puts the emphasis. "The rate of profit is the compelling power of capitalist production, and only such things are produced as yield a profit." "It comes to a standstill at a point determined by the production and realization of profit, not by the satisfaction of social needs." In the upswing of the business cycle profit comes not only or even mainly from producing consumer goods—shoes, furniture, books, etc.—but from producing machines and other means of production that capitalists sell to each other. The bulk of the profits thus derived they do not save or use for their own living but pour into still further production (the "accumulation" of capital) to make still more profit. But in time the new means of production produce consumption goods, piling them on top of what is already being produced. The resulting situation was later (1880) vividly described by Engels:

> We have seen that the ever-increasing perfectibility of modern machinery is, by the anarchy of social production, turned into a compulsory law that forces the individual industrial capitalist always to improve his machinery, always to increase its productive force. The bare possibility of extending the field of production is transformed for him into a similar compulsory law. The enormous expansive force of modern industry, compared with which that of gases is mere child's play, appears to us now as a necessity for expansion, both qualitative and quantitative, that laughs at all resistance. Such resistance is offered by consumption, by sales, by the markets for the products of modern industry. But the capacity for extension, extensive and intensive, of the markets is primarily governed by quite different laws that work much less energetically. The extension of the markets cannot keep pace with the extension of production. The collision becomes inevitable and as long as it does not break in pieces the capitalist mode of production, the collisions become periodic. Capitalist production has begotten another "vicious circle."

The "enormous expansive power of modern industry" is not, of course, self-generative but is the result of the competitive drive for profits, and its "enormity" results primarily from the production of means of production. This drive for profits is not a matter of free choice for the capitalists—although it may appear to be—but is inherent in capitalism as a system. Caught up in the economic tornado of competition the capitalists produce beyond "the market." Why beyond? In the first instance, obviously because the mass of consumers do not have the money to purchase all the goods produced. Why do they not have enough money? Although Engels was not in this passage intent on examining this question the answer clearly must lie in Marx's basic analysis of value and surplus value. In essence the market is limited because the exchange value of the goods produced is higher than the exchange value of the workers' laboring power. This differentiation lies beneath the gap between the total price of the goods produced and total purchasing power. As this gap grows a cyclical crisis develops—as described anew and in more detail by Engels in 1880, after some years of business experience:

> Commerce is at a standstill, the markets are glutted, products accumulate, as multitudinous as they are unsaleable, hard cash disappears, credit vanishes, factories are closed, the mass of the workers are in want of the means of subsistence, because they have produced too much of the means of subsistence: bankruptcy follows upon bankruptcy, execution upon execution. The stagnation lasts for years; productive forces and products are wasted and destroyed wholesale, until the accumulated mass of commodities finally filters off, more or less depreciated in value, until production and exchange gradually begin to move again. Little by little the pace quickens. It becomes a trot. The industrial trot breaks into a canter, the canter in turn grows into the headlong gallop of a perfect steeplechase of industry, commercial credit and speculation which finally, after breakneck leaps, ends where it began—in the ditch of a crisis.[13]

As Marx pointed out in his general statement in 1859, although people in each society build their means of production—from plows to factories—these means of production, once built, determine the economic structure of a society and it is this structure which basically determines the general nature and development of the society. So, too, with capitalist society and its economic system. The capitalist system was built over the centuries by capitalists, but once built the system itself was basically in control, the capitalist almost as much the puppet of its "anarchy" as the worker—as Engels, doubtless calling on his own experience, emphasized:

No one knows how much of his particular article is coming on the market, nor how much of it will be wanted. No one knows whether his individual product will meet an actual demand, whether he will be able to make good his costs of production or even to sell his commodity at all. Anarchy reigns in socialised production.

True, each capitalist operates his own business and seeks profit but in doing so he is primarily responding to the drive for profit inherent in the system as a whole. If, for instance, forseeing a crisis of overproduction, he slackens production, he can go under in the competitive struggle. If, on the other hand, he decides to chance it and continue production at a high level he can, equally, meet disaster. Nor can capitalists turn their inherently anarchic profit-driven system into a planned economy—as is shown by the fact that all attempts to introduce "price controls" are soon overwhelmed by the scramble for profits. To introduce a planned economy, they would have to cease to produce for profit and produce in accord with social need. In short, they would have to abolish capitalism, something they neither wish to do nor, in fact, can do.

Not only crises but the system as a whole, as Marx emphasized, depends on the private ownership of the means of production. There would be no "market" problem if it were not for surplus value; and if the means of production were not in capitalist hands there would be no surplus value. For what is it that the capitalists are investing as capital but the surplus value they have extracted from the worker's labor? Without surplus value there would be no finance, no investment, no profits, and no capitalist competition (and no millionaires or jet-set glitter).

"Capital," Marx wrote, "is not a thing, but rather a definite social production relation, belonging to a definite historical formation of society." Capital is not machines or goods as such but the "production relation" of exploitation based on the capitalists' ownership of the goods and machines. Machines and goods are converted into "capital" by this "relation"; in a future communist society, machines and goods will still exist but they will not be capital. They will not produce exploitive profit. The "formation of society" which creates capital is of a special nature and, like feudalism before it, will perish—even though its proponents wishfully bestow immortality upon it.[14]

If the movement of the capitalist system was simply cyclical (in crises) there would, of course, be no reason why it should not exist as long as society exists. But as the *Manifesto* noted, Marx and Engels believed that crises occur "each time more threateningly." And Engels in a later letter argued that a time was coming when the crises might "change from acute into chronic ones but at the same time lose nothing in intensity." Neither Marx nor Engels, however, state why this should be so. And in the first volume of *Capital* Marx seems to give a somewhat different account of the end of capitalism:

> Along with the constantly diminishing number of the magnates of capital grows the mass of misery, oppression, slavery, degradation, exploitation. . . . The monopoly of capital becomes a fetter upon the mode of production. . . . Centralization of the means of production and socialization of labor at last reach a point where they become incompatible with their capitalist integument. This integument is burst asunder. The knell of capitalist private property sounds. The expropriators are expropriated.

The implication here seems to be that the growing tendency to monopoly produces increased exploitation, which, in turn produces increased proletarian resistance and ultimately revolution, an explanation inherent, as we noted, in Engels' *Condition of the Working Class*. Marx and Engels certainly expected that this general historical panorama would include worsening cyclical crises but they do not specifically say so and do not anywhere, so far as I know, tie the two together as twin destroyers of capitalism. Again we come back to the question—and it is a basic one—of why? Why would the crises worsen? Why would monopoly increase exploitation?

Marx apparently believed—although this is not spelled out—that the basic factor at work behind all these phenomena of decline was what he called a tendency for the rate of profit to fall. This tendency, Marx argued, "breeds overproduction, speculation, crises and surplus capital alongside surplus population." The decline in the rate of profit leads to overproduction—and hence crisis—because the capitalists try to compensate for the decline in the rate of profit by increasing the mass of profits.

Why, however, does the rate of profit tend to decline? The answer, Marx contends, lies in the fact that capital falls into two parts, "constant capital," embodied in plant and machinery, and the "variable capital" paid out in wages. The capitalist drive is to increase "constant capital" at the expense of "variable capital," that is to say to introduce more machine power and less labor power. Surplus value, however, and the profit based upon it, as Marx had previously argued, are derived solely from labor power—"variable capital." As the capitalists's rate of profit (the total capitalist in the total system) depends on the amount of surplus value divided by the amount he spends on machines and other equipment—"constant capital"—the rate of profit will fall as the ratio of constant to variable capital increases.

The general mechanism that Marx had in mind and its end result were put succinctly by Engels in *Anti-Dühring:*

> It is the driving force of the social anarchy of production which transforms the infinite perfectibility of the machine in large-scale industry into a compulsory commandment for each individual industrial capitalist to make his machinery more and more perfect, under penalty of ruin. But the perfecting of machinery means rendering human labor superfluous. If the introduction and increase of machinery meant the displacement of millions of hand workers by a few machine workers, the improvement of machinery means the displacement of larger and larger numbers of machine workers themselves.[15]

Behind the falling tendency of the rate of profit, then, is the fact that each capitalist is driven to increase his profit by replacing workers by machinery. The result will be increasing unemployment and a consequent loss of purchasing power which will increasingly shrink "the market." Why, however, would it progress? Why, for instance, would it not stay about the same or simply move up and down with booms and busts? Neither Marx nor Engels seem to examine this question specifically but apparently they assume that this general capitalist drive for mechanization is so powerful that it will overwhelm worker opposition. That they were basically right is demonstrated in the present situation of capitalism—to be noted later—even though their explanations might be in some ways deficient.

Although the rate of profit tends to fall, it does not fall unimpeded. There are, Marx noted, "counteracting causes," one of which turned out to be more important than he anticipated:

> On the other hand, capitals invested in colonies, etc., may yield a higher rate of profit for the simple reason that the rate of profit is higher there on account of the backward development, and for the added reason, that slaves, coolies, etc., permit a better exploitation of labor. We see no reason, why these higher rates of profit realised by capitals invested in certain lines and sent home by them should not enter as elements into the average rate of profit and tend to keep it up to that extent.

Such counterbalancing forces, may, Marx noted, "check the fall in the rate of profit but they cannot prevent it altogether." They can retard the downward cycle of capitalism as a historical system, but they cannot stop it.[16]

Monopoly Capitalism

The capitalist system today clearly differs in some respects from that examined by Marx and Engels. Although there were great industrial and financial concerns, such as Carnegie Steel or the House of Rothschild in the nineteenth century, today's corporate units are not only larger but dominate the system. The export of capital (e.g., i.e., for building factories) to feudal nations in Asia and elsewhere that Marx noted in the late nineteenth century assumed monstrous proportions in the twentieth, and extracted massive superprofits from low-paid native workers. Corporations formed international cartels for the better exploitation of the world market. Since Lenin discussed some of these matters in *Imperialism* (1916), the big corporations have become even bigger, often developing into conglomerates, with assets in various fields, and international cartels have been supplemented by multinational corporations. To the export of capital to the so-called underdeveloped nations has been added a major export of capital into capitalist nations—United States capital into Europe, Japanese capital into the United States.

What would Marx say of these various changes? He would doubtless first note that he had predicted their general nature:

> One capitalist always kills many. Hand in hand with this centralization, or this expropriation of many capitalists by few, develop, on an ever extending scale, the cooperative form of the labor-process, the conscious technical application of science, the methodical cultivation of the soil, the transformation of the instruments of labor only usable in common, the economizing of all means of production of combined, socialized labour, the entanglement of all peoples in the net of the world-market, and with this, the international character of the capitalist regime.[17]

One "international" aspect of capitalism's drive towards "centralization" which Marx did not apparently foresee was that it applied between as well as within nations—the "uneven" development of world capitalism noted by Lenin. Following World War II this process elevated the United States to an absolute dominance among the capitalist nations, and this dominance although weakened in recent decades still exists. As a result, the economic situation in the United States vitally affects that in the rest of the capitalist world. This process, however, although affecting the form of world capitalist development does not affect the nature of capitalism itself. Nor has this been changed by the rise of imperialism in general.

Colonial (or neocolonial) profits and superprofits, Marx would point out, still come from the surplus value extracted from labor. Commodities are still exchanged at their values and exchange of itself still produces no value. Nothing basically different has been added by bigness, by the fact of capital concentration, by conglomerates, by multinational corporations by "third world" exploitation. Laboring power is still a commodity that the (collective) worker sells on the market, and the worth of this commodity is what it costs to keep the worker everywhere as a functioning machine, socially and biologically. And although what Engels called a labor "aristocracy" for a time expanded in capitalist nations (it is now declining) and received a greater share of surplus value (largely derived from colonial labor exploitation) than did nineteenth-century workers, Marx would doubtless see this as counterbalanced in the total system by the lesser share received by the colonial or neocolonial workers. The total exchange-value of this commodity (labor) he would see as still necessarily less than that of the exchange-value of the goods the worker produces (in the world-imperialist system). Even "aristocratic" workers are still workers and still exploited. Production is still for profit and still comes from surplus value.[18]

Marx, we might expect, would have little patience with the—essentially semantic—argument that with the rise of monopolies private "ownership" of the means of production was exchanged for corporate "control" and that this invalidated his general theory. Whether one called it ownership or control he would view as of little consequence, for the relationship was still basically the same: namely one that enabled the capitalist, corporate or individual, to extract surplus value from the worker. Capitalism still acted like capitalism—with its crises and polarization. Just as it mattered little to the feudal peasant whether he was exploited by an individual landlord or a group of landlords acting jointly, so it matters little to the worker whether he is exploited by an individual capitalist or by a large corporation. Capitalism is still capitalism.

Nor would Marx have much patience with the argument that with the rise of corporate capital competition has decreased or vanished. He would presumably point to the cannibalistic devouring of corporations by other corporations as indicating that competition is still there but the units involved are larger. And competition, Engels would doubtless emphasize, still drives capitalism to wild expansion beyond the capacity of the market. If there is—and this is doubtful—somewhat less total anarchy in production in monopoly capitalism, anarchy is still of its essence. The big corporations know little more than did the nineteenth-century capitalists of the actual extent of projected sales and have no basic control over the total market.

Great corporations flounder and go under just as the smaller ones did. The scenario is on a bigger scale but it is essentially the same scenario.

The social effects of capitalism are clearly still basically the same as when Engels saw them in 1845. The worker is still sold, as in the 1840s, "like a piece of goods." The masses are still doped with drink and religion, still fleeced by patent medicine firms, still thrown on the scrap heap when old; families are still riven by conflicts arising inevitably from exploitation and oppression; prostitution is still rife; crime rampant; the prisons full. Workers are still killed or maimed by the thousands in industrial accidents and slowly poisoned by chemicals at their work, probably at a higher rate than in Engels's day. To these horrors, monopoly capitalism had added those of massive war, whose half-human victims are hidden away by the millions in hospitals and psychiatric institutions; and it now threatens humanity with nuclear destruction and chemical and bacteriological warfare.

Turning from the general structure and functioning of capitalism to its evolutionary movement—which Marx was particularly interested in—let us look at a brief description of the capitalist system in the 1970s written by Paul M. Sweezy, a Marxist economist, in December 1979:

> The marked slowdown in average rates of growth accompanied by high and in some cases even rising inflation, both characteristics of the last five or six years, are not normal capitalist phenomena. Other ominous developments have been the enormous expansion of debts at both national and international levels, the growing instability of the international monetary system, the resurgence of protectionism in various forms, and a skyrocketing increase in the price of gold and other commodities thought to be relatively safe repositories of value. These are all signs that the global capitalist system has entered a time of troubles from which there is no obvious escape route.[19]

According to Sweezy (and Marxist economists in general) world capitalism began a general decline in the 1970's from which it will not recover. And events since then have confirmed this view. The crisis of the 1970's has continued—on a world-capitalist scale—in the early 1980's. The so-called "recovery" in the United States is essentially a matter of increased profits by the large corporations and clearly rests on shaky foundations. Production is still far below plant capacity and there is little long-term investment in new plant or equipment; the increased corporation profits come mainly from concessions wrung from the workers, and these will at some point be halted. Moreover this United States "recovery" is taking place in an unstable international economic situation. The growth rate of world capitalism has not only slowed but in some countries has become not a growth rate but a rate of decline. Whereas in the 1970s such capitalist nations as West Germany and Japan continued to flourish, in the early 1980s they too are being struck by crisis, as are France, Italy, and Britain. In Britain—as in the United States—inflation has been retarded by a deliberate slowing of the economy but this has resulted in massive unemployment and, hence, a decrease in purchasing power that will in time deepen the crisis. Both national and international debts have increased in the early 1980s and the international monetary system, with its imperialist investments, faces defaults of massive proportions, especially from third world nations, and perhaps also faces an international banking crisis. The "resurgence of protectionism" tends to become a panicky gallop as each national capitalism tries to save its own neck but is partly held in check by corporations with large international investments that trumpet patriotism as they undermine the national interest. These signs of decline are now so obvious that one does not need to be an economist to see them. Can these trends, however, now some ten years old, be reversed, say by the middle or late 1980s and a return made to the capitalist expansion of the 1950s and 1960s? To get perspective on this question we have to note the nature of this expansion and the decades that preceded it.

None of these decades, from the 1920s to the 1950s were exactly models of stability. Wild inflation and ruin followed World War I, and scarcely had capitalism begun to get on its feet—in part by reconstructing the mass of capital it had itself destroyed—than it was struck by the devastation of the greatest economic crisis of its history, the Great Depression of the early 1930s. Following the depression came World War II and, once again, capitalism recovered. This time, however, it did not slide into a major depression but followed a course of alternating booms and smaller depressions—"recessions." One key to this accomplishment was early perceived by the capitalists themselves, as noted in *U.S. News & World Report* in 1949:

> Government planners figure they have found the magic formula for almost endless good times. . . . Cold War is the catalyst. Cold War is an automatic pump primer. Turn a spigot, the public clamors for more arms spending. . . . Cold War demands, if fully exploited, are almost limitless.

As it turned out "cold war" was not enough, and slidings towards depression had to be reversed by "hot war," in Korea in the early 1950s and Vietnam,

Laos and Cambodia in the late 1960s and early 1970s, a "pump priming" with the blood of the peoples of East Asia. Cold war or hot war, however, the economic principle was the same: stimulate the economy with massive war spendings and seize international markets. If we consider the war spendings in the United States, the largest of the capitalist powers, it is apparent that if the war budget in, say, 1969 had been reduced to the level of 1929 the economy would have been in as severe a depression as that of the early 1930s. It was not, then, just a matter of clever businessmen learning how to increase their earnings by "pump priming" but a matter of capitalist survival. The capitalists were, to change the metaphor, at one and the same time trying to keep a leaky boat afloat and drive it at full speed.[20]

The economic expansion of the 1950s and 1960s—which was interlaced with recessions—was, then, largely due to artificial stimulation arising from unprecedented war spending. And this spending was continued into the 1970s even after the Vietnam war ended (with the defeat of the United States imperialist forces). Why, then, was this even greater pump priming not "limitless"? Why the financial crisis of the 1970s with its explosive inflation, mounting debts and wildly fluctuating gold and currency prices amid growing unemployment and falling wages? The answer apparently is that there is a limit to the power of governmental spending to stimulate a capitalist economy under conditions of general decline, a phenomenon which must ultimately be based on the nature of capitalism itself with its market limitations resulting from the existence of surplus value. To this general phenomenon has been added a specific one arising from the particular form of governmental spending under discussion, namely armament and military-maintenance spending.

Armament production and military spending in general, as Marxist and other economists have noted, are a major source of inflation because they pour money but not goods into the system. Producing armaments, in fact, is economically about the same as producing machines and factories and then dumping them in the ocean. For a time this process stimulates a wide section of the economy, but as it continues it creates an imbalance in the relation of goods to money. Furthermore, armaments and other war-spending and the vast military establishments connected with them are a major cause for the debt and credit explosion that is almost as alarming to some economists as is inflation. And, finally, war industry is so highly mechanized that it creates comparatively few jobs and hence provides relatively little increase in mass purchasing power.

How does the present situation and that of the preceding decades compare with the projections of Marx and Engels? The answer, in brief, is that the projections have proved to be correct in general but differ in certain secondary ways. As a result of intensive imperialist exploitation, war, and military spending, capitalism has lasted longer than Marx and Engels seem to have anticipated, although Engels in his later years clearly did not expect any imminent collapse. The cyclical crises have, as they both anticipated, gotten worse, but not in a simple declining series. They dropped all at once in the 1930s into an unprecedented economic hole from which war made escape possible and brought a series of recessions within a general expansion. Then in the 1970s the recessions began to take the form that Engels anticipated, namely that of chronic crises. Whether or not these events are accompanied by a declining tendency in the rate of profit is a matter of dispute among Marxist economists, some arguing that such a decline is demonstrably present. Certainly there can be no argument that the phenomenon Marx and Engels expected to accompany this decline is taking place, namely an increase in machinery in relation to human labor power, an increase which with the development of automation, computers, and robots has already reached monstrous proportions and threatens to increase still further. This phenomenon has clearly—as Engels predicted—contributed to the growing mass of the unemployed—with the consequent, depression-producing drop in consumer purchasing power. And ultimately, it has to be realized, the system rests on consumer purchasing. Capitalists cannot continue indefinitely to sell capital goods to each other.[21]

Finally, is the drama of the disintegration of capitalism ultimately a reflection of the "conflict" between the productive forces and the productive relationships that Marx saw as the basic determinant of historical development in all epochs? That the productive forces of capitalism are being held back by its productive relationships was first graphically demonstrated in the Great Depression with its deliberate destruction of farm and other products. And in spite of increases in production over the past decades and periods of "ups" as well as "downs" the fact that productivity is far below potential is shown by the increasing amount of idle productive forces.

As Marx noted in his polarization passage, economic developments are interconnected with social developments, and in projecting the future of capitalism this interconnection has to be taken into account. The attempt, most notably in the United States and in Great Britain, to shift the burden of the recession to the backs of the workers will be reversed only by social struggle. And the war-drives of capitalism are meeting massive resistance that will grow in the future. As a result of the development of the socialist nations there has been no world war or war between major powers for nearly forty years. Capitalism has been forced into the area of smaller—though often devastating—wars and even this area is closing down. These interconnections of economic and social forces, however, can best be considered— in the next chapter—in the total historical context of our era, which involves socialism as well as capitalism.

5

Communism

The Revolutionary Prelude

After discussing the increasing monopoly of capitalism in his "one capitalist kills many" polarization passage, Marx, as we have noted, went on to project future socioeconomic developments:

> Along with the constantly diminishing number of the magnates of capital, who usurp and monopolise all advantages of this process of transformation, grows the mass of misery, oppression, slavery, degradation, exploitation; but with this too grows the revolt of the working-class, a class always increasing in numbers, and disciplined, united, organized by the very mechanism of the process of capitalist production itself. The monopoly of capital becomes a fetter upon the mode of production, which has sprung up and flourished along with, and under it. Centralization of the means of production and socialization of labor at last reach a point where they become incompatible with their capitalist integument. This integument is burst asunder. The knell of capitalist private property sounds. The expropriators are expropriated.

The tendency of capitalism to concentrate in larger units would produce a parallel social concentration of the workers in these larger production units—which is what Marx means by "socialization." As at the same time "the mass of misery" would worsen (presumably in response to the decline of the rate of profit and other factors noted in *Capital*), the workers would increasingly rebel against capitalism as a system. The deeper historical process involved, as we have noted, Marx saw as that of the "conflict" between the productive forces and the productive relationships of capitalism. In the last such conflict the productive relationships of feudalism—based on land ownership—had held back the productive forces of developing capitalism. Now, however, the productive relationships of capitalism—based on the private ownership of capital—were retarding the productive forces developed by capitalism itself, and doing so with increasing pressure. In the previous feudal-capitalist conflict the capitalist class had won because it was able to free the productive forces for further development. Now, however, the capitalists must go down in their turn, for not they but the workers now occupy this position. The productive forces can be freed to expand only by the abolition of capitalism as a system and the seizure of these forces by the proletariat. Although this process would again take the form of a struggle for power between classes, with conflicting political leaders and ideas on both sides, it would again be rooted in objective historical process: "The appropriation is accomplished by the action of the immanent laws of capitalist production itself, by the centralization of capital."[1]

Although some modern economists treat the capitalist economic system as a virtually encapsulated entity whose movements can be determined by semi-algebraic formulae, it is clear that Marx did not do so. Although he saw economic movement as basic, he also saw it as inextricably interwoven with social movement. Thus a purely economic curve of capitalist demise would never touch bottom because before it did so social forces would intervene. In short the proletariat would expropriate the expropriators.

The proletariat would, however, not merely take over the means of production, it would operate them in a new form of society, one which had never before existed. Thus the working class could do something no mass oppressed class had done. In feudal and feudal-commercial societies in Europe and Asia, the peasants had many times rebelled and set up new regimes, such as that of the Heavenly Kingdom in China in Marx's day, but each time they had failed to achieve stability and collapsed, primarily because a peasantry is unable to put together an integrated economic system even when, as in the Heavenly Kingdom, it gets merchant support. So, too, with the slave revolts of Roman Italy, and with those of the city workers in commercial-feudal Europe.

Unlike the peasantry, the working class is, Marx emphasized, a concentrated class in a centralized economy, not one widely scattered in small units; a class engaged in collective and not individual competitive activity. Unlike the artisans or cottage industry and mill workers of commercial-feudal society, it operates the central means of production. It has connections through its network of trade unions with the economic system as a whole. It is a class that achieved literacy and has its own newspapers and periodicals. In short, it is a mass, exploited class with the potential to become a ruling class. To the argument that such a class could not operate the complex economic-financial structure left by capitalism Marx would have replied that it would not attempt to but would simply abolish this structure (although retaining the means of production) and build from the bottom up, organizing production and transportation in its own way, through its unions and other organizations, and creating whatever financial system was necessary for their operation (minus stock markets and brokerage houses).

It has been argued that Marx is projecting an inexorable "absolute impoverishment" in his polarization passage and this has not occurred. Marx, however, does not say this. Nor did Engels so interpret the passage. In 1885, in commenting on his *Condition of the Working Class in England,* written in 1844 and 1845, and after noting that a large section of the working class, those in the craft unions, had improved their conditions, he continued:

> But as to the great mass of working people, the state of misery and insecurity in which they live is as low as ever, if not lower. The East End of London is an ever-spreading pool of stagnant misery and desolation, of starvation when out of work, and degradation, physical and moral, when in work. And so in all other large towns—abstraction [separation] made of the privileged minority of the workers; and so in the smaller towns and in the agricultural districts.[2]

Engels, then, does not say that the workers in the 1880s were absolutely worse off than they were in the 1840s only that their condition was "as low" or "lower." He notes also that within this mass a less-exploited group of skilled workers has arisen—an improvement in conditions for some. And he realized that this group was living largely on the wealth extracted from India and other colonies. Today in estimating the "mass of misery" caused by capitalism as a world system, we would have to include the situation of these masses in colonial and other exploited nations. This total world-wide capitalist-created "mass of misery" appears to be greater than that in nineteenth-century capitalism, but, greater or less, the debate is, in any case, of little moment. As the history of the present century amply demonstrates, there is enough "misery" to form—in conjunction with other factors—an effective world revolutionary potential.

It has to be understood also that in this passage Marx was not attempting to project future events but to outline the underlying factors of a historical process. Although it is true that if the passage is read in isolation it can inadvertently convey the impression of two social armies lining up for a battle, Marx did not intend this. He was aware that future revolutionary struggles would be at least as complex as those of his own age. As he noted in his *Address to the Communist League* in 1850: "We say to the workers, 'You have got to go through, fifteen, twenty, fifty years of civil wars and national wars not merely to change your conditions but in order to change yourselves and become qualified for political power.' " And no doubt he would have shared the general prospect of future events that Engels so prophetically and vividly sketched out in 1887:

And finally no war is any longer possible for Prussia-Germany except a world war and a world war indeed of an extension and violence hitherto undreamt of. Eight to ten millions of soldiers will mutually massacre one another and in doing so devour the whole of Europe until they have stripped it barer than any swarm of locusts has ever done. The devastations of the Thirty Years' War compressed into three or four years, and spread over the whole Continent; famine, pestilence, general demoralization both of the armies and of the mass of the people produced by acute distress; hopeless confusion of our artificial machinery in trade, industry, and credit, ending in general bankruptcy; collapse of the old states and their traditional state wisdom to such an extent that crowns will roll by dozens on the pavement and there will be nobody to pick them up; absolute impossibility of foreseeing how it will all end and who will come out of the struggle as victor; only one result absolutely certain: general exhaustion and the establishment of the conditions for the ultimate victory of the working class. This is the prospect when the system of mutual outbidding in armaments, driven to extremities, at last bears its inevitable fruits. This, my lords, princes and statesmen, is where in your wisdom you have brought old Europe. And when nothing more remains to you but to open the last great war dance—that will suit us all right. The war may perhaps push us temporarily into the background, may wrench from us many a position already conquered. But when you have unfettered forces which you will then no longer be able again to control, things may go as they will: at the end of the tragedy you will be ruined and the victory of the proletariat will either be already achieved or at any rate inevitable.[3]

In making this prediction of the course of events, Engels was not simply guessing but making a projection from observable historical trends as analyzed by Marxism. Although here placing the emphasis on political factors, he was of course, aware of the underlying economic causes which Marx stressed. He took it for granted that his readers would understand that behind the "system of mutual outbidding in armaments" lay capitalist competition, and that behind the growing and "hopeless" disintegration of the economy, blending with political and social upheavals, lay the general processes of capitalist decay that he and Marx had elsewhere depicted. We might note, too, that Engels is projecting a long, complex struggle perhaps embracing several generations. He is envisaging not one but two or more major stages of development. In the first stage war will produce economic chaos and revolutions of various kinds, some antimonarchical—"crowns will roll by dozens"—and some primarily working class. These latter will not immediately result in the end of capitalism but only lay the basis for a future proletarian takeover: "conditions for the ultimate victory of the working class." Then will come the "last great war dance." This may end—after various ups and downs—in working class states or perhaps only make an advance toward them: "already achieved or at any rate inevitable." Working class revolutions could not, of course, occur if it were not for the particular nature of the class, its operating the capitalist means of production, its exploitation, and its concentration into increasingly larger economic units. Nor could such revolutions occur without the general decline of the capitalist system interlaced with the increasing cyclical cruises he and Marx had predicted. The basic revolutionary struggle Engels is projecting, that is to say, is that of the proletariat and the bourgeoisie, the bourgeoisie increasingly monopolistic, the proletariat increasingly exploited but also "increasing in numbers, and disciplined, united, organized by the very mechanism of process of capitalist production itself." This class will after many struggles take over the economic system and, in effect, run it without benefit of its capitalist masters. True, Marx and Engels do not anywhere put all the segments of their concept of immediate future development succinctly together in any one passage, but they were not, after all, writing a textbook. Their works arose in the main from urgent needs (to expose the nature of capitalism), from particular situations (the Paris Commune), or attacks on their views (as by Dühring), and they discuss in each work only what is relevant, sometimes expounding general theory, sometimes not. It is only by reading their works in some variety that we can begin to see the different facets of their world-view and their relevance to the whole. One form of attack on Marxism, in fact, is to take a particular passage—such as the polarization passage in *Capital*—and treat it as though it was the only thing that Marx wrote on the subject.

Although Engels in this passage was dealing with coming events in Europe, which he and Marx thought would be the prime center for world revolution because of its industrial development, they kept close contact with the situation in Asian and other colonial countries. The most general prediction of events in these areas came in a letter to the German socialist Karl Kautsky by Engels in 1882. In it Engels argued that working class revolt in the capitalist nations would be accompanied by nationalist revolt in the colonial world:

In my opinion the colonies proper, i.e., the countries occupied by a European population, Canada, the Cape, Australia, will all become independent; on the other hand the countries inhabited by a native population, which are simply subjugated, India, Algiers, the Dutch, Portuguese and Spanish possessions, must be taken over for the time being by the proletariat and led as rapidly as possible towards independence. How this process will develop is difficult to say. India will perhaps, indeed very probably, produce a revolution, and as the proletariat emancipating itself cannot conduct any colonial wars, this would have to be given full scope— it would not pass off without all sorts of destruction, of course, but that sort of thing is inseparable from all revolutions. The same might also take place elsewhere, e.g., in Algiers and Egypt, and would certainly be the best thing *for us*. We shall have enough to do at home. Once Europe is reorganised, and North America, that will furnish such colossal power and such an example that the semicivilised countries will follow in their wake of their own accord. Economic needs alone will be responsible for this. But as to what social and political phases these countries will then have to pass through before they likewise arrive at socialist organisation, we today can only advance rather idle hypotheses, I think. One thing alone is certain; the victorious proletariat can force no blessings of any kind upon any foreign nation without undermining its own victory by so doing. Which of course by no means excludes defensive wars of various kinds.[4]

Engels here projects a historical movement with several interlocking phases. In the first—implied rather than directly noted—the working class in the capitalist nations will take power. In the second the minor capitalist nations in the imperialist orbit will "become independent" and the "native population" in such "subjugated" colonies as India and Algeria will begin movements for independence, some of them revolutionary. At a first reading it might seem that Engels expected that these movements would be led by the working classes of the colonial countries, but it becomes apparent as we read on that by "the proletariat" he means the working class in the colony-holding nations, presumed to be already in revolt. This revolt would continue until European and American society was "reorganized," by which Engels intends Kautsky to understand "socialism." This socialist transformation of the previous main capitalist powers will lend impetus to the colonial revolutions both by "example" and economic assistance ("power"). Engels clearly did not believe that the working class in the colonial nations was then (1882) sufficiently developed to lead a socialist revolution or would be in the immediate future.

As the colonial nations struggle for independence the working class in the previous colony-holding nations must not attempt to suppress them, no matter how bloody the struggles become, but, on the contrary, "take them over" and assist in their revolutions. In doing so they will also help the movement towards socialism in their own nations ("the best thing *for us*"). This, however, is to be a temporary measure ("for the time being"), taken only until the "native population" develops sufficiently to take control itself. The colonial nations will in time move towards socialism through "social and political phases." This they must be allowed to do on their own.

Engels was clearly off the mark in some major respects (as Lenin in *Imperialism,* written some thirty-four years later, was not). Although the socialist revolution first took place in Europe and resulted in an industrialized, socialist state in the U.S.S.R., revolution in the colonial and semicolonial world—most notably in China—followed before west European capitalism (except in east Germany and Czechoslavakia) had collapsed, and it was a revolution led by native forces. But Engels's general outlook was, for the time, remarkably advanced. He saw something of the essence of coming developments, predicting massive colonial revolutions, although not their specific form, and this when Kautsky and other socialist leaders were almost obsessively Europe oriented. Furthermore, if we put these various passages from Marx and Engels together they give a remarkably true *general* picture of the major historical developments so far in the present century. Marx's view of increasing capitalist monopoly has clearly been borne out, and should be linked with his and Engels's prediction of worsening cyclical crises with general capitalist decline. As Engels foresaw in his "last great war dance" and other comments there has been "world war" followed by bourgeois, proletarian and colonial revolutions, some of which resulted in "the victory of the proletariat." Marx and Engels may at times have seen darkly through the glass but at least they saw, whereas the famed bourgeois "thinkers" of the later nineteenth century, from Carlyle to Nietzsche, saw nothing. Nor do such "thinkers" today.

The Two Phases of Communism

In the spring of 1875 the German socialist movement, which had been split into two sections, semi-Marxist and reformist, held a unity congress at the town of Gotha and produced a program which Engels considered "flabby and flavorless" and Marx condemned as full of "oratorical flourishes" about the "equal rights" of "all members of society" and lacking a realistic view of the coming communist society. It was important, they felt, to provide an antidote that would enable class-conscious workers to perceive the program's false perspective. This Marx proceeded to do in what he called a series of "marginal notes." These notes, which were suppressed at the time by the Social Democratic leadership and only published in 1891 after Engels unearthed a copy of them, constitute one of Marx's major theoretical writings, his most extensive commentary, in fact, on the future communist society. In them he condemns the Gotha socialists' woolly abstractions and discusses communism as an actual social system that would emerge from current developments. He indicated, as he had before, that a period of turbulent revolutionary struggle—not, as the Gotha program implied, a mere parliamentary "transition"—would advance into communism, a system antithetical to capitalism:

> Between capitalist and communist society lies a period of revolutionary transformation from one to the other. There corresponds also to this a political transition period during which the state can be nothing else than the revolutionary dictatorship of the proletariat.

Communist society would go from a lower phase into a higher one. In the lower phase there would be not a Utopia with "equal rights" for all but a society circumscribed by unavoidable limitations:

> What we have to deal with here is a communist society, not as if it had developed on a basis of its own, but on the contrary as it emerges from capitalist society, which is thus in every respect tainted economically, morally and intellectually with the hereditary diseases of the old society from whose womb it is emerging.

In this society there would be no absolute equality nor absolute rights:

> But one man will excel another physically or intellectually and so con-
> tributes in the same time more labor, or can labor for a longer time; and
> labor, to serve as a measure, must be defined by its duration or intensity,
> otherwise it ceases to be a standard measure. This equal right is an unequal
> right for unequal work. It recognizes no class differences because every
> worker ranks as a worker like his fellows, but it tacitly recognises unequal
> individual endowment, and thus capacities for production, as natural priv-
> ileges.

Thus there will in this first phase still be inequalities of income, although
not those of the extremes of capitalism, inequalities between higher and
lower paid workers, not between millionaires and slum-dwellers. "These
deficiencies," Marx continued, "are unavoidable in the first phase of communist society when it is just emerging after prolonged birthpangs from
capitalist society. Right can never be higher than the economic structure
and the cultural development of society conditioned by it."

In the higher stage of communist society these various "deficiencies"
will vanish, not because one wishes them to but because the working class
will create the socioeconomic base to make it possible:

> In a higher phase of communist society, after the tyrannical subordination
> of labor and thereby also the distinction between manual and intellectual
> work, have disappeared, after labor has become not merely a means to live
> but is in itself the first necessity of living, after the powers of production
> have also increased and all the springs of cooperative wealth are gushing
> more freely together with the all-round development of the individual,
> then and then only can the narrow bourgeois horizon of rights be left far
> behind and society will inscribe on its banner: "From each according to
> his capacity, to each according to his need."

This "higher phase" could not, of course, have developed if the workers had
not already expropriated the expropriators and substituted for the "anarchy"
of capitalist production a planned economic system.

In the first phase of communism, then, Marx expected that some
economic inequalities and "the distinction between manual and intellectual
work" would continue. Under "intellectual work" he must have intended
to include all needed professional skills—from accountants to architects—
and presumably he expected that this form of labor would be one of those
which would be highly compensated. It is not possible in this still relatively

undeveloped economy to pay "each according to his need." Instead "the individual producer receives back again from society, with deductions, exactly what he gives," that is to say the equivalent of "his individual amount of labor." The "deductions" include "reserve or insurance funds," taxes for school and health services, and monies to be used for "the extension of production" and "replacement for the means of production used up." Thus not only will there be a considerable spread in wages but these wages will necessarily be reduced in general by hidden or open deductions.[5]

Although Marx's comments on the Gotha Program are more specific than his or Engels's other comments on the communist future they do not differ from them, and, like them, follow from their "world view." For instance Marx had written in 1852 of the "transition period" (after stating that he had not "discovered" the class struggle as such):

> What I did that was new was to prove: (1) that the existence of classes is only bound up with particular, historic phases in the development of production; (2) that the class struggle necessarily leads to the dictatorship of the proletariat; (3) that this dictatorship itself only constitutes the transition to the abolition of all classes and to a classless society.

In the *Gotha Program* Marx makes it clear that the "dictatorship" is part of the "revolutionary transformation" of society from its capitalist to its communist stage, a period of "prolonged birth pangs." It was the form which "the state" would then assume. And this period must be the same as that of the "civil wars and national wars" during which the proletariat would not only change society but change itself and "become qualified for political power." Marx is, of course, projecting a major historical epoch and not brief or blocked-off steps. He did not imply a rigid line between the transition period and the "first phase" of communism. Clearly the "revolutionary transformation" would include the expropriation of the expropriators and this could hardly be done without being simultaneously consolidated by a proletarian dictatorship. And this movement and its accompanying dictatorship must blend into the "first phase" of communism. Marx did not spell out these interpenetrations because he was concentrating on the stages themselves but his depiction in his general statement (1859) of the previous "epoch" of transition, from feudalism to capitalism, suffices to show that he anticipated them, in fact assumed that his readers, realizing the historical scope of the picture, would take them for granted.[6]

The transition period was envisaged as one of wars and revolutions and the first phase of communism as one in which the evils of the old society, the manner of birth of the new, and a still comparatively low level of productivity would unite to make for the continuation of inequalities and injustices of various kinds. The writers of the *Gotha Program,* on the other hand, Marx implies, were not realistically thinking of their "socialist" state as historically emerging from capitalism but were simply creating fantasies. What they were actually proposing was to reform capitalism and project vague antiestablishment threats to gain concessions for the higher-paid workers and the middle class. In the course of this process they took isolated fragments from Marx and fitted them into a reform-of-capitalism perspective. A truly Marxist political program would have concentrated first on the dictatorship of the proletariat, the political force that would shape the new society.

How did Marx and Engels visualize this "dictatorship?" It would, Engels tells us, be very similar to the Paris Commune of 1871, when the Paris workers seized power following the Franco-Prussian war:

> Of late [1891] the Social-Democratic philistine has once more been filled with wholesome terror at the words: Dictatorship of the Proletariat. Well and good, gentlemen, do you want to know what this dictatorship looks like? Look at the Paris Commune. That was the Dictatorship of the Proletariat.

Engels, then, believed that the Commune foreshadowed the State in the transition period between capitalism and communism. Marx, who would doubtless have agreed, described the government of the Commune as follows, giving, in effect, a general picture of what he believed the future era of the dictatorship of the proletariat would be like:

> The Commune was formed of the municipal councillors, chosen by universal suffrage in various wards of the town, responsible and revocable at short terms. The majority of its members were naturally working men, or acknowledged representatives of the working class. The Commune was to be a working, not a parliamentary body, executive and legislative at the same time. Instead of continuing to be the agent of the Central Government, the police was at once stripped of its political attributes, and turned into the responsible and at all times revocable agent of the Commune. So were the officials of all other branches of the Administration. From the members of the Commune downwards, the public service had to be done at workmen's wages. The vested interests and the representation allowances of the high dignitaries of State disappeared along with the high dignitaries themselves. Public functions ceased to be the private property

of the tools of the Central Government. Not only municipal administration, but the whole initiative hitherto exercised by the State was laid into the hands of the Commune.

Having once got rid of the standing army and the police, the physical force elements of the old Government, the Commune was anxious to break the spiritual force of repression, the "parson-power," by the disestablishment and disendowment of all churches as proprietary bodies. The priests were sent back to the recess of private life, there to feed upon the alms of the faithful in imitation of their predecessors, the Apostles. The whole of the educational institutions were opened to the people gratuitously, and at the same time cleared of all interference of Church and State. . . . Like the rest of public servants, magistrates and judges were to be elective, responsible and revocable.

The leaders of the Paris Commune wished the commune system to spread throughout France, with Communes in every city and "rural communes" in "every district." The country was to be run by a network of communes, all basically similar to that of Paris.[7]

Marx had direct connection with the Commune through his leadership of the International, a sizeable bloc of whose members were elected to its leading body. These and other leaders of the Commune were well aware that they were taking over State power in a kind of city state and selected the key sources of this power: the government, the armed forces, the judiciary, Church, and the educational system. The Commune broke the armed forces of its opponents by substituting for them its own National Guard. The legal power was remolded by the "election" of magistrates subject to popular "recall." "Communal officials" of all kinds were to be similarly elected and subject to recall. Education was removed from the hands of the clergy.

The Commune's statement of economic reform was more cautious than the political and bears the imprint of compromise: "to universalize power and property in accordance with the needs of the moment, the wishes of those interested and the results of experience." As a beginning the unions were to draw up a list of factories abandoned by their owners (but not those still in operation) and then to run them "by the cooperative association of the workers employed in them." The Commune abolished fines in factories and night work in bakeries, declared a moratorium on rents, and, for three years, on debts, and began a program for the regulation of wages.

In order to carry out its program the Commune appointed nine commissions: war, finance, supplies, foreign affairs, education, justice, police, labor and exchange, and public services.

As in previous revolutions in France and elsewhere women seized the opportunity both to advance their own and the general political interest. In the Commune they showed disciplined militancy—there was a Women's Battalion in the National Guard—and advanced into the general leadership. One of these leaders, Louise Michel, was a socialist.

The Commune's only hope for survival would have been supportive revolts by the workers in Germany, Britain and other countries but this proved impossible, for nowhere else was there the revolutionary situation that the war had produced in (defeated) France. For two months the people of Paris held out, but, in the end an armed force of 70,000 broke through the defences and after eight days of bloody fighting the Commune came to an end. Thirty thousand men, women, and children were executed. "The ground," reported Louis Thiers, President of the Third French Republic, in a telegram to his government, "is paved with their corpses; this terrible spectacle will be a lesson to them." Outside the Polytechnic School alone there was a pile of corpses 100 yards long by 3 yards high. The existing graveyard facilities could not even begin to handle the situation. But the problem was solved. "Buses, char-a-banc, any vehicle which would hold the bodies, many of them far gone in decomposition, were requisitioned. The cemeteries were crammed. Great ditches were filled. The trenches dug during the war . . . were crammed too. But still there were too many. On the Buttes-Chaumont . . . they built a huge pyre. For days and days, a cloud of stinking smoke hung low over eastern Paris."[8]

Twenty years after the defeat of the Commune, Engels in preparing a new edition of Marx's *Address* added to Marx's comments in a Preface (1891). The workers, he tells us, were planning—just a month before the Commune was destroyed—to reorganize not only the State but also the economic system:

> By 1871, large-scale industry had already so much ceased to be an exceptional case even in Paris, the centre of artistic handicrafts, that by far the most important decree of the Commune instituted an organisation of large-scale industry and even of manufacture which was not only to be based on the association of the workers in each factory, but also to combine all these associations in one great union; in short, an organisation which, as Marx quite rightly says in *The Civil War*, must necessarily have led in the end to communism, that is to say, the direct opposite of the Proudhon doctrine.[9]

If the Commune as described by Marx and Engels does not sound much like a dictatorship this is because they were using the word dictatorship in the broad historical sense of the rule of a class and not in the narrowly political one of a dictatorial government. They considered bourgeois "democracy" a class dictatorship in which the real reins of power remained in bourgeois hands despite voting rights and parliaments. So, too, with a working-class State. Political power would be in the hands of the working class; as the class was both large itself and would seek allies among the middle class and peasants—the Commune's "victory" was the peasant's "only hope"—its State, Marx expected, would be a mass democracy. It would, however, be repressive in relation to its class enemies: "a reign of labor." Hence it was a democracy for the workers and their allies, but a dictatorship in relation to the bourgeoisie, an aspect of power that would decline as the bourgeoisie itself declined. This kind of mass revolutionary State, Marx believed, would prevail in the transition period between capitalism and communism.

One of Engels' main objections to the Gotha Program was its failure to emphasize the trade union movement, which is, he wrote, "the real class organization of the proletariat, in which it fights out its daily battle with capital, in which it trains itself." And Marx, looking ahead, saw the trade unions as an instrument for the transition from capitalism to communism:

> If the Trades' Unions are required for the guerilla fights between capital and labor, they are still more important as organized agencies for superseding the very system of wages labour and capital rule. . . . Apart from their original purposes, they must now learn to act deliberately as organizing centers of the working class in the broad interest of its complete emancipation. They must aid every social and political movement tending in that direction. Considering themselves and acting as the champions and representatives of the whole working class, they cannot fail to enlist the nonsociety men into their ranks. They must look carefully after the interests of the worst paid trades, such as the agricultural labourers, rendered powerless by exceptional circumstances. They must convince the world at large that their efforts, far from being narrow and selfish, aim at the emancipation of the downtrodden millions.

Marx, then, obviously expected the trade unions to be a major force in the dictatorship of the proletariat, especially in the economic sphere.[10]

Although the Commune was basically working class this was not reflected adequately in its political structure. Only twenty-one members of its Communal Council of ninety-two were workers; thirty were professionals and thirteen were small businessmen. As a result the Council was unable to put its plans for economic reorganization into effect. Influenced by Proudhon reformism they had failed to seize the reins of economic power. "The hardest thing to understand," Engels commented, "is certainly the holy awe with which they remained standing respectfully outside the gates of the Bank of France. This was also a serious political mistake. The bank in the hands of the Commune—this would have been worth more than ten thousand hostages." Obviously, then, during the projected future period of proletarian dictatorship Engels expected that banks and other economic units would be taken over as the revolution moved towards the first phase of communism. This would require political repression by the workers:

> A revolution is certainly the most authoritarian thing there is; it is the act whereby one part of the population imposes its will upon the other part by means of rifles, bayonets and cannon—authoritarian means, if such there be at all; and if the victorious party does not want to have fought in vain, it must maintain this rule by means of the terror which its arms inspire in the reactionaries. Would the Paris Commune have lasted a single day if it had not made use of this authority of the armed people against the bourgeois? Should we not, on the contrary, reproach it for not having used it freely enough?

The workers would, of course, not only use force but all aspects of State power. They would do so, however, not within the old State structure but within that of a new mass, revolutionary State similar to the Commune:

> From the very outset the Commune was compelled to recognise that the working class, once come to power, could not go on managing with the old state machine; that in order not to lose again its only just conquered supremacy, this working class must, on the one hand, do away with all the old repressive machinery previously used against itself, and, on the other, safeguard itself against its own deputies and officials, by declaring them all, without exception, subject to recall at any moment.

And in his Preface to the German 1872 edition of the *Communist Manifesto,* Engels noted (quoting Marx): "One thing especially was proved by the Commune, viz., that 'the working class cannot simply lay hold of the ready-made State machinery, and wield it for its own purposes.' " "The Commune," as Marx also commented, "was to be a working, not a parliamentary body, executive and legislative at the same time." The political body of the State in the dictatorship of the proletariat, then, was not to be a parliamentary talk-shop but an active entity which like that of the Commune, would embrace mass organizations and encourage their participation at all levels of government. As "the expropriators" were "expropriated," the political repression of the enemies of the working class would continue; a new State would develop; political and economic change would go hand in hand.[11]

The initial material basis for communist society would be the concentrated means of industrial production developed by capitalism. These the workers would not destroy but develop further—as the Chartists had earlier argued. They would develop them, however, not for private profit or amid the anarchy decreed by a competitive market but as part of a planned, cooperative economy:

> Crises will cease to be; the extended production, which in the present system of society spells overproduction and is such a mighty cause of misery, will then not even suffice and have to be further expanded. Instead of bringing misery in its wake, overproduction exceeding the immediate needs of society, will satisfy the needs of all, will create new needs and simultaneously the means for their gratification. It will become the condition and stimulus of further progress, it will achieve progress, without, as heretofore, always involving the social order in confusion. Once liberated from the yoke of private ownership, large-scale industry will develop on a scale that will make its present level of development seem as paltry as seems the manufacturing system compared with large-scale industry of our time.

The new order which Engels is here envisaging is clearly the same as or at least blending into Marx's "higher phase of communist society." In this phase Marx projected "the abolition of all classes" and the creation of "a classless society," the result of high economic productivity in a communally planned economy. A general community of people of diverse skills would arise as "the distinction between manual and intellectual work" disappeared.

As classes disappeared so, too, Engels emphasized, would the State:

> As soon as there is no longer any class of society to be held in subjection; as soon as, along with class domination and the struggle for individual existence based on the former anarchy of production, the collisions and excesses arising from these have also been abolished, there is nothing more to be repressed which would make a special repressive force, a state, necessary. The first act in which the state really comes forward as the representative of society as a whole—the taking possession of the means of production in the name of society—is at the same time its last inde-

pendent act as a state. The interference of the state power in social relations becomes superfluous in one sphere after another, and then ceases of itself. The government of persons is replaced by the administration of things and the direction of the processes of production. The state is not "abolished," *it withers away.*

Engels does not, of course, mean that governmental administration will be abolished (Marx's comments on the Gotha Program imply a considerable administrative force):

All Socialists are agreed that the political state, and with it political authority, will disappear as a result of the coming social revolution, that is, that public functions will lose their political character and be transformed into the simple administrative functions of watching over the true interests of society.

What would disappear would be the repressive aspect of the State, the aspect which, Marx and Engels contended, was its essence. Once that was gone the State would be no longer a State but simply government (whose main function would be running the socialized economy).[12]

Engels, like Marx, is clearly thinking of a long historical process, of which he is here only expressing the essence. He obviously did not envisage any one period in which the means of production of the capitalist world would be seized by the proletariat, and the repressive aspect of the State "wither away." The proletariat would not, as he notes, abandon its State so long as there were antagonistic classes to repress.

In time, the distinction between town and country would disappear:

The abolition of the separation between town and country is therefore not utopian, even in so far as it presupposes the most equal distribution possible of large-scale industry over the whole country. It is true that in the huge towns civilization has bequeathed us a heritage to rid ourselves of which will take such time and trouble. But this heritage must and will be got rid of, however protracted the process may be . . . . the great towns will perish.

People, in communist society, will assume a variety of tasks: "the man who for half an hour gives instructions as an architect will also push a barrow for a period." Consequently, "each individual" will be given "the opportunity to develop and exercise all his faculties, physical and mental, in all directions." Marriage and family life will be transformed:

It [communist society] will make the relations between the sexes a purely private affair which concerns only the persons involved, and calls for no interferences by society. It is able to do this because it abolishes private property and educates children communally, destroying thereby the two foundation stones of hitherto existing marriage—the dependence of the wife upon her husband and of the children upon the parents conditioned by private property.[13]

Marx and Engels expected that communist society would be the last form of human society, for once the world's productive forces were communally owned no other form could arise. They anticipated that it would last not merely for thousands but for millions of years. It would not, however, last forever. In discussing Hegel's view of life as "endless ascendency from the lower to the higher," Engels commented:

It is not necessary, here, to go into the question of whether this mode of outlook is thoroughly in accord with the present position of natural science which predicts a possible end for the earth, and for its habitability a fairly certain one; which therefore recognizes that for the history of humanity also there is not only an ascending but also a descending branch.[14]

In considering these various projections of the future by Marx and Engels we have to distinguish between those which are an extrapolation from historical forces and those which are more speculative. The growing monopolization of capitalism, the coming of major wars between the great capitalist powers to be followed by revolutions, the rise of working-class revolutionary States blending into a growing world communism are such extrapolations. But predictions on such matters as the abolition of legal marriage, the communal bringing up of children, or the disappearance of cities—made primarily by Engels—are simply based on a general concept of what might happen when private property is abolished. Marx and Engels clearly regarded their projections on the dictatorship of the proletariat and the two phases of communist society as basic, the inevitable consequences of socioeconomic conditions already existing, a projection, in fact, simply one stage further than that of growing capitalist monopoly, war and revolution. As we have seen, these latter predictions have proved to be correct in general. What, then, of the others? Do the countries generally known today as socialist, primarily the U.S.S.R., represent the dictatorship of the proletariat and the first phase of communism?

The Socialist World

"The Russians," Engels noted in 1885, "are approaching their 1789." As the comment shows, Engels was thinking of a revolution of the bourgeoisie in the urban areas and the peasants in the country, directed at overthrowing the feudal power—as in France in 1789. This appeared to be so at the time but economic advance soon radically changed the picture.

In the 1890s Russian industry began to move forward rapidly. By 1913 Russia was producing 40 million tons of coal and 10 million tons of oil and had the largest oil center in the world at Baku (in Stalin's native Georgia). An industrial proletariat necessarily arose with the industry—as a startled world discovered when in the course of the 1905 revolution there occurred the most massive strike movement in European labor history to that time: three million strikers. On the eve of the March 1917 revolution the Russian aristocracy, shaken by the 1905 revolution, was in decline, penetrated by capitalist interests, foreign and domestic, and the peasantry, although massive and socially important, was of secondary historical significance. The basic political struggle, as events were soon to demonstrate, was that between the bourgeoisie and proletariat. In July 1917 an all-Russian Conference of Trade Unions registered nearly one-and-a-half million members in 976 unions. The metal workers' union in Petrograd had 16,000 members in March, 70,000 in June, 138,000 in August. Paralleling this increase in economic organization during the months of ferment leading to the November revolution was political organization in the Soviets (councils) of Workers, Soldiers, and Peasant Deputies. In August there were 600 soviets in Russia, representing 23 million workers and peasants. The workers' delegates to the soviets were mainly elected directly from the factory, each delegate representing 100 workers. The peasants elected two delegates from each township to each district soviet. As the dynamic center of the revolution was in the cities this meant that the core of the revolutionary bodies was proletarian.[15]

The Russian Social Democratic Party, with some of whose early leaders Engels had been in touch, had split in 1903 into a Bolshevik (majority) and a Menshevik (minority) faction. As the revolution progressed, the workers and their trade union and other organizations turned more and more to the Bolsheviks, led by Lenin, with their platform of working-class seizure of power.

The actual seizure of power in Petrograd was under the direction of a Revolutionary Military Committee appointed by the Petrograd Soviet. In addition to soldiers and sailors it contained representatives of the "railway men's union, post and telegraph union, soviets of factory and mill committees, soviet of labor unions." When this committee seized the key points of power, including the parliament, it handed power over to the All-Russian Congress of Soviets, a body in which the majority of the delegates were by then Bolshevik members or followers, a majority achieved in some nine months of bitter social and political struggle. The Congress elected a Council of People's Commissaries to conduct the government's business, a council revocable at its demand. This Council became the executive governmental body, and its central core consisted of Bolsheviks.

One of the first orders of business of the Council was to dismantle the old State. The old parliament was a mere shell. The next step was to replace the old legal system with a new one. "District courts, courts of appeal . . . military and naval courts" were "abolished" and were to be replaced by "courts established on the basis of democratic elections." The banking system was nationalized: "All banking business is declared a state monopoly." The basic industrial plants were nationalized, including 215 metal plants, 311 textile, 99 mineral fuel, 57 mines, 40 electrical plants, and 40 cement. Their overall production was in the hand of a Supreme Economic Council. In actuality the nationalization decrees followed actual plant seizures by the workers. Of 513 enterprises taken over by June 1918, 413 were taken over locally. These plants were placed under workers' control: "In the interests of a systematic regulation of national economy, Workers' Control is introduced in all industrial, commercial, agricultural (and similar) enterprises." The plants were to be run locally by "factory and shop committees," and overall district planning to be in the hands of district soviets. In all these actions, as Lenin later noted, the trade unions played a vital role: "without their hearty support and self-sacrificing work . . . it would, of course, have been impossible for us to govern the country." The constitution, adopted in July 1918, gave the right to vote to all citizens "without distinction of sex, religion, or nationality." "It is essential," Lenin wrote, "that women workers take an ever-increasing part in the administration of public enterprises and in the administration of the state." If we add to all this the fact that one of the first acts of the new government was to hand over the land—including the great feudal estates—to the peasants it is hard to deny that this is indeed an example of the "expropriation of the expropriators" that Marx foresaw. And the new state clearly had even more characteristics of what Marx and Engels considered the dictatorship of the proletariat than did the Paris Commune. The November 1917 Revolution in Russia, that is to say, was essentially a proletarian revolution of the type that Marx and Engels had anticipated. This has been disputed in part because of the bourgeois-feudal conflict, which some view as the basic one, and the massive peasant economy. But Russia's industrial development, as we have noted, was sufficient to provide proletarian dominance, and this is the essential factor in determining the nature of the revolution. The fact that the bourgeois revolution laid a base for the proletarian revolution eased its way, but did not determine its nature or that of the society that followed. The proletarian revolution triumphed comparatively easily because the bourgeoisie was comparatively weak, but it was still proletarian.[16]

If the new, soviet society was, then, both the result of an expropriation of the expropriators and an example of proletariat dictatorship, does it also represent what Marx considered the "first phase" of communism and was later called—by Lenin and others—socialism? In considering this question we have again to distinguish between primary and secondary factors. The primary factor is the general nature of the society. On this there has been wide and heated debate, but the following characteristics are clear, even to gross observation: the economy—unlike that in capitalist countries—is planned and balanced; economic development steady, if sometimes slow, with bust-and-boom crises eliminated, along with unemployment and extremes of wealth and poverty; housing provided for all at a minimal rent; medical and social services and education free or virtually so; and women widely employed in the trades and professions and possessing full legal rights. There are wage differences but these are minor compared to those of capitalism. There are no millionaires and no paupers. The industrial means of production are owned by the State. Agriculture is collectivized. The emphasis in production is on mass necessities with few luxury items. In short, it is a mass-oriented society that generally reflects Marx's "first phase" and Engels's depictions of the early stages of the new order. The arguments that it does not are varied, one of the most common being that a "new bourgeoisie" has arisen, taken control of the economic system, and is operating it for profit and its own material comfort. Hence, the U.S.S.R. has "returned to capitalism." That the U.S.S.R. is not capitalist, however, is sufficiently shown by the basic economic facts that its economy is centrally planned, does not go through capitalist boom-and-bust cycles, and operates without unemployment. Thus, whatever the "new bourgeoisie" does, it does not run a capitalist system. Is there, however, in fact a new bourgeoise? Clearly not in any meaningful sense, for a bourgeoisie without capitalism is not a bourgeoisie. What there is, however, is what was designated by

Lenin, Stalin, and others as an "intelligentsia," that is to say a group of top professionals whose special skills are necessary for the operation of the society. This was early noted by Lenin who advocated the employment of specialists "to direct the labor process and the organization of production, for there are no other people who have practical experience in this business." These professionals—at first mainly from the old society but now from the new— have in the interest of increasing production been granted higher average wages than workers; but Marx, as we saw, expected that there would be considerable wage differential in his "first phase." And some professionals have also—for the same reason—been granted special privileges in housing, shopping, and other fields. This, however, is clearly not at all the same kind of thing as a bourgeoisie that owns a nation's economic system and runs it for profit.[17]

Fundamentally—although designated by Stalin and others as a "stratum"—this group is the upper segment of a new class. In feudal and capitalist societies the professionals are part of either the middle class—along with small business people; or the bourgeoisie—along with the large capitalists, whose economic and other interests they serve. But with the rise of socialist society with its complex planned economy and its massive social services an actual—and large—class of professionals was needed. This class, whose lower segment blends into the working class, works on the whole in the proletarian interests, but its upper echelons have at times attempted to invade the proletarian power, notably under Nikita Khrushchev; but that the proletarian power remained, and remains, essentially intact is shown by the general nature of the society, the emphasis upon socialist industrialization, and the political structure, whose composition has been becoming increasingly proletarian in recent decades. Marx and Engels did not specifically anticipate the creation of a professional class in socialist society but they would hardly have been surprised by it in view of the social and economic needs Marx projected in his *Gotha Program.*

It has also been argued that the U.S.S.R. cannot be considered a socialist nation of the kind envisaged by Marx because its political structure is dominated by a political party of a highly disciplined nature and comparatively small membership. But obviously a revolution cannot run itself, nor can a socialist state. The basic question is whether or not this party has on the whole acted in the interests of the proletariat. And here the record seems clear. It was the party which did the practical organizing of the revolution, overthrew both feudal and capitalist power, and went on to win a bitter civil war and then to build a great industrial state on a planned economy basis. Otherwise, it would still be an exploitive capitalist state with feudal trimmings. It was the party that rallied the people to victory over invading German imperialism. These accomplishments have, some argue, to be balanced by the "purges" of the later 1930s. But it has also to be recorded that these purges were called forth by massive antisocialist sabotage and that many observors at the time—as now seems conveniently forgotten—including the United States ambassador, Joseph E. Davis, who attended the trials, believed that most or all of the accused leaders were guilty—as Davis noted in his *Mission to Moscow*. And if the leaders were guilty most of their followers must have been also. It is clear, too, that the Party and Stalin in the following years had overwhelming popular support. In considering anti-Sovietism in general, however, we have to realize that we are not dealing primarily with facts but with villification reflecting the antiproletariat hysteria of the world bourgeoisie, a villification tied up with a "mad monster" caricature of Stalin and a stereotype of the Soviet people as robots.

That there are deficiencies in Soviet society is obvious. The most serious of these, including lags in labor productivity resulting from slackness and absenteeism, the Soviet authorities are trying to correct. And although there have been great cultural advances there should have been more. Soviet writers on historical and dialectical materialism, for instance, have developed a semidogmatic approach that virtually precludes advance in the realm of general theory. In considering such deficiencies, however, Marxists have to see them in Marxist terms. What Marx would have said of such deficiencies is clear from the *Gotha Program*. He would have regarded them in general as the inevitable consequences of a society but shortly emerged from capitalism (and feudalism)—and existing in a still dominantly capitalist world. He would have seen that whatever its faults, this society is on the whole the best that history can produce at present and that those who lamentingly parade Utopian blueprints are trying not to help but to hinder. He would have seen also that it is a vigorous and growing social organism, and that if we had a world of nations like the U.S.S.R., there would be neither war nor imperialism, neither exploitation nor mass oppression, and no threat of nuclear annihilation.

Projection and Reality

Although Engels' "last great war dance" with its accompanying revolutions generally fits events after World War I does it fit those following

World War II? During that war some eastern European nations, such as Rumania, Hungary and Bulgaria, supported German imperialism, others, such as Albania and Czechoslovakia, resisted it. In the final stage of the war the Soviet armies drove the German forces from the soil of some east European nations and assisted in the overthrow of the governments by the people, and the Soviet Communist Party helped to construct new governments from a mixed assortment of radical groups and parties. In some of these nations, notably Czechoslovakia and east Germany, which had industrial bases, proletarian dictatorships similar to those in the U.S.S.R. emerged, and the same was true of Albania, where the revolution cut deep as the people fought Fascist and Nazi armies in a bloody revolutionary war. Some of these nations, such as Poland, Rumania, Bulgaria, and Hungary, had been largely feudal with but slight capitalist development. In them the proletarian forces were less well defined. Nevertheless in all of them the property of the feudal landowners was seized and so were factories and financial institutions. These revolutions, then, differ from Engels's picture in that some of them were materially assisted by an outside proletarian power and some were without any substantial industrial base. Although Engels did not specifically predict that some proletarian nations would assist others he would hardly have been surprised by it. And, as his letter to Kautsky indicates, he expected revolutions to develop in nonindustrialized nations and that the workers in the (socialist) industrialized ones would assist them. These events, then, also fit within the general framework of Engels's projection. And this is, of course, the essential point. We are not dealing with clairvoyance but with a correct general projection of socioevolutionary trends; and only Marxists have been able to do this.

Engels, however, did not anticipate that nations with little industrial development would be among the first to move towards socialism and that this lack of development would leave some of them vulnerable to retrograde movement. In some east European nations, notably Poland and Yugoslavia, the peasants were mainly permitted to keep their land, and little collectivization took place, thus leaving a large section of the economy open to private trade. And in most of them it proved more difficult to establish a proletarian dictatorship and build a socialist economy than it had been in Russia. Although this total block of nations exhibits considerable variations in development levels, nevertheless, in most of them we find the basic qualities we noted for the U.S.S.R.: a planned economy; State ownership of the industrial means of production; steady economic development without depressions or recessions; collectivized agriculture; full employment; nationwide free social, medical and educational services; wide employment of women in the trades and professions—in short, a mass society geared for mass needs.

These general characteristics apply also to a range of other nations— China, Vietnam, Laos, Kampuchea, North Korea and Cuba—that were previously colonies or semicolonies with little industrial base. And some socialist structures are rising in such previously feudal condition states as Ethiopia and Nicaragua.

Marx and Engels did not anticipate that while socialism was being built a large bloc of powerful capitalist nations would still be in existence. These nations have made war against the socialist nations, including the German invasion of the U.S.S.R., the Japanese invasion of Soviet China, and the United States's attack on north Vietnam. In addition it is partly because these capitalist nations have constantly exerted economic, political, and cultural pressures on the socialist bloc that some retrograde movements have taken place, for instance, in Rumania, Yugoslavia, and Poland (which is some $25 billion in debt to the United States and other capitalist nations).

These retrograde movements, however, have not become dominant for the central historical movement within this bloc of nations is one of socialist advance. True, this advance has not yet involved the major capitalist powers and this has disturbed some modern Marxists; for instance, the following from Bertell Ollman's *Social and Sexual Revolution: Essays on Marx and Reich:*

> What has gone wrong? Until socialists begin to examine the failure of the proletariat to perform its historically appointed task in light of their own excessive optimism, there is little reason to believe that on this matter at least the future will cease to resemble the past.

Or, more recently, Paul Sweezy in the *Monthly Review:* "To begin with, in the advanced capitalist countries there have been no revolutions despite expectations derived from the theory of capitalist development expounded in *Capital.*" Consequently:

> Today, a hundred years after Marx's death, it is impossible to make out a reasonable case for the view which has been so long at the heart of Marxism, i.e., that the proletariat in the advanced countries is destined to be the agent of revolutionary change.

"The true proletarians in the original Marxist sense," Sweezy continues, "are the rapidly increasing masses of dehumanized humanity in what is now popularly called the Third World." He argues also that the Russian revolution "was in essence much closer to a Third World revolution than to the kind of proletarian revolution originally envisaged by Marxism."

Thus Sweezy's prospect is for more Third World revolutions by "dehumanizes" masses and a continuing capitalism in the major capitalist states. None of this, however, has much to do with Marxism. Revolutions and societies have to be examined in class terms. Clearly there is no such thing as a "Third World revolution." The revolution in China, for instance, was not accomplished by "dehumanized masses" but by a combination of proletarian, peasant, and antiimperialist bourgeois forces. The Russian revolution, as I have tried to show, was basically proletarian. And so, too, obviously were the Czechoslovakian, the east German; and so, too, the other European revolutions even though the proletarian forces were at first weak. Furthermore, the revolution in China (and Vietnam, and North Korea) has resulted in a socialist state in which the proletarian forces have been gaining increased power as is shown by increasing industrialization. What we have seen, in fact, is an extraordinary advance of proletarian power, until it has become the dominant force in more than one-third of the world.

On the other hand, it is true that except for Czechoslovakia and East Germany no "advanced" capitalist nation has yet had a proletarian revolution, and in these nations the process was assisted by an already existing socialist state. But in considering this problem we cannot mechanically extrapolate the economic views expressed in *Capital*. As Marx and Engels made clear— they believed that many factors were involved, including colonial exploitation with its creation of an "aristocracy of labor" and capitalist rivalries leading to war and revolution. And these various factors, Engels specifically put into a long time-frame with various stages. If there have not yet been revolutions in the United States, Great Britain, West Germany, France, Italy and Japan this is not because capitalism in these nations has acquired immortality but because the conditions for its overthrow have not yet come about. That Sweezy does not think they will—at least in the foreseeable future—is surprising in view of his analysis of the deepening capitalist crisis. Part of the problem is, perhaps, that some Marxist economists tend to think in terms of more restricted social processes than those of history. It is, after all, only sixty-six years since the Russian revolution—a trifle in the timetable of history.

The pessimism of Ollman (and others) has a somewhat different rationale, namely the social and psychological deficiencies of the proletariat. Ollman finds the proletariat irrational, "submissive," and "uncritical," possessing "authoritarian character structures"—resulting in part from sexual repression—which make it virtually impossible for them to rebel. This is based in part on the Freudian (and basically male-chauvinist) theories of Wilhelm Reich, one of the founders of the "Frankfort School," who established psychoanalytic clinics in pre-Hitler Germany to enable workers to release their sexual repressions as a necessary prelude to revolution. Another Frankfort School protégé, Herbert Marcuse, emigrating to the United States, likewise mixes Freud and Marx in an eclectic jumble and concludes that the proletariat has lost its revolutionary potential. Eugene Genovese and, in Europe, Jean-Paul Sartre, have come to similar conclusions about proletarian impotency but with varying rationales.[18]

When we consider the consistently positive view of Marx and Engels in a period when there was no socialist state anywhere in the world, when the Paris Commune had been destroyed and capitalism was supreme, this debilitating pessimism suggests a penetration of bourgeois thinking into Marxist circles. It reflects not only an inability to grasp the difference between current events and the cycles of history, but between psychological and social phenomena. Marx and Engels certainly did not idealize the proletariat—as appears at the outset in Engels *Condition of the Working Class in England* with its grim picture of the moral and psychological havoc wrought by exploitation. Nor did they confuse these things with the historical potential of the class. Furthermore, in spite of the demoralizing effects of capitalist exploitation the working class has been able to develop its own inherent qualities. The characteristics it has shown in the revolutions of the present century are not at all irrationality, submission, or conservatism, but realism, heroism, and vision.

It has been argued that the Marxist projection has turned out to be wrong because Marx and Engels did not believe that socialism could come about in one country alone. This argument is based mainly on an early statement (1847) by Engels in a draft for *The Communist Manifesto* (in which it was not included). Although Marx and Engels in their later statements seemed to assume that socialism would arise in several capitalist nations at about the same time they were not explicit on the matter. Engels implied— in 1895—that Germany was more advanced along the road to socialism than was France or Britain. In another place he seemed to assume that socialism could arise in the United States without European assistance. Again, however, the question is of secondary import. The main thing is that socialism did arise—as Marx and Engels said it would—not whether it arose in one or several countries.[19]

In 1872, Marx, first speaking at the Hague Congress of the International, was reported as saying:

> We do not deny that there are countries such as America, England, and I would add Holland if I knew your institutions better, where the working people may achieve their goal by peaceful means. If that is true, we must also recognise that in most of the continental countries it is force that will have to be the lever of our revolutions; it is force that we shall some day have to resort to in order to establish a reign of labor.

This comment has sometimes been taken to mean that Marx expected a transition to communism by parliamentary means in the United States, Great Britain and other capitalist countries. But this cannot be so. For one thing, in the *Civil War in France,* written in May 1871, he wrote that "the working class cannot simply take hold of the ready-made state machinery, and wield it for its own purposes." And the State of the Commune as he described it was almost the reverse of the bourgeois State. What, then, did he mean when he suggested that in some circumstances it "may" be possible to "achieve" the "goal" of the working class "by peaceful means?"

In 1870 the International and Marx were widely attacked as the instigators of the "violence" of the Paris Commune, by which was meant the seizure of power by the workers, not the subsequent wholesale slaughter of the workers by French reaction. In 1871, the year before his Hague speech, Marx was interviewed by two United States journalists who were interested in his supposed ties to the "violence" of the Commune; one journalist from the *New York World,* the other from the *New York Herald.* When the *Herald* interviewer asked him if the transition to communism would be violent in England Marx replied:

> We do not intend to make war. We hope to be able to gain our rights in a legal and lawful way by act of Parliament, and it is the aristocracy and the moneyed men who will rebel. It is they who will attempt a revolution. But we have the force of numbers. We shall have the strength of intelligence and discipline.

And he answered the *World* reporter similarly:

> The English middle class has always shown itself willing enough to accept the verdict of the majority, so long as it enjoyed the monopoly of voting power. But mark me, as soon as it finds itself outvoted on what it considers vital questions we shall see here a new slaveowners' war.

By the "middle class," Marx, following the custom of the day—the "upper class" was the aristocracy—meant the capitalist class, the "moneyed men." Marx, then, implies that in Britain the working class might acquire control of parliament but that this would only be the beginning of the struggle for power. As soon as the workers acted to "establish a reign of labor," bourgeois counterrevolutionary action would begin and this would certainly include military violence—as he noted in 1870: "Ireland is the only pretext the English Government has for retaining a big standing army, which if need be, as has happened before, can be used against the English workers after having done its military training in Ireland." To such attacks, the workers would have no choice but to reply with massive but disciplined revolutionary action.[20]

In 1891, Engels, in rejecting the view that socialism could be achieved "peacefully" in Germany, whose parliament he saw as controlled by the dictatorial, semifeudal regime established by Bismarck, did not rule out such a possibility for other capitalist countries:

> One can conceive that the old society may develop peacefully into the new one in countries where the representatives of the people concentrate all power in their hands, where, if one has the support of the majority of the people, one can do as one sees fit in a constitutional way: in democratic republics such as France and the U.S.A., in monarchies such as Britain, where the imminent abdication of the dynasty [monarchy] in return for financial compensation is discussed in the press daily and where this dynasty is powerless against the people.

Engels certainly seems to go further here than Marx in his view of a peaceful transition but this seems to be partly a matter of language. That he did not expect any easy or primarily parliamentary transition to the new order is apparent from his other writings of the time.

In 1895—the last year of his life—Engels argued that the great political successes of such parties as the German Social Democratic Party opened new ways to the transformation of society:

> With this successful utilization of universal suffrage, an entirely new mode of proletarian struggle came into force, and this quickly developed further. It was found that the state institutions, in which the rule of the bourgeoisie is organised, offer still further opportunities for the working class to fight these very state institutions.

His concept was not, however, one of relying on parliamentary action but of combining socialist penetration of the political, legal, and other organs of the State with social struggle. And this struggle would be revolutionary— in spite of the fact that the 1848 "barricade" tactics had been rendered obsolete by the construction of wide, expansive city streets:

> The revolutionary would have to be mad, who himself chose the working class districts in the North and East of Berlin for the barricade fight. Does that mean that in the future the street fight will play no further role? Certainly not. It only means that the conditions since 1848 have become far more unfavourable for civil fights, far more favorable for the military. A future street fight can therefore only be victorious when this unfavourable situation is compensated by other factors. Accordingly, it will occur more seldom in the beginning of a great revolution than in its further progress, and will have to be undertaken with greater forces. These, however, may then well prefer, as in the whole Great French Revolution on September 4 and October 31, 1870, in Paris, the open attack to the passive barricade tactics.

Engels, then, in stating that one could "do as one sees fit in a constitutional way" if "one has the support of the people" was not thinking of a simple parliamentary majority but a mass of socially as well as politically active people, primarily, as he implies in other statements, those of the working class and its trade union core. Similarly he was not, as other comments show, thinking in regard to the United States of the old two-party system, the Republicans with their "big industry" core and the Democrats representing the "big landowners of the south," but of a mass movement with new political formations. On the other hand, Engels seems to have exaggerated the importance of such feudal remnants as the British monarchy or Bismarkian absolutism. The demise of the British monarchy would then have done little to undermine British capitalism.[21]

The question, then, as Marx and Engels saw it, was essentially one not of parliamentary actions but of social struggle. The form of transition to the "dictatorship of the proletariat" would depend on the ebb and flow of this struggle and the relative strengths of the opponents as it continued. Marx's comments to the journalists have been borne out in their basic outline by the Russian revolutions of 1917. Neither revolution, March nor November, involved much violence. In March, the Czarist government was quickly overwhelmed by mass action. The violence came when the bourgeois-feudal government that emerged struck back in the summer. In November, there was little military action except in Moscow and even that was minimal. The real violence came when the overthrown bourgeois and feudal classes began civil war and the capitalist powers sent in armies of intervention. As we have seen, Engels expected that the revolution in the oppressed countries would be violent; and this has indeed come true. The Chinese people could uproot their feudal and imperialist masters only through civil war and the Vietnamese through an anti-imperialistic revolutionary war. The question, then, as Marx saw, is not one that depends upon the prosocialist forces and their "intentions" but upon the ruling classes. On the whole, the transition to socialism has taken place with much more violence—with war, revolution, and revolutionary wars sometimes intermingled (in East Europe as well as Asia)—than Marx and Engels seem to have anticipated. And the indication is that this will continue. However, the advance of socialism, which has become the dominant historical force of our century, will likewise continue and the bourgeoisie will in time everywhere go under in spite of its terrorist savagery. Masses in action, as Iran also showed—even though the revolution there has been temporarily diverted by native bourgeois and feudal interests—can very rapidly erode State foundations, which, after all, consist of people. And a ruling class cannot effectively strike back if it is isolated from the modes of power: "The elements obey me not."

What, however, of nuclear and other weapons of mass destruction? Will they prevent future revolutions? Can they and do they seriously threaten human life on our planet? Marx and Engels did not have to face this problem, but they faced the general one of which it is part. The German philosopher Eugen Dühring had argued that "force" plays the decisive role in history. Engels, in *Anti-Dühring,* answered as follows:

> And when the bourgeoisie now make their appeal to force in order to save the collapsing "economic order" from the final crash, by so doing they only show that they are caught in the same illusion as Herr Dühring: the illusion that "political conditions are the decisive cause of the economic order;" they show that they imagine, just as Herr Dühring does, that by making use of the "primitive phenomenon," "direct political force," they can remodel those "facts of the second order," the economic order and its inevitable development; and that therefore the economic consequences of the steam engine and the modern machinery driven by it, of world trade and banking and credit developments of the present day, can be blown out of existence with Krupp guns and Mauser rifles.[22]

If Engels's contention was right in regard to military force and history in general, it must still apply, even when that force includes nuclear and other weapons of mass destruction. Making war is a political decision and such decisions are determined by class forces. The vision of world nuclear war being started by a mad button-pusher is a bourgeois fantasy designed to demoralize the peace forces. Major political decisions, such as that of launching a world war, are not the result of sudden impulse but arise as the final step in a back-and-forth socio-political struggle with mounting stages. That the working class and its allies in the capitalist nations will not allow the situations necessary for such a decision to arise is shown by the massive antinuclear weapons demonstrations and political pressures that have begun, especially in Europe, to effect political actions. And these actions will not only grow but take new form in the social turmoil produced by the general crises of capitalism, and perhaps at some point will be spurred on by nuclear disaster. The basic fact is that the international proletariat—in its socialist and capitalist sections combined—is the controlling force in world history today and that it and its allies will not permit widespread nuclear destruction.

6

Women and Society

In the late eighteenth century at the same time as an understanding of class oppression was developing, understanding of another kind of oppression was developing also. "Marriage," William Godwin bluntly declared in 1793, "is law, and the worst of all laws . . . an affair of property and the worst of all properties." He urged its abolition as a legal entity. His wife, Mary Wollstonecraft, in her pioneering book, *The Rights of Woman* in 1792, although defending marriage, in some respects went further than he did. "The very men who are the slaves of their mistresses," she wrote, "tyrannize over their sisters, wives and daughters." She proposed that women should be prepared to assert their rights by a proper education:

> Strengthen the female mind by enlarging it, and there will be an end to blind obedience; but as blind obedience is ever fought for by power, tyrants and sensualists are in the right when they endeavour to keep women in the dark because the former only want slaves and the latter a plaything.

The views of Godwin and Wollstonecraft were taken further by their son-in-law, Percy Bysshe Shelley, who pointed to the economic roots of sexual oppression:

> Women therefore, in rude ages and in rude countries have been considered as the property of men, because they are the materials of usefulness or pleasure. They were valuable to them in the same manner as their flocks and herds were valuable, and it was as important to their interests that they should retain undisturbed possession.

And Shelley's line from his strongly feminist epic, *Laon and Cyntha*—"Can man be free if woman be a slave?"—struck a note in the hearts of later feminists and other radicals, including Marx's daughter, Eleanor.[1]

Although Godwin, Wollstonecraft, and Shelley spoke of women in general, they were thinking primarily of upper and middle class women. The assertion of the rights of working class women in Britain first came from working-class women themselves. In the early 1800s we find women's contingents in the marches and demonstrations for parliamentary reform—essentially extension of the franchise—and Female Reform Societies were established in a number of towns. About 1819 a new development was noted by Samuel Bamford, weaver and poet: "and ever from that time females voted with the men at the Radical meetings. . . . It became the practice, female political unions were formed, with their chairwomen, committees and other officials." Women were prominent in the massive reform demonstration at Manchester in 1819, which became known as the Manchester Massacre when it was attacked by cavalry. But little is yet known of these early working class women's movements. In the 1830s and 1840s women were active in unions and this continued then and later in the Chartist and Owenite movements. In the United States the feminist movement was linked to antislavery activity (when the women abolitionists found themselves discriminated against by the men). The first prominent working class feminist was the Frenchwoman, Flora Tristan. "I have," she wrote shortly before her death, in 1844, "nearly the whole world against me. Men because I demand the emancipation of women, the owners because I demand the emancipation of wage-earners."[2]

Marx and Engels, like most radicals of the time, were well acquainted with the feminist movement, as well as with the writings of Godwin and Shelley, and in *The Communist Manifesto* in 1848 they presented their own views:

> On what foundation is the present family, the bourgeois family, based? On capital, on private gain. In its completely developed form this family exists only among the bourgeoisie. But this state of things finds its complement in the practical absence of the family among the proletarians, and in public prostitution.

The unbalancing of the working class family by exploitation and oppression, with accompanying child labor, poverty and drink, Engels had graphically depicted in *The Condition of the Working Class in England* in 1845. As for bourgeois marriage: "The bourgeois sees in his wife a mere instrument of production." It was not really monogamy, as was claimed, but "monogamy, supplemented by adultery and prostitution."[3]

In 1868, Marx praised "the American 'Labor Union' " for affording equality to its women members, in contrast to the British and French with their "spirit of narrow-mindedness." And he added: "Anybody who knows anything of history knows that the great social changes are impossible without the feminine ferment." He strongly supported feminist causes and encouraged his daughters in their intellectual and radical interests, but he was most particularly concerned with the economic exploitation of women workers;

> Mary Anne Walkley had worked without intermission for twenty-six-and-a-half hours, with sixty other girls, thirty in one room that only afforded one-third of the cubic feet of air required for them. At night they slept in pairs in one of the stifling holes into which the bedroom was divided by partitions of board. And this was one of the best millinery establishments in London. Mary Anne Walkley fell ill on the Friday, died on Sunday, without, to the astonishment of Madame Elise, having previously completed the work in hand.[4]

The Origin of the Family

The development of the Marxist view on the oppression of women was mainly left to Engels, Marx concentrating on economics and the International. Engels examined the subject historically and theoretically in *The Origin of the Family, Private Property and the State* in 1884. Although, he argued, the oppression of women first arose with the development of classes and was connected with class factors it had other roots also:

> The first class opposition [antagonism] that appears in history coincides with the development of the antagonism between man and woman in monogamous marriage, and the first class oppression coincides with that of the female sex by the male.

In preclass society, Engels believed—following the anthropology of his day—there had been matriarchal societies in which women were dominant. This dominance they lost with the rise of animal farming because herding and animal tending were men's work. There were also various forms of "group" sexual relations and marriage. Marriage took a monogamous form with the development of private property, and it was a monogamy favoring men:

> Monogamy arose from the concentration of considerable wealth in the hands of a single individual—a man—and from the need to bequeath this wealth to the children of that man and of no other. For this purpose, the monogamy of the woman was required, not that of the man, so this monogamy of the woman did not in any way interfere with open or concealed polygamy on the part of the man.

With capitalism came the "marriage of convenience" arranged on a primarily financial basis by the bourgeois parents of the bride and groom. Prostitution he regarded as more widely destructive for men than for women:

> Among women, prostitution degrades only the unfortunate ones who become its victims, and even these by no means to the extent commonly believed. But it degrades the character of the whole male world.

Within the bourgeois family the dominance of the husband is ultimately based on capitalism itself, which gives the man an economic advantage: "Within the family he is the bourgeois and the wife represents the proletariat." There are also, as in feudal societies, discriminatory laws. Here, too, the basic explanation is not to be sought within the area of discrimination itself but in the underlying economic structure: "The legal inequality of the two partners, bequeathed to us from earlier social conditions, is not the cause but the effect of the economic oppression of the woman." As a result of these factors, upper class marriages cannot be primarily based on sexual love. The situation in the lower classes is different, and the future will be more different still:

> Sex-love in the relationship with a woman becomes, and can only become, the real rule among the oppressed classes, which means today among the proletariat—whether this relation is officially sanctioned or not. . . . Here there is no property, for the preservation and inheritance of which monogamy and male supremacy were established; hence there is no incentive to make this male supremacy effective. . . . Having arisen from economic causes, will monogamy then disappear when these causes disappear?
>
> One might answer, not without reason: far from disappearing, it will, on the contrary, be realized completely. For with the transformation of the means of production into social property there will disappear also wage-

labor, the proletariat, and therefore the necessity for a certain—statistically calculable—number of women to surrender themselves for money. Prostitution disappears; monogamy, instead of collapsing, at last becomes a reality—also for men.[5]

Again Engels emphasizes the economic base. Prostitution does not arise from psychological or moral causes but primarily from the fact that upper class men are able to purchase working-class women for sexual gratification, in short to exploit them sexually as well as economically. Prostitution, Engels implies, will continue as long as capitalism exists. It will disappear only as the general social evils of capitalism are eradicated with the eradication of the economic base that sustains them. Only then can a true monogamy—with equal rights for men and women—emerge. Whether this new monogamy will include a legal contract, Engels does not say but he expected that it would be dominated by a love relationship of a new kind:

> What we can now conjecture about the way in which sexual relations will be ordered after the impending overthrow of capitalist production is mainly of a negative character, limited for the most part to what will disappear. But what will there be new? That will be answered when a new generation has grown up: a generation of men who never in their lives have known what it is to buy a woman's surrender with money or any other social instrument of power; a generation of women who have never known what it is to give themselves to a man from any other consideration than real love or to refuse to give themselves to their lover from fear of the economic consequences. When these people are in the world, they will care precious little what anybody today thinks they ought to do; they will make their own practice and their corresponding public opinion about the practice of each individual—and that will be the end of it.

Men and women, Engels implies, have potentials for sexual love that cannot be realized in capitalist—or, we should add, feudal—society, which corrupts and distorts. What, however, is this potential? And what is the basis for it? The essence of sexual love, Engels believed, lay in the interaction of the general human qualities shared by men and women alike with the differing specific qualities of each sex. As he wrote in 1891 to his young friend, Conrad Schmidt, who was about to marry:

> At the same time you can always make the thing clear to yourself by concrete examples; for instance, you, as a bridegroom, have a striking example of the inseparability of identity and difference in yourself and

your bride. It is absolutely impossible to decide whether sexual love is pleasure in the identity in difference or in the difference in identity. Take away the difference (in this case of sex) or the identity (the human nature of both) and what have you got left? I remember how much this very inseparability of identity and difference worried me at first, although we can never take a step without stumbling upon it.[6]

As we consider these views of Engels it becomes apparent that his approach is basically different from that of the feminists, largely stemming in his day from Mary Wollstonecraft. He did not regard the exploitation or oppression of women as a unique phenomenon but as part of the general patterns of capitalist society. Working-class women were economically exploited more than men, receiving less pay for the same or similar work. This, however, was still part of a general pattern of capitalist exploitation. Prostitution was still part of this pattern although at first it might appear to be different. The question, then, was basically one of degree, of the greater exploitation and oppression of women than of men in a generally exploitive and oppressive society. Hence, no major advances could take place until the society itself was fundamentally changed.

The Historical Record

Engels, then, whether one agrees with his view or not, was certainly attempting to examine the relations of women and society in a broader social framework than had previously been proposed. Nevertheless, there are clearly deficiencies in his view, many of them due to the level of knowledge in his day, especially in anthropology and social history.

Although, to judge from those hunter-gathering and early-type farming societies that have survived into civilized society times, women had roughly equal economic and social status with men, there is no evidence of a matriarchal stage in which women were dominant. In such societies community affairs are conducted primarily by men, often operating through a council of older males, an embryonic political structure. That women lost some community power with the development of farming may be true but if so it was probably not primarily due to animal herding—most farming societies were apparently based on agriculture not on herding—but, as we have seen, more likely to the rise of the male professional potter and weaver and the coming of war, which, in general, advances male power.

Engels's contention that in preclass societies there were various forms of group marriage—as argued by Lewis Henry Morgan and others—and that monogamy developed only with the rise of private property has not been borne out by later anthropological research. In hunter-gathering and early-type farming communities which have been examined, marriage is monogamous, and the probability is that monogamy was the main form of marriage from the beginnings of human society and formed the core for the family whether that of the parents and children only or the extended family which included other relatives. One basic reason for this is that there is roughly the same number of men and women in any society. It is no doubt true that as private property arose in later-farming societies—apparently about 4,000 B.C.—monogamy assumed a new role, namely that of assuring paternal succession, and that this placed restrictions, legal and social, upon women, but this clearly was of more limited scope than Engels assumes. In the first place it would apply only to families whose men owned property—individual or State—and these were but a small fraction of the population. In the second place the restrictions on women that we find as early feudal societies arose—first about 3,000 B.C. in Sumer and Egypt—seem not so much rooted in private property as such as in the general land-grabbing and profit drives of these societies, in most of which joint (State) great landowning was dominant, including the land of the Church and the Military. We are now able to examine these societies concretely because of historical research in recent decades. When we do it becomes apparent that we cannot speak of the exploitation or oppression of women in general but must distinguish between women of the upper and lower classes, and that class depends primarily not on private but State (feudal) property. Although there are some qualities in common between the oppression of women in both classes these are of secondary significance. The rights and life style of a woman were determined primarily not by the fact that she was a woman but by her social status—whether she was a serf or the mistress of an estate.

With the rise of the first civilized (feudal) societies in Sumer and Egypt we find that a small number of women, the women of the upper classes, were elevated, for the first time in history, above the mass of men. These women had some property rights and could in some states will property to their offspring, but they did not have at all the extent of property or power over property of upper class men and they were subject to restrictive laws. In neither Sumer nor Egypt were women educated or admitted into the professions. These restrictions, however, must have held little interest for the mass of women, who were either serfs or slaves.

As feudal societies arose throughout Asia in the next 2,000 years, the same social patterns for women grew up everywhere. And this was not a matter of imitation but of similar socioeconomic structures producing similar effects. In India, upper class women could own some property but the husband had certain rights over it and could sell it in an emergency. They had few legal rights, being generally regarded under the law as wards of their husbands or fathers. They were not, however, in pre-Moslem India or Arabia "secluded," that is to say restricted to certain areas of the house and not allowed in theatres and other public places. Although they were not formally educated, some women became educated, and we hear of women poets and philosophers. The mass of the women were again, however, serfs and slaves. Prostitution in India became a massive State industry, exploiting lower class women under the control of a government Superintendent of Prostitution. In China upper class women were largely secluded and generally did not appear on public occasions. Again, some upper class women became educated and there were women writers and poets. And in Japan we have Lady Murasaki with her magnificent *The Tale of Genji*, the first true novel. Chinese peasant women had certain property rights, for instance, over furniture, and were considered to be in charge of the house. There were great masses of women household slaves and prostitution was as widespread and organized as in India. Women slaves could be executed at the will of their mistress and were sexually available for their master, and the "concubinage" system became general.

When we turn to the slave-commercial societies of Greece and Rome the story is similar. In Athens upper class women were secluded and did not appear at public events. They had few legal rights, even in property, and were excluded from the professions. They did, however, as elsewhere, have household slaves under their control. As in feudal China prostitution and concubinage were general. Roman upper class women, unlike those in Athens, were not secluded and attended the theatre and sporting events—as Ovid noted with interest. Upper class girls as well as boys were educated and there were some women in the professions. Although women did not have the vote they had social clubs and engaged in electoral activity. How these advances came about is not clear but they must—as always—have resulted directly from organized struggles by women, in this case primarily by upper class women. There were still great masses of women slaves, not only in households but in textile and other manufacturing. Slave girls could be purchased for sexual exploitation and rich young Romans bought them as such men would today buy a new car. Brothels were legal, prostitution massive and highly organized. Every inn on every highway in Roman Italy apparently had its quota of prostitutes.

Whereas in feudal and slave-commercial societies there was but a small middle class, in European commercial-feudal society—which preceeded capitalism—it apparently became larger; and some of the privileges which had previously been the exclusive right of upper class women were gained by middle class women. The "great lady" of an estate had—as in earlier feudal societies—considerable power within the bounds of the estate and certain property rights. But with the spread of manufacturing and commerce we find an increasing number of women as owners of businesses, such as Chaucer's Wife of Bath. We also find women, both in France and England, joining trade guilds. But neither upper nor middle class women had political rights, their legal rights were very limited, and they were barred from the professions. Queens and aristocratic ladies, however, often had considerable actual power. But, again, these matters had little relevance for the mass of women—peasant and working class. Feudal peasant women toiled, as ever, in the fields with the men, and like the men had neither legal nor political rights. Their children were referred to in legal documents not as *familia* but as *sequela*—brood or litter. Some working class women worked, either in factories or in "home industry," and in general shared the exploitive lot of the men of their class. But they were also oppressed as women. The ferocity of the oppression of lower class women may be gauged from the fact that between 1250 and 1400 some thirty thousand women were burned alive by the Church's Holy Office as witches.[7]

With the rise of industrial capitalism in the nineteenth century a large number of women—for the first time in history—worked for pay in factories. Upper and middle class women—some of whom owned small businesses— began a persistent drive for legal rights and admission into the professions and universities (as reflected in Tennyson's *The Princess*), a drive that by the end of the century—when Engels died—had made but moderate progress. The throwing of working-class women into the labor market was, as Engels noted in 1845, of mixed value. It moved women from the narrow social circle of the home into the larger one of competitive struggle and unionization, but these women were doubly exploited, and the long hours they worked—twelve or more a day—left them little time for their children or family life.

The oppression endured by women throughout history was not passively endured. Women seem everywhere to have fought back as well as they could.

Sometimes this rebellion took organized form. Much of the evidence on this has been irretrievably lost as historians have neglected to record or have skimmed over the story of women's struggles just as they have those of the working masses, for instance, the great slave revolt led by Spartacus. But some records exist and research will produce others.

There is indication, for instance in China, of women struggling in early farming society against rising male dominance. In 195 B.C., the Roman women marched on the Forum to demand repeal of a discriminatory law and denounced the reactionary Cato. Peasant women took part in peasant revolts in Germany, England, and China, such as the great Heavenly Kingdom revolution in nineteenth-century China in which women made obvious advances—to the dismay of some Western observers. And women took part also in the European bourgeois revolutions, first in the British revolution in the 1640s when, according to a contemporary poet, they "Marched rank and file, with drum and ensign," and they presented mass petitions to Parliament. In the French Revolution we have the famed march of the women of Paris to Versailles. Women were among the leaders of the Paris Commune of 1870, one of them, Madame Andre Leo, declaring: "The Revolution . . . means liberty and responsibility for every human being, with common rights as their only limit and without any privilege of race or sex." The women of Petrograd helped to spark the March 1917 revolution as they defied and then won over the soldiers of the Czar.[8]

In general, too, historians, past and present, have obscured the social and cultural contributions of women to society. These become apparent when we turn from the historical to the literary and artistic record, from the Japanese annals to Lady Murasaki, from the medieval chroniclers to Chaucer and Boccaccio, with their vibrant intellectual women, from the Renaissance historians to Shakespeare or Castiglione. Nor must we forget the folk arts and crafts with which women over the centuries have enriched life. In general the pattern seems to have been that women, particularly upper class women, could acquire considerable social status and cultural expression but were shut out from the State and the professions, from political power, ecclestical power, the military, and the legal structure. It is largely from a failure to observe this distinction in social areas that we get diverse pictures of the status of women by modern historians, the antifeminists stressing one aspect, the profeminists another. The basic picture, however, remains one of exploitation and oppression.

In considering these matters we have to remember also that during the long centuries of recorded history most women during their child-bearing years appear to have been almost constantly pregnant; nursing and nurturing, grief-stricken by the frequent deaths of infants, and running households without benefit of labor-saving machines. The mass of women were obviously at a considerable disadvantage in the realm of social action, which in part explains why what is usually called history, with its parliaments and kings, its wars and oppression, has been primarily a male phenomenon—although it is not presented as such.

As we look back over the past historical panorama of women's exploitation and oppression, most of which was unknown to Engels, it becomes apparent that his approach was in some respects too narrow. As in his treatment of monogamy he tends to concentrate on upper class, particularly bourgeois, women.

His comments on the status of women and related matters in capitalist society—on the "marriage of convenience," on prostitution, on the economic basis for the legal and social domination of the male—have wider application than he realized. The "marriage of convenience" is not a bourgeois phenomenon but part of a general pattern—which includes dowry and bride-price customs—that was dominant among the upper classes in the long centuries of feudal society in Asia, Europe and elsewhere, and is still dominant in such societies today, sometimes resulting in the virtual sale of young women and girls. Neither Marx nor Engels nor anyone else at the time seems to have known of the extent of the exploitation and oppression of women in feudal societies—of mass slavery, sexual exploitation, and Church terrorism. Prostitution in feudalism or capitalism is not mainly a matter of a number of "unfortunate ones" who were not degraded "to the extent commonly believed" but of untold millions of women whose lives were shattered by organized exploitation, brutalization, abortions, venereal diseases, psychological destruction, and social ostracism. Woman slaves, peasants, and others were periodically subjected to mass rape in war, often herded like animals by cavalry and other troops; mass rapes, which, as Susan Brownmiller has shown, constituted a weapon for tribal or national subjugation.

In considering these conditions, we have to consider also that those of the mass of men—serfs and slaves and proletarians—were not much better. It might be noted, too, that men have also, in a way, been sexually exploited. Ruling classes throughout history have distorted and utilized male aggressiveness and sexual drives for their own purposes in war and oppression, turning average moral men—as in Vietnam—into killers, racists and rapists. That there are class differences in sexual relations has been demonstrated by Alfred C. Kinsey and others but that these relations are, as Engels contends, more based on love among the proletariat seems doubtful. As Engels pointed out in his *Condition of the Working Class in England,* the working class family is often weakened by the necessity of the wife's working—the children left to "grow up like wild weeds"—and by pressures which lead to alcoholism and wife-beating. The truth seems to be that the tensions of an exploitive society affect all classes, although in different ways, and distort sexual love by "male supremacy" and other factors on all social levels.[9]

The Two Faces of Oppression

> The first class opposition that appears in history coincides with the development of the antagonism between man and woman in monogamous marriage, and the first class oppression coincides with that of the female sex by the male.

This is by no means an easy statement to follow. Did Engels believe that the oppression of women was the oppression of one whole sex by the other as a sex? If so why did it first arise with class society? Did he think that the root cause of the "antagonism" between men and women lay in the monogamous form of marriage? If so, what of such antagonisms in other than marriage relationships?

What Engels does not make clear is that we are dealing with two different but related phenomena: the oppression of women by exploiting classes and the oppression of women by men. In capitalism today, for instance, the monopoly bourgeoisie uses the State and other instruments of rule to continue the special exploitation and oppression of women. Legislative bodies churn out laws discriminating against women. The political and economic systems exclude women from real power; so, too, do the church and educational establishments. The news media, novels, plays, films, television, and advertising continue to present stereotypes tending to sustain this subordination. True, the exploiters of female labor are overwhelmingly men, but that they act as they do, not primarily because they are antifeminist, but to increase their profits and maintain their power is shown by the fact that they similarly overexploit racial and other minorities. And the legal, political and cultural instruments of rule also are similarly used against these minorities. Some of the consequences of this exploitation and oppression were noted by Marx:

> The average English worker hates the Irish worker as a competitor who lowers wages and the standard of life. He feels national and religious antipathies for him. He regards him somewhat like the poor whites of the Southern States of North America regard their black slaves. This antagonism among the proletarians of England is artificially nourished and supported by the bourgeoisie. It knows that this scission [split] is the true secret of maintaining its power.[10]

Some of the sociopsychological processes at work in these matters will be examined in the next chapter. In the meantime we should note that in relation to women there seems throughout history to have been a kind of "understanding"—usually not directly expressed—by male rulers that women present a danger to their power, a feeling that early found eloquent expression in the Athenian drama with its array of "evil" women rebels.

In addition to the social oppression of women, an oppression similar to racial and national oppression, there is also an oppression of women by men. This takes place not on a national or State scale but between individuals and on a family or community level. It includes wife-beating, rape—including gang rape and rape within marriage—sodomy, incest—especially between fathers and daughers—excessive child-bearing, and general abuse, physical and verbal. Some of the roots, biological and social, for this area we can better discuss later in another context. Engels, however, was not referring to this area alone in speaking of "male" oppression of "the female sex" but to all oppression of women, including State oppression. That there is a connection between the two is apparent from the fact that where social oppression of women is high, oppression by men is high also, as, for instance, in Saudi Arabia and other partly feudal countries today. In general an exploitive and oppressive society breeds personal antagonism between men and women, and gives economic, legal, and other advantages to men in the ensuing conflicts. However if we regard all oppression of women as that "of the female sex by the male" we obscure the social causes of such oppression and can hamper the struggle against it.

Not only the social but the sexual relations between men and women are, Engels argues, affected by the corrupting influences of capitalism. "Sexual love" could be distorted by "the marriage of convenience," by economic pressures, by prostitution, by "male supremacy." Engels' assumption in these comments is that men and women have a natural potential for sexual love—which he differentiates from "sexual desire"—and that this potential is based on the "inseparability of identity and difference" of male and female. In a communist society, this potential will be fully realized and will take forms which it is at present difficult to visualize.[11]

Neither Marx nor Engels place the same emphasis on the sexual as on the class division of society. The reason for this is that whereas the class struggle of the proletariat will destroy capitalism and shape the coming communist society, the struggle for women's rights (or minority rights) can of itself produce only reforms within a basically explotative system. Hence the struggle for women's rights has basic historical significance only insofar as it becomes part of and strengthens the general revolutionary struggle.

In the present century we have seen this projection begin to come true. The bourgeois feminist movement in Czarist Russia, active though it was, would on its own have achieved little but concessions from Czarism, but the total Russian feminist movement, proletarian and bourgeois, by allying itself with the mass revolutionary forces, achieved an unprecedented historical advance. And in the intervening decades this advance has occurred also in China, in East Europe, in Cuba and elsewhere.

As an example of the nature of this advance, let us take the German Democratic Republic (East Germany). One of the first decrees passed was that of equal pay for equal work. Women make up half the membership of the trade unions and hold about half the trade union posts, including those on the national executive board. Women hold more than one-third of the seats in the national parliament. About half the judges and one-quarter of the mayors are women. Maternity leave is twenty-six weeks, abortion is on demand in the first twelve weeks of pregnancy. In 1949 there were but eight nursery school places for every 1,000 children, by the late 1970s there were places for 60 percent of the children. In contrast only 7.5 percent of the seats in the West German parliament are held by women and only 13 percent of the working women are organized.

In spite of the advances made in the socialist world in the status of women further advances are needed and are being struggled for. As Margrit Pittman points out, in the German Democratic Republic, women, although holding a large number of executive posts, do not equally share the "top jobs" with men. And a high divorce rate indicates domestic maladjustments, some of which must be related to remnants of male chauvinism. It has, as various socialist leaders have pointed out, been found easier to vanguish old institutions than old ideas. In this regard we might note the number of historical and other works that continue to come out of socialist countries using "man" or "men" where they should use "people" or "humanity."[12]

Neither these advances nor their present limitations would have surprised Marx and Engels. The present socialist societies represent what they considered the first phase of communism, in which, as Marx noted in his *Critique of the Gotha Program,* many "taints" would necessarily still remain from the old society. And these, in the present situation, have been compounded by the threat of antisocialist imperialist aggression.

Today the most savage oppression of women occurs in feudal and semifeudal societies, in Asia, Africa, and Latin-Indian America. Although Engels does not seem to have had much information available on this situation, which has changed little over the centuries, he did expect—as he told Karl Kautsky in 1895—massive colonial revolutions, and both he and Marx would have anticipated that the "feminine ferment" would be part of them. And this has indeed happened. The women of China played a vital part in the revolutionary civil war and in Vietnam in the anti-imperialist revolutionary war. It is but a matter of time before the women of India or Mexico advance with and help to direct the anti-imperialist revolutionary tide.

In the United States and other capitalist countries recent decades have witnessed a resurgence of feminism in a primarily bourgeois "women's liberation" movement which has made some feminist views part of the national consciousness and has sometimes advanced these views in bold new ways. Marx and Engels would certainly have rejoiced in this movement even as they would wish that it had greater proletarian and Marxist components.

7

Class, Ideas, and Art

The Realm of Ideas

In a period of "social revolution" arising from economic change, Marx noted in his 1859 general statement, "ideological forms" undergo a "transformation." This is because these forms—"legal, political, religious, aesthetic or philosophic"—arise from the socioeconomic "basis." What, however, are the specific ways in which this dependency works? How do ideologies grow up? How conscious are the ideologists of their function? Did literature and the other arts arise in the same way as ideology? Engels was aware that he and Marx "failed to lay stress enough" on these matters (as he informed Franz Mehring—later to become Marx's biographer—in 1893) as they were intent on establishing the "derivation" as such; and he continued:

Ideology is a process accomplished by the so-called thinker consciously, indeed, but with a false consciousness. The real motives impelling him remain unknown to him, otherwise it would not be an ideological process at all. Hence he imagines false or apparent motives. Because it is a process of thought he derives both its form and its content from pure thought, either his own or that of his predecessors. He works with mere thought material which he accepts without examination as the product of thought, he does not investigate further for a more remote process independent of thought. . . . And since the bourgeois illusion of the eternity and the finality of capitalist production has been added as well, even the victory of the physiocrats and Adam Smith over the mercantilists is accounted as

137

a sheer victory of thought; not as the reflection in thought of changed economic facts but as the finally achieved correct understanding of actual conditions subsisting always and everywhere—in fact if Richard Coeur-de-Lion and Philip Augustus had introduced free trade instead of getting mixed up in the crusades we should have been spared five hundred years of misery and stupidity.

If Engels exaggerates, he does not exaggerate by much. As we have seen, few historians today discuss general theory, and when they examine the problem of the relationship of thought to social evolution they leave the impression that thought is somehow the motivating force. Nor has the addition of psychiatric concepts—"Alexander [I of Russia] . . . exhibited signs of schizophrenia"—to the old standbys of ambition, pride and greed changed the picture.[1]

Engels's comments, however, have to be put into a class context. The "so-called thinker" who ends up with an ideological theory of history or culture is clearly not a Marxist. Nor is he a working-class thinker of the Chartist variety or of those associated with the International. Both Marx and Engels at times while speaking of such matters are really thinking of bourgeois ideology—as is Marx in his 1859 general statement.

According to the *Communist Manifesto,* "The ruling ideas of each age have ever been the ideas of the ruling class." However, if each age thus produces its ideas, why is there a general continuity of basic views, from, say, slave-commercial Athens to capitalist North America? The answer is as obvious as it is theoretically significant. (And here we might add that many Marxist views are obviously true, some of them almost simple statements of facts—which is why the opponents of Marxism have to struggle so deviously to refute them.)

> But whatever form they may have taken, one fact is common to all past ages, viz., the exploitation of one part of society by the other. No wonder, then, that the social consciousness of past ages, despite all of the multiplicity and variety it displays, moves within certain common forms, or general ideas, which cannot completely vanish except with the total disappearance of class antagonisms.

What, then, is usually considered as "the thought" of "civilized society" and regarded as an absolute and self-generating entity is in reality, according to Marx and Engels, socially determined and limited. This thought moves within "certain common forms" not because these forms are "universals" but because the exploiting classes in each civilization have common interests and objectives. Only with the "disappearance of class antagonisms" will human thought—and artistic creation—be free to develop its potentials, and the period in history which this "disappearance" will usher in, that of communist society, will last as long as the planet is inhabitable. The past is, indeed, but prologue, intellectually as well as socially, and its "great thinkers" have to be viewed in relation to this wider perspective. True, on the whole, there has been great advance, and many have struggled heroically against ruling class oppression to grasp segments of the social truth and assist humanity. Others, such as Galileo, have fought for truth in natural science. All this advance, however, has been within the perimeters of a society in which the few live on the backs of the many and this necessarily imposes limitations.[2]

The views of Marx and Engels on the class basis for dominant ideologies have sometimes been oversimplified. They did not see such ideologies as arising directly from each class but as part of a vortex of "class antagonisms." Hence they contained a mixture of class elements, some dominant, some subordinate, as seen, for instance, in the infusion of feudal concepts into bourgeois thought and in distortions in reaction to mass pressures (as, for instance, upper classes become infected by their own superstitions). Furthermore, the general ideas of upper classes on philosophy, theology, history, and so on are not formed by the class as a whole but by a group of intellectuals within it or associated with it. These intellectuals, too, are caught up in the swirl of "class antagonisms," often tossed between conflicting upper class interests and uneasily conscious of the stirrings of the working mass, peasant, slave or proletarian.

Marxists have long noted that modern liberal intellectuals fall into predictable patterns. Not perceiving the underlying forces of capitalist society, they see each event—a strike, a colonial revolt, a war—as a separate phenomenon arising from a particular "evil" or "injustice." And they support "justice" against "injustice" so long as "justice" only makes for a temporary "easing of tensions" and does not threaten to end the oppressive system as such. In effect, they counsel the bourgeoisie on the degree of concession needed to survive. When they inadvertently help to release mass forces which acquire their own momentum, they advocate retreat, urging the working mass not to go beyond a "reasonable" alleviation of their "misfortunes." This basic pattern, however, did not arise with capitalism. The role of the intellectual attached to a ruling class has been the same for some three thousand years and reflects the integration of professionals economically dependent on a property-owning system into the ruling class, where they act in general as a moderating force to counter the possibly self-destructive conservatism of the basic-property owners (of land or capital).

Confucius and Aristotle, for instance, alike specialized in urging "moderation" on the ruling class. But Confucius agreed with the basic outlook of the feudal great landowners: "The relations between superiors and inferiors is like that between the wind and the grass. The grass must bend, when the wind blows across it." And Aristotle supported the slave-owning Athenian bourgeoisie: "Some men are by nature free, and others slaves." Plato's "ideal" Republic, as modern scholarship has demonstrated, was based on slave and serf labor—the disdained "many." It was a "republic" for the aristocracy only, indeed, only for the male aristocracy (the exalted "guardians"). Thus whatever "liberal" views intellectuals in feudal or slave-commercial societies might have expressed the general social framework of their thought reflected the interests of the dominant classes, whether they were aware of it or not. In all such cases there is a strong element of class determination that is "understood," often without examination of its roots.

So, too, in other civilized societies. John Locke, no matter what he thought he was doing, was not formulating a philosophy for humanity but for the commercial bourgeoisie of seventeenth-century England. "The end of government," he declared, "is the good of mankind." However, the "chief" function of government he considered to be "the preservation of their [mankinds] property." Unlike the (feudal) Catholic Churchmen he was for religious "toleration," but this toleration excluded atheists: "those are not to be tolerated who deny the being of God." Thus both his social and intellectual perimeters were narrow. Voltaire and Rousseau opposed the French feudal regime but had no intention of supporting a peasant revolution. Similarly, modern liberals support working-class reforms but not a proletarian revolution. In attempting to assess such thought today the basic question is—as with Confucius, Aristotle, and Locke—to define its perimeters and perspectives. And it is not only what modern bourgeois thinkers say but what they do not say that determines these things. They lament an individual "injustice" but fail to note that "injustice" is of the essence of the system, thus spreading the illusion that each "injustice" is an anomaly. They omit the basic fact that capitalist societies are built on mass exploitation and are held together not only by force but by an elaborate network of lies and deception. Once they omit this as a foundational concept or utilize it but fragmentarily, their works, whether social studies or novels, in effect support capitalism and imperialism. And this is aided by their failure to provide any future perspective beyond a fantasized version of capitalist society deprived of its "worst excesses." It is sometimes aided also by a melange of antisocialist and anti-Marxist distortions which are sometimes based—with breezy indifference—on ignorance and sometimes on malice.[3]

As we examine the so-called "great thinkers" of exploitive societies, past and present, it becomes clear that their ideas not only serve upper class interests but in the main are shallow and distorted. The very fact that the ideology of a ruling class is basically determined by "the exploitation of one part of society by the other" necessarily sets limits on the degree to which it can reflect reality. Some such limitations are immediately visible. For instance, a dominant class develops attitudes which virtually exclude the mass of humanity from human form, as reflected in the class, racial, sexual and other stereotypes which it uses as justification for exploitation and oppression. (The term *nigger*, for instance, implies part-animal status.) This basic antihuman perversion then subtly penetrates the whole fabric of the society and forms the often unstated framework for thought. Upper classes regard the working mass as "naturally" inferior and themselves as "naturally" superior (as Aristotle frankly stated). Their fear of this mass evokes paralyzing aversion to basic change:

> *Those who consume these fruits through*
> *these grow fat,*
> *Those who produce these fruits through*
> *these grow lean,*
> *Whatever change takes place, oh, stick to that!*
> *And let things be as they have ever been.*

This fear of change today clearly pervades all forms of bourgeois ideology, often in devious and indirect ways: history with its static or circular views of the past; sociology, economics, and politics with their similar views of the present; philosophy with its lifeless categorizations and vision of celestial changelessness. Dominant-class thought, in short, is an inferior form of thought, generally limited in depth and scope, static and fragmented. It has been able to some degree to transcend these limitations only in periods of bourgeois ascendency over great landowning interests, as in Europe and North America in the period of bourgeois revolutions. Even so, however, such thought was limited to groups on the bourgeois periphery. Later, as capitalism consolidated and then moved into its monopoly stage, its only major contributions to thought came from natural science (which the bourgeoisie needed), but, as we shall see, even this thought was prevented from achieving its philosophical potential. In its social thought the class has gone backward from its revolutionary days, how far backward is dramatically shown when its State assumes fascist form, as in Germany or Italy, whose thinking was not a unique phenomenon but an intensification of general bourgeois patterns.[4]

As we consider the upper class thought of feudal, slave and capitalist societies, it becomes apparent that it is not only narrow but implies a distortion of reality. Capitalism, for instance—as Engels early documented—is a system of ruthless exploitation and class oppression, which, in the present century is not only disintegrating economically but has developed inherent drives to imperialist and antisocialist (essentially antiproletarian) war, drives which now have a "nuclear component." These realities, however, are transformed in the telling. A monopoly-dominated economic system is converted into one that in spite of admitted "deficiencies" still champions "free enterprise" and has potential "upward mobility" for all. Capitalism's inherent imperialist war drives become a matter of "national defence" against (nonexistent) Soviet and other "menaces." The hatreds of the world's people for United States bankers and "counter-insurgent" killers become attacks on "the nation" by irrational rebels often of implied inferior races. The phenomenon is one of a basic structure of lies with a mottled superstructure of fragmented distortions.

Although Marx and Engels examined the class and other roots of ideology and showed how various events, for instance, the 1848 revolutions, molded particular views, as Engels noted they did little specific analysis on the sociopsychological process by which ideology is shaped. For instance, Marx considered "parson power" as much a form of state rule as "physical force," the educational system as important a repressant as the legal system. But these matters involve difficult questions, including that of how the views that cement the system are actually formed. The lines of power whereby policy is made and decisions arrived at have been described in various works: for instance, in William Domroff's *The Higher Circles: The Governing Class in America*. These "circles," Domroff shows, are almost all men and are largely known to each other, directly or indirectly. They form a network that controls corporations, universities, foundations, and other institutions, including the communication media, and indirectly through them and directly through their political associates have " dominance" over the "political process." Big business in the United States has particular influence in key organizations ranging from the National Security Council to the Rand Corporation and including the National Association of Manufacturers and the

United States Chamber of Commerce. Such are the lines of power. The basic processes behind policy formulation, however, are far from simple.[5]

On investigation, even the simplest of these processes, such as that involved in a war crisis, are seen to be more complex than they appear on the surface. Certain views and prejudices are, as it were, whipped up almost overnight. A nation, such as Germany in 1914, which the day before was a "friend" to "Britain"—and after years of mutual mass slaughter will again become a "friend"—suddenly becomes an enemy, enveloped in a frenzy of chauvinist hysteria, and those who oppose war are metamorphosed into instant traitors. Clearly deliberate decisions are made in this process by political and other leaders, but the rapid coordination of all the instrumentalities of rule, from press to pulpit, shows that we are not dealing basically with a deliberate or deliberative process but with a kind of network of sociopsychological reactions—conscious and unconscious—on various levels. No one group, economic or political, makes general policy and simply hands it down to the newsmedia, the church, the educational system, and so on. Decisions seem to be arrived at through a sort of psychological milling around by the ruling big bourgeois groups in and between each field, primarily economic and political but also social and cultural. These seem designed to subordinate particular interests to the basic class interest; in part, a kind of class self-disciplining procedure, which is "understood" rather than openly acknowledged. In all these procedures, however, as well as in the day-to-day functioning of rule, the process is complicated by the fact that the big bourgeoisie often has to clarify its own ideas at the same time as it continues to delude other classes, primarily the working class. Hence, in public statements it makes use of an already existing symbolic language that conveys meaning within the class but distorts it outside.

An even more complex process is that involved in the formation of the underlying sustaining foundation of the general ideas, prejudices and superstitions of an exploitive society. These are not deliberately contrived or consciously implemented but are mostly inherited from the past, their nature and use often rather intuited than directly understood. They constitute the foundational molds whose variations make up both the general concepts, prejudices, stereotypes, or superstitions of particular societies and those needed for specific situations.

In discussing dialectical materialism, Engels argued that the essence of nature is not to be found in "things" but in "processes." And the same is true of society. The functioning of particular individuals or groups within a class does not provide a general explanation of the formation of upper class ideology. True, the State is run by dominant individuals and some groups have more power than others but both rule as such and the ideology connected with it are essentially processes. The individuals and groups can be sloughed off and one ruling class can be succeeded by another (for instance, feudal by bourgeois) but the process as such, which is basically beyond conscious control, continues.

What Marx and Engels did in the 1840s was to take that portion of the outlook of the working class which is rooted in its own social situation—of exploitation—separate it from that infused into it by the bourgeoisie, and shape it into a world-view. In doing so, they were continuing what the Chartists and others had begun but did not complete.

A mass exploited class, unlike an exploiting class, assumes the natural oneness and equality of humanity even as it resents their perversion:

> *When Adam delved, and Eve span,*
> *Who was then a gentleman?*

When John Ball uttered these words during the English Peasant Revolt in 1381, he was expressing the views of the peasantry. As the class showed during that revolt and in similar revolts in Germany, China and elsewhere, it not only hated its exploiters (a hatred, which like that among the slaves, earlier and later, was generally hidden from them) but had considerable cohesion as a class and something of a communal outlook. As the city working class grew up in commercial-feudal and commercial capitalist societies, the cohesion was strengthened and the hatred more sharply focused, as shown in frequent bitter—sometimes citywide—strikes and revolts.[6]

With the dismantling of the cottage industry system and the rise of the industrial working class, this general and mass communal outlook began to take a definitely proletarian form—even as it was mixed with bourgeois components. Both aspects of the class's outlook became more obvious because, unlike the working masses of the past, it achieved literacy (through social struggle). The old mass assumption of equality was transformed into a reasoned doctrine. Communal values became class values—daily expressed in strikes, meetings and demonstrations. Antireligious views developed among the most sophisticated members of the class, aware—as shown in O'Brien's comment on the clerical exploitation of the workers—of the socially reactionary aspect of organized religion. Some, such as Richard Carlile in England or Joseph Dietzgen in Germany, actively propagated an anticlerical viewpoint. Furthermore, unlike previous exploited classes, the industrial working class had a historical perspective. Harney and O'Brien believed their class could move society forward and establish a "socialist" order on a world scale to take the place of capitalism, yet retaining and developing the productive forces created by capitalism.

When Marx and Engels spoke of the ideology of a class they did not, of course, mean that all members shared all its aspects. There were, for instance, in the bourgeoisie obviously divergent views on many matters; but there was also a core of ideas which although changing to some degree with circumstances remained as a core. With an exploited class such as the proletariat the situation is more complex partly because of its size but primarily because of the wide penetration into it of views alien to its interests. And only a small proportion of the class—in contrast to the bourgeoisie—has in normal circumstances an unadulterated class philosophy. That, nevertheless, a core of basically proletarian views is always present becomes manifest by their sudden proliferation in revolutionary situations, as in the Paris Commune or the Russian Revolution. These views appear also, although in more restricted form, in strikes and other working class actions, particularly in general strikes. In massive proletarian actions the whole apparently well-narcotized mass appears to the shaken bourgeoisie as overnight transformed into communists, for, like the slave owners or feudal lords of the past, they had not realized the degree either of its resentment or its social understanding.

Although Marx and Engels never formulated it in quite this way, their implication is that what they discovered when they synthesized the essence of proletarian thought was that this thought was not restricted, as was that of an exploiting class, by the exigencies of oppressive rule but was theoretically capable of uncovering reality in all its aspects, social as well as natural. For instance, although workers often have to lie in order to survive, deception is not of the essence of their way of life, as it necessarily is with an exploitive or ruling class. Their inherent materialism, partly based on daily working with and changing the forms of matter, is potentially wider in scope than any previous materialism. And their constant social struggles predispose them to think in dynamic rather than static terms. It is, however, also clear that the class could not by itself have properly developed its ideological potential. The formation of any class ideology is a complex sociopsychological process and that of a mass, exploited class is especially difficult.

A rounded class ideology was apparently first formed by groups of intellectuals associated with the feudal ruling class and commercial interests in Sumer and Egypt about 3,000 B.C. Although some of the thinking of these intellectuals, as we shall see, had antiestablishment overtones it was basically set within a feudal framework. As similar feudal societies with commercial enclaves grew up in the succeeding centuries in Ásia, similar thinking grew with them, primarily emerging from each new society but influenced by others, the Chinese by the (earlier) Indian for example. There was no basic development of these patterns, particularly in social thought. They remained essentially static from Sumer to the China of Confucius or the India of Buddha or to modern feudal states. As slave-commercial societies began to form in Greece and Roman Italy and powerful (slave-owning) commercial interests fought for and at times achieved, State power, a form of bourgeois thought arose, expressed in social thinking in writers from Aristotle to Cicero and in philosophy from Democritus to Lucretius. But certain basic patterns of social thought inherited from the feudal past and needed for rule in slave-owning conditions continued, as we noted in regard to Plato and Aristotle. Greek and Roman philosophy also had roots in the past; Plato in Hinduism, for instance, and the materialists in the Jains of India. When feudalism arose in Europe, feudal ideology arose with it and as commercialism developed within feudal society bourgeois views began to form. These first became a cohesive body of thought in the centuries of the bourgeoisie's development in Europe—from about 1600 on—and then in North America. Its shapers were people—from Bacon to Madison—who, although often engaged in social struggles, had leisure for writing, were educated and had the knowledge of their age and of past ages at their disposal. Furthermore, as they were part of an exploiting class, they could take over many of the concepts of the commercial-feudal society in whose · midst they had arisen as well as those of past feudal or slave-commercial societies—the "classics." This was the more easily done because, also like the feudal intellectuals (largely Churchmen), bourgeois intellectuals were not shaping knowledge toward the fullest possible correlation between idea and reality but only—whether they were aware of it or not—toward sufficient correlation to enable the bourgeoisie to advance its class interests. They were also held back for a time by an admixture of feudal thought, which reflects itself as an ambivalence toward bourgeois values, visible in thinkers from Descarte to Jefferson even though the main thrust of their actions was toward the advancement of bourgeois society, or in Hegel, whose philosophy of change reflected the growing bourgeois forces in the Germany of his day, his mysticism and abstractionism the feudal.

By the time of Shelley and Byron, a new cultural phenomenon appeared: the first stirrings of working class thought were added to the upper-class intellectual complex. Byron vigorously defended the Luddite rioters—"Will the famished wretch who has braved your bayonets be appalled by your gibbets?"—and Shelley wrote in *Song to the Men of England* (1818):

> *Men of England, wherefore plough*
> *For the lords who lay ye low?*
> *Wherefore weave with toil and care,*
> *The rich robes your tyrants wear?*

Byron, however, also wrote a maudlin lament on the death of the King's daughter, and Shelley viewed with some trepidation a possible mass revolution even though he felt it was justified: "The last resort of resistance is undoubtedly insurrection." Both poets supported the democratization of parliament and hailed antifeudal revolutions on the Continent; and Byron gave his life in the Greek bourgeois nationalist struggle against feudal Turkish domination.[7]

The difficulties in the formation of previous class ideologies were compounded many times for the proletariat. The workers had neither leisure nor wide education. Their leaders had to fight for knowledge. The creation of ideology was not, as it was for the feudal aristocracy and the bourgeoisie, among its trades. It was not a ruling class or one with its own area of dominance such as the bourgeoisie had had in feudal, slave-commercial and commercial-feudal societies, but was an exploited class subjected to an omnipresent ideological blizzard of falsehood, prejudice, and superstition. Nor could it, as could the bourgeoisie, take over substantial parts of an ideological base from a kindred class, past or present. As a majority, nonexploitive, nonoppressive class, it had no such direct historical kin, although it did have roots in the ideas developed by peasant and artisan leaders in the past, such as, for instance, in Britain, the seventeenth-century "diggers" and "levellers," but these did not provide a major ideological base comparable to that handed down to the bourgeoisie. It was a large and widely scattered class lacking the compact coherence of either an aristocracy or a bourgeoisie. Although increasingly literate, its members did not have the wide range of knowledge necessary to form a world-view. For these various reasons, its world-view could only properly be formed by people who both had confident command of this knowledge and were unreservedly one with the class and its struggles. If Marx and Engels had not formed this view—on the basis of the class's own efforts—others would certainly have done so. It would doubtless have taken longer but sooner or later it would have been formed.

And once the essence of this view was created it did not need to be created again, although like any living body of thought, it requires constant development. In time this development will change certain aspects of the essence, a process similar to that seen in the history of the natural sciences.

One question which Marx and Engels did not discuss, except fragmentarily, was that of the relation of class ideology to ideology in general. That all ideology is not class-determined is clear from the fact that ideology existed before classes; and, according to the projections of Marxism, class ideology will not exist in a future world communist society.

What ideas people held in hunter-gathering and early-farming societies can be determined in general by investigations of similar societies existing into the present, for the same social structures produce the same ideas in all times and places—from the Germanic, early-farming society tribes observed by Caesar and Tacitus, to similar societies examined by modern anthropologists. In making such anthropological investigations we have of course, to separate ideas native to the society from those coming from "the outside world," but this does not present the difficulties which the layman would expect. The general ideas of peoples in the hunter-gathering and early-farming communities that have been examined in the present century have shown comparatively little outside influence, the basic stock of ideas arising from social conditions many centuries old and generally remaining as unchanging as the societies themselves. Ideas from outside form a generally easily detectable overlay. In these societies ideas arise primarily from work and social activities, particularly those with a biological basis—the family, childbirth, child care, courting, puberty, aging, illness, and death—but also from community problems and conflicts between communities. On some of these subjects, sexual differences in viewpoints are apparent, some of them arising from the differing social roles of the sexes. In the wealthier of such societies differences in status produce embryonic class differences in outlook but there is no major dichotomy.

When classes arose first in later-type farming societies—about 4,000 B.C.—and then in the first feudal civilizations, some of these earlier ideas were perverted for the use of class rule, for instance, religious superstitions, which were remolded in the new State religions, and new ideas, such as that of the inherent, indeed, divinely bestowed, superiority of the upper classes and their "leader." But a great mass of ideas were carried along from the old society, particularly among the peasantry, for their life styles did not change as much as those of the new dominant classes, and as new knowledge was obtained they were mostly shut out from it. Marx and Engels were certainly right when they contended that in class societies class factors pervade almost all thinking, affecting people's views not only directly but indirectly in a multitude of unseen ways and in a whirl of conflicting interests. But the impact of class is less directly felt in the area of ideas arising from community and family life than from economic or political life, and although the bourgeoisie and proletariat differ in many regards in their ideas in this sphere there is also an area, especially in the general form of ideas, which classes share in common.

The fact that industrial working-class views are often not obtrusive, as in the United States today, sometimes gives liberals and others the impression that they do not exist. However, once we become aware of them we can see that they exist all around us. They are particularly apparent—on various levels—in capitalist nations where the workers have their own political parties. They are expressed of course, in a variety of forms, ranging from trade union periodicals—which most intellectuals, for instance, never see—to party newspapers. And they become dramatically obvious, as we have noted, in revolutionary situations or general strikes—as in San Francisco or Terre Haute in the Depression.

In all capitalist nations today, a segment of the working class has acquired some Marxist understanding. This understanding, however, clearly exists in varying degrees and cannot achieve its potential because of the limitations imposed upon the class by capitalism. The Marxist world-view is no easier to grasp than are the complex realities it attempts to reflect. But what we might call the viable essence of Marxism, that is to say, the degree of Marxist understanding necessary to overthrow capitalism is clearly quite attainable by large masses of workers and others. Marxism, like everything else, is not a set entity but a process, with a core, conflicting forces, and a volatile periphery.

Marx and Engels on Literature

Marx and Engels made no systematic study of art or its relation to society. (I use the word art to signify all the creative arts including literature and the drama.) Their comments on the subject—mostly on literature— come largely in their letters. It is, however, clear that they believed that art arose in the same general ways as did ideas, even though it encompasses more than ideas and has its own essence. As Engels succinctly noted in 1894: "Political, judicial, philosophical, religious, literary, artistic, etc., development is based on economic development. But all these react upon one another and also upon the economic base." The phrasing "literary, artistic, etc., development" in place of Marx's "ideological forms." perhaps indicates that Engels felt that Marx intended to include the arts, and that the ideological superstructure was actually a cultural superstructure. The thing that is missing in Engels's comment—which continues—is, however, as in his 1890 letter to Bloch, a clear reference to the class struggle as the central determinant force in class societies operating between the economic foundation and the cultural superstructure. And the same omission brings some confusion also into some of Marx's comments on the subject, for example:

> It is well known that certain periods of highest development of art stand in no direct connection with the general development of society, nor with the material basis and the skeleton structure of its organization. Witness the example of the Greeks as compared with modern art or even Shakespeare.

Marx is apparently arguing that "modern art" or the plays of Shakespeare are inferior to the Greek—primarily fifth-century Athens—although the economy was more highly developed in Britain in the mid-nineteenth or the early seventeenth century. The problem, however, must not be viewed in absolute but in relative terms. For its time the economic power of Athens was unprecedented and unique. Athens was a bustling commercial city-state with considerable industry, including rich silver mines, and a colonial empire. The resulting wealth produced a concentrated bourgeoisie that challenged the landowners for power. In this class struggle, which involved artisans and small merchants as well as the bourgeoisie, an active balance of upper class forces created political democracy for these classes. It also stirred up a general social turmoil that took an already existing cultural tradition and transformed it, as shown in the Athenian drama with its tumultuous reflections of class and sexual conflicts and its humanist views. Thus although Athenian economic production was well below that of nineteenth-century Britain, it was of a nature that could produce social turbulence and it was out of this turbulence and not a general economic level that its art arose. And this is generally true; art of high quality in class society has arisen from class conflict. There was, then in slave-commercial society Athens as "direct" a link between culture and "the material [i.e., the economic] basis" as in any exploitive class society, namely that of the class struggle.

This link is, of course, always there and provides the same general connection between economic and cultural forces in all such societies.[8]

The arts, then, are part of the general cultural aspect of society. What, however, is art? How does it differ from ideology? Marx and Engels do not go into these matters in any detail, and indeed, in the nineteenth century there was not much known about them. Nor in certain respects is there today. Marx's often-quoted early views on some of these things in the 1844 manuscripts, written before he was fully a Marxist, are insightful but fragmentary. He there speaks of "the laws of beauty" but does not examine them or speculate on their possible origin. He believed that "an eye for beauty of form" was part of the "richness of man's essential being" including his "senses" and was not a unique entity. In 1859 he wrote: "The sensation of color is, generally speaking, the most popular form of aesthetic sense." Marx, then, believed that people possessed an "aesthetic sense," but he did not go into its nature or roots, perhaps, feeling that too little was known about it for useful speculation. In *Capital* (1867) he wrote that "many a human architect is put to shame by the bee in the construction of its wax cells," but he does not seem to feel that there is any evolutionary connection between the two phenomena: "However, the poorest architect is categorically distinguished from the best of bees by the fact that before he builds a cell in wax, he has built it in his head." Engels, in discussing the evolution of the hand notes that chimpanzees "construct roofs between the branches for protection against the weather" and "seize hold of clubs to defend themselves" but he concludes: "No simian hand has ever fashioned even the crudest of stone knives." Thus although Engels believed that the human brain and hand evolved from that of the ape, he does not mention possible evolutionary roots for craftsmanship.[9]

It is, however, becoming apparent today that what Marx called an "aesthetic sense" does indeed have evolutionary roots. Chimpanzees can be taught to paint and they not only achieve design and color sense but take a kind of pride in their work. When we see a film of monkeys at play, for instance turning somersaults, it is apparent that they have a sense of rhythm and enjoy their accomplishments. And still deeper roots are to be found in the mating dances of birds and in bird songs, both of which display complex rhythm and pattern, truly "unpremeditated art" as Shelley said the skylark's song. The segments of the brain and hormonal system that are connected with these activities have begun to be explored.

It is apparent that while each art has its separate identity, it shares a general character with all art. Rhythm, melody and harmony in music, song or dance, pattern in sculpture or painting, rhythm in writing—in prose as well as poetry—are clearly all basically the same phenomenon and connected with "the aesthetic sense," whatever it is and whatever its roots, neurological or evolutionary. The aesthetic sense does not, as Marx also suggested, live alone but in conjunction with the senses and the "essential being," including the emotions. Finally, as many writers and other artists have recognized, the ideas and other components of a work of art do not come primarily from conscious effort but emerge from the unconscious in an emotional vortex. Although some works of literature, such as in Goethe's *Faust* or Shelley's *Prometheus Unbound,* are intellectual and critical, their ideas do not arise primarily from conscious thought but in the creative process mingled with emotion and rhythm and shaping "before unapprehended relations."[10]

The continuity of ideology in civilization Marx and Engels attributed to the continuity of similar classes, particularly dominant classes. What of the arts? Why are people today able to respond to the great works of art of the past, the Greek drama, for instance? The answer must basically be the same as for ideology. Not only the general class outlooks but the general emotional responses and general aesthetic frameworks of explotive and other classes continue through feudal, slave-commercial and capitalist societies. But in regard to art another factor is particularly involved namely that of the general social area of the family and community life, and of the relations of the sexes, an area which, as we have noted, does not in certain respects respond to economic change but has social (ultimately biological) roots. And in this area some of the forms of living—no matter how different their specific content—are the same in different strata of society. It is this general social area, the area of what we might call everyday living, that poets, artists, and musicians primarily reflect. Thus the frustrations and exaltations of Romeo are in their general form the same as those of lovers in all classes in all ages and they can to varying degrees respond to them. So, too, with some works with political or philosophical content. Both liberals and radical workers can empathise in varying degrees with the Prometheus of Aeschylus in his rebellion against authority, for even though the rebellion arose from the class struggles of slave-commercial Athens the utterances of rebellion against oppressive rule are generally similar in any society. So, too, with the sexual rebellion of Lysistrata.

On the other hand there are clearly limitations. Romeo was, after all, an upper class lover and many of his values would be rejected as alien by a worker. The rebellion of Prometheus is essentially a personal rebellion and hence can elicit but a limited response from a class-conscious worker today.

And *Lysistrata* contains a strong anti-feminist streak. Thus while all such works can still have a strong appeal to the upper classes their appeal to the working class and others is more restricted.

Both Marx and Engels were remarkably well read in European literature, usually reading the writers in their native languages. Some of their comments are well known and appear in convenient form in several anthologies. It might be helpful to consider some of these in chronological order so they can be viewed against their historical backgrounds.

Marx and Engels begin their comments on art with the Greek Homeric period, which, as we have seen, Engels perceived as a rather primitive society instead of the slave-commercial civilization that in fact it was. And Marx was similarly mistaken, both of them necessarily so in view of what was then known. The Homeric "epos" Marx regarded as the expression of "an undeveloped stage of art development." And the Athenian Greeks he regarded as under the spell of a primitive "mythology" which was no longer possible as a framework for art: "Where does Vulcan come in as against Roberts & Co. . . ?" The Homeric epics were highly developed works of art, the Greek dramatists were as sophisticated as Plato and Aristotle. They used mythology primarily for dramatic purposes and not because they believed in it. That Greek mythology could still serve as the material for art in the nineteenth century although given new meanings was shown in the *Prometheus Unbound* of Shelley. And the same is true today, not only of Greek but of all mythology.[11]

As we have seen, nothing was known in the nineteenth century of Sumer, and hence of the first art of a civilized state. Sumerian literature, 2,500 years before the Athenian, contained some of the basic qualities of all that was to follow: some of it philosophical; some of it social, "Not all the households of the poor are equally submissive"; some personal,

> *Bridegroom let me caress you,*
> *My precious caress is more savory than honey;*

some satirical, as a would-be bride speculates;

> *Who is well provided, who is rich?*
> *For whom shall I hold my love?*

The major work was the philosophical, adventure epic, *Gilgamesh:*

When the gods created mankind
they alloted to mankind Death,
but life they witheld in their own hands.

Little was known in nineteenth-century Europe of succeeding Asian literature from the Indian epics to Lady Murasaki's novel the *Tale of Genji,* and Marx and Engels do not seem to refer to this literature. [12]

Following their comments on Greek literature, the next major writer noted was Dante, of whom Engels wrote:

> The close of the feudal Middle Ages and the onset of the modern capitalistic era are marked by a figure of grandiose stature: it is an Italian, Dante, who is both the last poet of the Middle Ages and the first modern poet.

Without this general historical perspective, the deeper significance of Dante, particularly the *Inferno,* cannot be grasped; but such phrasing as "Middle Ages" and "modern poet" obscure the specific class forces that molded Dante, and should not be used by Marxists today. Dante arose out of the class struggles in Florence between feudal and commercial interests. His works mix elements from both but their essence has its roots in the developing commercialism of Italy at the time. [13]

The commercial capitalism of feudal Europe was of limited scope, being confined largely to port cities and operating within a dominant feudal economy. It was not until the sixteenth century that it began to become a central economic force and bore on its back the cultural movement known as the Renaissance. In examining the rise of science in the Introduction (1875–1876) to his *Dialectics of Nature* Engels discussed the Renaissance:

> In Italy, France, and Germany, a new literature arose, the first modern literature; shortly afterwards came the classical epochs of English and Spanish literature. . . . It was the greatest progressive revolution that mankind has so far experienced, a time which called for giants and produced giants—giants in power of thought, passion, and character, in universality and learning. The men who founded the modern rule of the bourgeoisie had anything but bourgeois limitations.

Once again, Engels hits the essence of the subject but once again his secondary concepts and phrasing are open to question. By "modern" Engels again means primarily the literature of the bourgeoisie. And although the thinkers, writers and artists of the Renaissance—Engels mentions Leonardo and

Dürer—were indeed great, they were molded by and part of the rise of commercial capitalism and there was no way in which they could transcend its perimeters. Engels is using the term *bourgeois* too narrowly, perhaps unconsciously having the settled industrial bourgeoisie of the later nineteenth century in mind. But the bourgeoisie in its rise and later in its revolutionary epoch had heroic attributes and farsighted vision. The general point, however, is that no group of thinkers, writers or artists can develop beyond the confines of the social forces that produce them. It might be emphasized, too, although Engels clearly implies this, that the Renaissance writers and artists were "giants" not primarily because of an inherent "genius" but because of the social forces acting upon them. The amount of potential human talent is the same in any population in any society—as Shelley long ago pointed out.[14]

It is true that in England following the Renaissance (with such writers as Shakespeare, Spenser, Raleigh and Milton), a classical trend (Dryden and Pope) developed, but it gives a sense of things "just happening" to state that it simply "came." Following the weakening of the bourgeois revolutionary forces of Cromwell and his associates a balance of bourgeois and feudal power was consolidated, and it was basically the feudal aspect that was expressed in the classical movement, a movement mainly in poetry (with its pony trot of the "heroic couplet"). It was balanced by the bourgeois movement in the novel (Richardson, Fielding, and Smollet) and by the satiric vision of Swift.

According to Marx's son-in-law, Paul Lafargue, Marx's two favorite Renaissance writers were Shakespeare and Cervantes. Marx, he tells us, "made a detailed study" of Shakespeare's works "and knew even the least important of his characters." Marx's daughter Eleanor tells us that her father read the whole of *Don Quixote* to her; and "As to Shakespeare he was the Bible of our house, seldom out of our hands or mouths." That Marx would revel in Cervantes with his rollicking, satiric undermining of feudalism is to be expected, but why the fascination with Shakespeare? There is certainly little overtly progressive for his time in Shakespeare as there is, for instance, in Bacon, with his championing of science and his materialist outlook. The answer is that Shakespeare grew out of the same movement that produced Bacon, namely that particular advance of the bourgeoisie that was some half-century later to produce the British Revolution, led by Cromwell and supported by Milton, but that this movement was reflected differently in Shakespeare than in Bacon because he was a creative writer and not a philosopher. It was apparent, for instance, directly in his admiration for the commercial aristocracy, demonstrated in his Henry V, an admiration which was shared by other poets of the day, notably Spenser and Sidney. But Shakespeare also has a quality which Bacon did not, namely a feeling for the common people, for Shakespeare came from a middle class background whereas Bacon was part of the commercial aristocracy. The London theatre, of which Shakespeare—along with Ben Jonson, a former bricklayer—was part was primarily a middle class phenomenon. These qualities in Shakespeare, plus his religious scepticism, which he shared with Marlowe, his keen psychological insights and the power of his language, must have appealed to Marx. Yet on the other hand, Shakespeare was a product of an exploitive society and shared many of its prejudices, including an acceptance of rank and privilege. And, unlike Bacon, he had little vision of the future.[15]

Of the early nineteenth-century writers, Marx and Engels seem to have favored Balzac and Shelley, again sharply contrasting figures. Although Balzac supported the feudal regime, Engels notes, "his satire is never keener" than when he depicts "the very men and women with whom he sympathizes most deeply—the nobles." And, strangely, he admired their bourgeois revolutionary "antagonists." Engels concludes:

> That Balzac thus was compelled to go against his own class sympathies and political prejudices, that he saw the necessity of the downfall of his favorite nobles, and described them as people deserving no better fate; and that he saw the real men of the future where, for the time being, they alone were to be found—that I consider one of the greatest triumphs of Realism, and one of the grandest features in old Balzac.[16]

Engels's comments again bring out the fact that class attitudes are not a simple matter of direct reflection, but arise in the interactive whirl of "class antagonisms," usually in writers as in people in general with the views of one class dominant but with admixtures from others. We might note, however, that Balzac, for all his admiration for "the nobles" was himself of middle class origin and was a businessman before he was a writer. His attitude towards the aristocracy was clearly ambivalent, with his bourgeois origins exerting more influence, perhaps mostly unconsciously, than Engels recognized. We might object also to "old Balzac." Balzac was in his thirties when he wrote some of his best novels, including *Eugenie Grandet* and *Father Goriot*. The common habit of referring to those in the past as "old" obscures the continuity of life and the life cycle in the historical process.

As we have noted, both Marx and Engels were Shelley enthusiasts. Eleanor quoted her father as follows:

The real difference between Byron and Shelley lies in the following: Those who understand and cherish them, consider it fortunate that Byron died in his thirty-sixth year, since if he had lived longer he would have become a reactionary bourgeois. On the other hand, they regret that Shelley died at twenty-nine, since he was a thoroughgoing revolutionary and would always have belonged to the Socialist vanguard.

In making the comment Marx was doubtless thinking of such working-class-oriented poems by Shelley as *Song to the Men of England* and *The Masque of Anarchy* and perhaps mainly of Byron's then popular *Childe Harold's Pilgrimage* with its mixture of bourgeois-revolutionary and aristocratic attitudes. Shelley, too, felt that for all his progressive views and his courage Byron suffered from "the canker of aristocracy." The reason for the difference between the two poets doubtless ultimately stemmed from the fact that Shelley came from a "squirearchy" family with trading interests and Byron from the aristocracy (including a castle). Although Byron supported bourgeois liberation causes, such as that in Greece, he had little use for Shelley's egalitarian projections—as in *Prometheus Unbound*—having, for all his generally advanced views no concept of a future society beyond that of a bourgeois democratic republic. It is unlikely that Byron would have become a "reactionary bourgeois" (and it is not, of course, certain that Eleanor was quoting her father exactly). He would, in Victorian England, have more likely been a liberal reformer, although he would not, as Shelley doubtless would, have become a socialist. Byron, for all his aristocratic nostalgia and self-deprecating irony, was staunchly and courageously in the forefront of the bourgeois revolutionary movement and, especially after his death in the Greek cause, became a symbol for struggle against oppression everywhere.[17]

In the nineteenth century works by working-class and socialist writers first began to appear. The Chartist journals carried poems, which Engels read, and proletarian poets arose, notably George Weerth, a member of the Communist League, whom Engels called "the first and most important poet of the German proletariat." The rise of socialist writers raised problems on how their views were to be integrated into creative writing. In 1858–59 the German socialist leader, Ferdinand Lassalle, wrote a play, *Franz von Sickingen,* on a sixteenth-century revolt of the lower German aristocracy, the "knights," against the great aristocrats in which he embodied material reflecting nineteenth century struggles. Marx wrote to Lassalle as follows:

In this case, then, the noble representatives of revolution—behind whose slogans of unity and liberty the hope of the old imperial power and fistic right is concealed—should not take up all the interest as in your play, but the representatives of the peasantry (especially them) and the revolutionary elements in the cities should have provided an important and active background for your play. Then you could have expressed in much greater measure the most modern ideas in their purest form. As it is the major theme of your play, together with religious freedom, remains civil unity. You would then have Shakespearized more; at present, there is too much Schillerism, which means making individuals into mere mouthpieces of the spirit of the times, and this is your main fault.[18]

Marx, then, objects to Lassalle's play on two counts: Lassalle placed too much emphasis on the knights and neglected the peasantry and the rebelling city merchants and artisans; he failed to have his material develop naturally in individualized dialogue—as did Shakespeare—but instead used generalized views which he twisted to give them contemporary significance. The socialist writer, then, Marx is contending, must be first of all a writer and not a propagandist. His ideas must be expressed only in so far as they fit the characters and situation (as in O'Casey's plays in the present century). And Engels took a similar position. As he wrote to Minna Kautsky, the mother of Karl Kautsky, of a socialist-oriented novel she had written:

Evidently you felt the need in this book to declare publicly for your party, to bear witness before the whole world and show your convictions. Now you have done this; you have it behind you and have no need to do so again in this form. I am not at all an opponent of tendentious writing [Tendenzpoesie] as such. . . . But I believe the tendency must spring forth from the situation and the action itself, without explicit attention called to it; the writer is not obliged to offer to the reader the future historical solution of the social conflicts he depicts.

Engels also struck out at presumed proletarian fiction which, like much such literature today, depicted only the oppression of the working class but not its positive power:

In the "City Girl" the working class figures as a passive mass, unable to help itself and not even making any attempt at striving to help itself. All attempts to drag it out of its torpid misery come from without, from above. Now if this was a correct description about 1800 or 1810, in the days of Saint Simon and Robert Owen, it cannot appear so in 1887 to a man who for nearly fifty years has had the honour of sharing in most of the fights of the militant proletariat.[19]

The great contribution that Marx and Engels made to our understanding of art, particularly literature, does not, of course, lie only or even primarily in their specific comments on the subject but in their general theory of sociocultural development. Unless we perceive the social, especially class, foundations of culture that Marx and Engels uncovered, the history of the arts seems a series of miracles depending on chance showers of "genius." Nor can an individual writer be fully understood unless we perceive the historical roots of the time. People can, of course, respond, and respond passionately, to writers without such knowledge, but with it new perspectives open. In short, Marx and Engels provided a basic framework for the understanding of art, and hence, for deepening our appreciation of it.

As we have seen, Marx and Engels were unaware that feudalism prevailed from Sumer in 3,000 B.C. into nineteenth-century Europe. Thus they failed to perceive the unity of the ideological patterns arising from feudal society in this vast period and area, particularly from the conflicts between landowning and commercial interests. And so, too, with art. The Sumerian poems and the *Inferno* reflect the same general feudal-commercial conflict. Nor did the slave-commercial society of Athens and Rome change the basic situation although it produced new content and form—from Aeschylus to Lucretius. The Athenian and the Elizabethan drama alike arose from the struggle of commercial against landowning interests. So, too, the poems of Byron and Shelley, with the newly added element of a rising industrial capitalism. There was, that is to say, a common pattern to the development of both idology and art in world civilizations of which Marx and Engels were but faintly aware. Marx and Engels seem also to have known little of folk art—song and dance, tales and pot making, music and woodcarving and embroidery—a vast reservoir of art stemming from hunter-gathering societies and continued by peasants and workers, and especially by women.

As all history so far has been but prologue, so too, with art. Art in the past was the product of exploitive and oppressive societies. This means that not only was there a massive repression of talent but that this art was, to a greater or lesser degree in differing situations, limited and distorted. It was limited in its concepts of the general relations of humanity to society and to nature. Neither Dante nor Shakespeare, neither Goethe nor Tolstoy, had any real understanding of society, its structures and motive forces, its movement and development, and this necessarily limited their vision. And even the most humanitarian of these writers and other artists were afflicted by the antihuman prejudices of exploitive society, sometimes in subtle and indirect ways. As society advances into a highly developed world communism, their—then long past—limitations and distortions will become more obvious. Nevertheless, as their reception in socialist countries today shows, people in communist society will continue to make allowances for their defects and respond to their insights into people in their everyday life as well as to the broad vision of such poets as Lucretius and Shelley. And so, too, with the progressive-minded writers of capitalist society in general.

In the present century, we have witnessed a development unique in the history of art, namely the rise of Marxist creative writers and other artists, not only in capitalist but in socialist and exploited "third world" countries. Their works, arising in varying circumstances—as witness Neruda, O'Casey, Brecht, Rivera, Shostakovich, Sholokhov—are of varying forms and merits, the analysis of them a special task. But some of them will clearly also be appreciated in communist society for many centuries. And all of them, along with the great progressive figures of the past, play a vital part in the struggles of humanity today for a new world.

Just as Marx and Engels did not much investigate the specific socio-psychological ways in which ideologies arose, they did not much investigate the even more complex ways in which individual art is shaped by social forces, more complex because art is not primarily a matter of conscious reasoning but of unconscious creation. The general social process at work, as we have noted, must be the same for art as for ideology, namely creation in class societies in a whirl of primarily class influences, in which, in time, some become dominant. There is, however, clearly a field here which is still largely unexplored, although some beginnings—including my own work on Shelley—have been made. And, as we have seen, further investigation is still needed into the psychological and aesthetic processes at work.

In studying a major writer such as Shelley various levels of understanding and appreciation are possible. One can respond to his poetry on a personal level, knowing nothing of his life or times, and revel in the beauties of his lyrics. This appreciation can be given more depth by learning something of his life and seeing the circumstances of composition. Still more understanding can come from also reading his contemporaries, such as Byron or Keats, and seeing the values, social and esthetic, they all shared. But even with all this the basic framework is still missing, namely a study of the social forces which produced not only Shelley but the literature of his age. This framework not only assists in understanding his political poetry but all his poetry (and prose). The personal and the esthetic acquire new significance as we perceive interconnections. So with his relations to his contemporaries. We can, for instance, see that underneath its mythological symbolism *Prometheus Unbound* is essentially a poem of social revolution, a projection into the future. Without this insight the essential meaning of the poem is lost and the reader is left—as the history of the criticism of the drama abundantly reveals—with aesthetic and emotional responses in a cultural vacuum. It is this kind of basic framework that Marx and Engels made possible—which, of course, does absolve us from investigating every situation independently and discovering its particular characteristics.

As we have seen, Marx and Engels, in addition to supplying the basic framework for understanding art, also made insightful examinations of particular authors, sometimes, as in Marx's comments on Lassalle, of striking brilliance. Neither of them, however, concentrated primarily on literature or the other arts, but on social and philosophical analysis. They were clearly wrong on some things, partly because of the lack of knowledge at the time, as on Homer and the Greek drama. But usually when they made false judgements it was the result of their not properly applying their own general views.

8

Nature and Society

Dialectical Materialism

When Marx and Engels met in Brussels in 1845 they intended not only to put together a social philosophy but what Engels later called a "new world outlook," a general philosophy examining the relation of humanity to nature as well as to society. In the part of this world-view which later came to be called dialectical materialism they were primarily concerned with the former. Although they jointly laid the foundation for dialectical materialism, its development was left almost entirely to Engels, Marx being occupied by *Capital* and his work with the *International*. They clearly intended, however, for both aspects of their "world outlook" to be considered together. Engels, for instance, in his eulogy at Marx's grave noted Marx's interest in natural as well as social science, an interest which is apparent in their correspondence. The importance of this emphasis on the scope of their total "outlook" is especially clear today when the natural sciences are revealing new links between nature, people, and society. As a result of this research it has become apparent that to understand society in depth, we have to investigate its roots in nature to an even greater degree than Marx and Engels realized. The chain from the atom to humanity is in fact unbroken and more of its links are becoming visible.[1]

"The great basic question of all philosophy," Engels wrote in *Feuerbach* in 1888, is that of "the relation of thinking and being." In religious controversy this relation had been "sharpened into this: Did God create the world or has the world been in existence eternally?"

162

The answers which philosophers gave to this question split them into two great camps. Those who asserted the primacy of spirit to nature and, therefore, in the last instance, assumed world creation in some form or other . . . comprised the camp of idealism. The others, who regarded nature as primary, belong to the various schools of materialism.

Although it is suggested in some Marxist studies that these two—idealism and materialism—are the only major "camps" of philosophy, Engels also lists a third, namely scepticism: "In addition there is yet a set of different philosophers—those who question the possibility of any cognition, or at least of an exhaustive cognition, of the world." In the first camp were such "idealists" (*Idea*-ists) as Plato, Berkeley, and Hegel, as well as all theologians, for they all, philosophers or priests, had in common the view that a hypothetical cosmic mind created matter, regardless of whether they called this mind God, the Absolute, the One or the Idea. Marx wrote his Ph.D. thesis on the Greek materialists, whose views—surviving mainly in fragments—were later embodied and further developed by the Roman poet Lucretius in his philosophical epic *The Nature of Things*, a work that provided the main intellectual base for the French eighteenth-century materialists, Diderot and Holbach. Of the sceptics the most prominent was the Scottish philosopher David Hume, who doubted the very existence of either matter or mind, reducing all to a passive stream of "sensations" of undetermined origin. And Engels also included Kant among the skeptics for Kant argued that "things-in-themselves" are unknowable, and in effect, reduced reality to mental "categories."[2]

In considering dialectical materialism, we have to emphasise at the outset that it is fundamentally materialism, a materialist philosophy, and not dialectics. Its dialectical aspect arises from the fact that matter acts in dialectical ways. It is for this reason that the influence of Hegel in the shaping of dialectical materialism, important though it was, was of a secondary and not a primary nature. Hegel perceived some of the dialectical patterns of reality but he saw reality as a manifestation not of matter but of God, and his method of thought was shaped by the fact that he viewed this God as a developing entity; in contrast to Plato's unchanging One he had a changing One. It is for this reason also that discussions of dialectical materialism should begin with an examination of its materialist aspect and its roots in previous materialism. Otherwise the "dialectic" appears as a kind of disembodied molding force both in matter and in dialectical materialism.

Lucretius, basing himself on earlier Greek materialists and on Greek and Roman science, argued that the universe had existed from eternity, that it first consisted of "atoms and the void" and, in an extraordinary general anticipation of the modern view—in the biological as well as the physical sciences—argued that the universe and life had been formed by chance combinations among an infinitely large number of "atoms": "But multitudinous atoms, swept along in multitudinous courses through infinite time by mutual clashes and their own weight, have come together in every possible way and realized everything that could be formed by their combinations." There is no God, no creation, no heaven, no "murky pit of Hell," no immortality; the mind dies with the body: "Death is necessary so that life may exist." Lucretius argued—nearly 2,000 years before Darwin—that life forms were affected by a kind of natural selection: "In those days again many species must have died out altogether and failed to reproduce their kind. Every species that you now see drawing the breath of life has been protected and preserved from the beginning of the world either by cunning or by prowess or by speed." Biological matter, like physical matter, consists of atoms; so too do the emotions and the mind, which is composed of more refined atoms linked to the atoms of the body by intermediate atoms.

"The universe," wrote Holbach, consists only of "matter and motion", a concept followed by Engels. There was the visible motion of physical objects, the invisible motion of atoms, manifested, in living matter, in fermentation and growth, and, in the human body, in thought. Life had emerged from matter "combined of particular modes." "The essence of matter," Holbach wrote, "is to act." Hence, there was no dichotomy between matter and motion, no need for Aristotle's Prime Mover (God) to infuse motion into matter. Diderot, as we have seen, speculated on evolution, but neither he nor Holbach had any explanation for the origin of Man, Diderot, rather desperately, suggesting that there were "perhaps men upon earth from eternity."[3]

Although Marx and Engels rejected certain aspects of these previous materialisms they accepted most of their basic premises: matter is primary, Mind derivitive; the world was not created but has existed eternally; there is no God and no immortality. Like the earlier materialists (and such deists as Voltaire and Paine) they attacked the reactionary historical role of organized religion and denounced its theology as fantasy but they recognized that religion as a narcotic was a necessary accompaniment of exploitation and oppression, as Marx noted in 1843, before he was really a Marxist: "Religion is the sigh of the oppressed creature, the sentiment of a heartless world, as it is the soul of soulless conditions. It is the opium of the people."

Like the earlier materialists also, Marx and Engels saw mind as an expression of matter, but with the development of the theory of evolution they no longer had to resort to crude analogies with fermentation but perceived that mind also had evolved:

> But if the further question is raised: what then are thought and consciousness, and whence they come, it becomes apparent that they are products of the human brain and that man himself is a product of Nature, which has been developed in and along with its environment.[4]

The materialism of Diderot and Holbach, based primarily on the physics of mechanical bodies, failed, Engels felt, to take interactivity and development properly into account:

> The materialism of the last century was predominantly mechanical, because at that time, of all natural sciences, mechanics and indeed only the mechanics of solid bodies—celestial and terrestrial—in short, the mechanics of gravity, had come to any definite close. Chemistry at that time existed only in its infantile, phlogistic form. Biology still lay in swaddling clothes. . . . The second specific limitation of this materialism lay in its inability to comprehend the universe as a process—as matter developing in an historical [evolutionary] process. This was in accordance with the level of the natural science of that time, and with the metaphysical, i.e., antidialectical manner of philosophizing connected with it.

By *metaphysical* here Engels does not mean *mystical*, but uses the word, as Hegel did, to designate the division of reality into "categories," particularly those of Kant, and the static logic that went with it.

Although the French materialists had considerable understanding of nature they had little of history:

> Old materialism looked upon all previous history as a crude heap of irrationality and violence; modern materialism sees in it the process of evolution of humanity, and aims at discovering the laws thereof.

The French materialists, then, in spite of their progressive social views still saw history as resulting from ambition, intrigue, violence, and so on. They had no concept of objective historical process, and hence were unable to formulate a true "world outlook," one which embraced both nature and society.

And finally, as Marx pointed out, the old materialism—like all previous philosophy—had a false concept of mind: "the chief defect of all hitherto existing materialism—that of Feuerbach included—is that the thing, reality, sensuousness, is conceived only in the form of the *object* or *of contemplation* but not as *human sensuous activity, practice,* not subjectively."

The comment, of course, is more than a critique of earlier materialism, for it implies that there is no such thing as "the mind," an abstract isolate that throughout the centuries had formed the base for epistemology. Whereas, Plato argued, matter is material, transient, and evil, mind is spiritual, eternal and good, the two being antithetical entities. The human body is connected with matter, the human mind with the Divine Mind— as Plato laid the basis of arguments both for immortality and asceticism (antifeminism). Even when this mystical idealism was rejected by materialists, something of the mind-matter dichotomy inherent in it remained. Although the connection between body and mind was accepted by Lucretius and stressed by Holbach, the French materialists and others, including Feuerbach, saw mind as essentially reflective. We must, Marx continued, reject "contemplative materialism, i.e., materialism which does not understand sensuousness as practical activity." What we have in reality, Marx is arguing, is not a static mind-body dichotomy but an interactive complex of the senses ("sensuousness"), body, mind and action. Or, as Engels might have put it, the base for "knowing" is not a "thing" but a "process," a concept beyond the mechanical logic of the metaphysicians. Seeing the base for knowing in process Marx found the test for truth not in logic but in practice: "The dispute over the reality or nonreality of thinking which is isolated from practice is a purely *scholastic* question." The French materialists, especially Diderot, were greatly interested in science but in their philosophical works they still placed the emphasis not so much on experimental evidence as upon abstract "reason."[5]

Engels accepted and then went beyond the French materialists' concept of the relations of matter and motion:

> Motion is the mode of existence of matter. Never anywhere has there been matter without motion, nor can there be. Motion in cosmic space, mechanical motion of smaller masses on the various celestial bodies, the motion of molecules as heat or as electrical or magnetic currents, chemical combination or disintegration, organic life—at each given moment each individual atom of matter in the world is in one or other of these forms of motion, or in several forms of them at once. All rest, all equilibrium, is only relative, and only has meaning in relation to one or other definite form of motion.

"Time and space," Engels declared, are "but forms of the existence of matter." They are "nothing without matter, empty concepts, abstractions which exist only in our minds." There was, then, no such thing as time before the universe existed and there is no absolute space, no eternity or infinity. Space and time are relative entities dependent for their being on matter. As the essence of matter is motion, at various levels, there is no absolute equilibrium of forces.

These are admittedly difficult concepts but they have on the whole been borne out by modern science. Engels was able to make this advance in part because of the advance of science itself, but that this was not the basic factor involved is shown by the fact that other nineteenth-century thinkers, such as Thomas Henry Huxley, also had these advances at their disposal but got no further than a semi-Kantian "agnosticism." Even Darwin, who considered himself a materialist, made no effort to develop the general concepts of materialism as a philosophy, being stifled, whether he knew it or not, by the bourgeois reaction around him. He and Huxley were sheltered by their class positions—in a kind of social greenhouse—from the swirl and aspirations of the proletarian movement from which Marx and Engels received their inspiration. The basic factor, then, in the creation of dialectical materialism, as of Marxism, was social and not intellectual. And this was shown also by the development of dialectical materialism by Lenin in *Materialism and Empirio-Criticism* and the *Philosophical Notebooks*.

The French materialists were associated with a bourgeoisie deep in an antifeudal struggle in which it was in its interest to undermine the feudal Church and advance natural science. But it necessarily had no basic perspective for humanity beyond the establishment of capitalist exploitation in the place of feudal. The proletariat, however, had no such social limitations and some of its early leaders, as we have seen, had, both in Britain and on the Continent, advanced not only to socialist radicalism but into an anticlericalism that was directed against bourgeois as well as feudal religion.[6]

In one respect Marx and Engels found that Hegel, even though an idealist, marked an advance over the French materialists, namely in breaking with what Engels called their "metaphysical" or "mechanical" method. The "great basic thought that the world is not to be comprehended as a complex of ready-made things but as a complex of processes," had, Engels believed, its roots in Hegel. These processes acted through a series of "contradictions" between interpenetrating "opposite" elements:

So long as we consider things as static and lifeless, each one by itself, alongside of and after each other, it is true that we do not run up against any contradictions in them. . . . But the position is quite different as soon as we consider things in their motion, their change, their life, their reciprocal influence on one another. Then we immediately become involved in contradictions.

As an example of these "contradictions," Hegel cited negative and positive electricity or the opposite poles of a magnet, or, in a different field, "debts and assets," but he tended in general to view matters in the abstract. On the basis of this inherently "contradictory" process change resulting in new forms ("quality") came about by the addition of previously existing factors ("quantity") and these changes tended to take place rapidly at certain "nodal points," of which Hegel gave as examples the change of water to ice at one nodal point and to steam at another. Hegel then went further and argued that in addition to quantity producing quality, a certain quality could be "negated" and emerge in a new and higher form, for example, a seed was "negated" as it changed into a plant, and then it emerged again as a number of seeds. This "law" of dialectics he called "the negation of the negation."[7]

These concepts, it should be noted, are by no means as clear in Hegel as in Engels. Engels extracted them from the often almost impenetratable fog of Hegelian abstraction, an abstraction based not, like that of Marx, upon facts, but, like that of Kant, on "pure" logic." However, Hegel did provide a basis for a new way of thinking, dialectical—in terms of process— rather than mechanical, in terms of "things" (or static Kantian categories). Marx acknowledged his debt to Hegel in this regard at the same time as he discarded Hegel's mysticism:

> My dialectic method is not only different from the Hegelian, but is its direct opposite. To Hegel, the life-process of the human brain, i.e., the process of thinking, which, under the name of "the Idea," he even transforms into an independent subject, is the *demiurgos* of the real world, and the real world is only the external, phenomenal form of "the Idea." With me, on the contrary, the ideal is nothing else than the material world reflected by the human mind, and translated into forms of thought.

In spite of his "dialectic," Hegel's overall view is the same as Plato's: the human mind is a reflection of the Divine Mind that determines the patterns of reality. In actuality, Marx responds, the so-called Divine Mind is but a fantastic projection of the human mind; and ideas reflect reality. In another passage, attacking the French bourgeois "socialist," Pierre Joseph

Proudhon, with his concept of "God" or "Universal reason" directing history, Marx commented: "In short, it is not history but old Hegelian junk." In another comment on Proudhon Marx further denounced his dialectics in-a-vacuum and emphasised the materialist base of dialectical reasoning. Proudhon, studying dialectics, "learned to play with his own contradictions and developed them according to circumstances into striking, spectacular, now scandalous, now brilliant paradoxes." This, Marx commented, was not "scientific dialectics" but "sophistry." At present when we are hearing much of "dialectics" but little of materialism Marx's comments are particularly apt. "Dialectics" (unqualified) usually turn out to be idealist and not materialist.

In his *Dialectics of Nature* and other works, Engels argued that quantity-quality change is a general process everywhere apparent in nature: for instance, in the table of the elements, in which simple increase in "atomic weight" resulted in a new element; or in the production of compounds from elements, for instance, water from uniting the molecules of oxygen and hydrogen. He speculated also that not just increase in quantity but "a change in position" of "molecules" might in "allotropic" and other reactions produce new forms. And he and Marx noted that when something new was about to emerge the "opposites" in the "contradiction" interpenetrated more intensely and tended to speed up in a final spurt, a concept that was later elaborated by the Russian Marxist, G.V. Plekhanov. Engels also accepted the "negation of the negation" concept from Hegel; and Marx did also, applying it, for instance to the feudal-capitalist-communist sequence, for which he was attacked by Dühring and defended by Engels.[8]

Modern Science and Nature

Engels made his last major comments on science and dialectics in the 1880s. Although there have been great advances since then, these do not, as some seem to think, simply take the place of nineteenth-century science but grow on its foundations. Engels singled out three advances in the nineteenth century as most significant: the discovery of the biological cell, the theory of evolution by natural selection, and the law of the conservation and transformation of energy (for instance, from mechanical to chemical to electrical). All three are still basically valid today, as are other scientific theories from the past, even though often valid in somewhat different forms (for instance the conservation of energy on the elementary particle level). By the nineteenth century, in short, science had revealed certain truths about the universe and life, and Engels' general speculations based on these truths are still largely valid. And in a broader context his and Marx's view of the inherently materialistic and dialectical nature of reality has been further confirmed by modern scientific discoveries, indeed to a greater degree than most Marxists today seem to realize. So, too, with his and Marx's general philosophical views; for example, the following from Einstein: "They used to think that if all things in the world disappeared, space and time would remain; and in accordance with the theory of relativity, with the disappearance of all things, space and time too must disappear." Einstein had doubtless not heard of Engels' similar view of more than half a century previously when he wrote these lines, but he is, whether he intended it or not, philosophically reducing the problem to one of matter. Time and space began with matter and depend on matter for their continued existence.[9]

As even the most sketchy account of modern science suffices to show, its findings have provided detailed confirmation of materialism. It is becoming clear that from physical matter to the human brain the same material particles and atoms are at work and nothing else is present except them and their compounds. Stephen Jay Gould and other scientists are beginning to note also—although in a fragmentary way—that underneath the complexities of matter and life certain general processes are at work which involve the change of quantity to quality and a speeding up as qualitative change approaches. These processes involve all fields and occur on all levels. In short, the specifics of the dialectical-materialist picture are being filled in.

In view of the ideological—ultimately theological—confusion that is spread about the philosophical implications of science, it is important to stress that its findings are providing, little by little, the material for the actual explanation for the universe and life—and us. There is no "something else." Complexity is gradually being broken down into its component parts and the parts fit into a total emerging picture, the main outlines of which seem rather simple. And, it might be emphasized, it is *one* picture—from the universe to society. So, too, is the Marxist "world outlook." We really cannot understand living matter or life without understanding matter, with its atoms and particles, mass and energy, and we cannot really understand society without understanding life, molecular, animal and human.

When Engels wrote, little was actually known of the constitution of matter. The electron had not been discovered, nor had the proton, and the neutron was not discovered until 1932. And since then, numerous elementary particles have been found or created (in accelerators). The atom, however, is still seen as functioning primarily through the interactions of its protons, neutrons and electrons, the more solid neutrons and protons in the nucleus, the nimble electrons in orbits circling it. The protons and neutrons interact through a tight nuclear "force" or—preferably—"reaction" (visible in nuclear explosions). The protons interact with the whirling electrons through an electric reaction (visible in lightning). Atoms cling to each other or repel each other in response to their electrical charges, protons being positively charged, electrons negatively, both having equal charges. (The neutron has no charge.) As positive repels positive and negative repels negative, whereas positive and negative attract each other, atoms are in a constant, indeed, frenzied state of imbalanced agitation. This arises not only from their internal interactions but from their interactions with each other, particularly through the interchange of electrons in the outer orbits. These interchanges make for rapid switches in the total charge of an atom from positive to negative to positive, atoms clinging or separating in billions of interactions in billionths of a second. This basically simple positive-negative electric reaction provides the key not only to the functioning of atomic matter but, as we shall note, of biological matter and life as well.

In addition to atomic matter, physics has discovered particle matter, notably electricity and radiation (light). That visible light and all other forms of "radiation," from X-rays to radio waves, are not, as is sometimes suggested, nonmaterial but are also forms of matter is dramatically shown in the destructive action of the laser beam. Furthermore, all forms of radiation consist of the same elementary particle (in different degrees of intensity)— the photon. What we see as light is not a continuity but a massive stream of photons.

Matter, it now appears, and as Engels did not know, consists of two contradictory general components, mass and energy, which interpenetrate and can be interactively converted one into the other. Such minute and agile particles as electrons and photons are essentially energy, protons and neutrons essentially mass. And all are interconnected; photons can arise from the interactions of electrons and other charged particles as in X-rays and they can, in turn, affect these particles.

So far science has discovered about 100 different elements—hydrogen, oxygen, carbon, and so on—which differ from each other primarily in the number of their protons and electrons. Hydrogen, the simplest element, has one proton and one electron, uranium has 92 of each. ("Isotopes" of an element are made by the simple addition of neutrons, which are normally the same in number as the protons. The difference which this simple quantitative factor makes, however, may be gauged by the fact that three neutrons taken from uranium make nuclear explosion possible—as uranium 238 is changed to uranium 235.) The elements above hydrogen, as was unknown when Engels wrote, are compounded in the stars in high-energy interactions. Even the simplest of them, the fusion of hydrogen atoms to make helium atoms constitutes the fire of the sun, and those of more complexity, such as iron, with 26 protons and electrons per atom, result from the sudden collapse of immense stars.

By means of their negative and positive charges, atoms can cling together to form molecules, and groups of the molecules of different atoms constitute "compounds," such as water, ammonia and methane (all of which have been detected in space). Nor is there any break in the chain when we come to living matter, which consists primarily of six atoms, all found in matter, those of hydrogen, oxygen, nitrogen, carbon, phosphorus and sulphur, plus those of certain metals, including sodium, potassium, iron and magnesium. It is primarily carbon which, because of its electrons' arrangement, is able to combine other elements into large "chain" molecules (or "macromolecules"), sometimes with millions of atoms, and it is these chain molecules that primarily differentiate living matter from matter. In the functioning of living matter, the chain molecules of two basic substances, protein and the nucleic acids (which shape protein patterns and regulate heredity) interact. Both molecules, however, consist of the same atoms— hydrogen, oxygen, nitrogen, carbon—except that the nucleic acid molecules contain phosphorus and some proteins contain sulphur. These chain molecules, although not themselves living, give life to the cell through their combinations, and nothing else.

As is becoming more and more apparent, matter is contradictory in its essence. All particles, with the exception of the photon, have antiparticles—the neutrino and the antineutrino, and so on—and the photon's actions can only be explained by the physicists by theorizing that it acts as its own antiparticle. Not only, however, do all particles have their opposites, but the atom itself operates as a kind of machine based on the interpenetration of opposites, namely the proton and neutron in the nucleus and the proton and the electron with their positive and negative electric charges in the total atom. The balances and imbalances of these opposite charges create all the elements and compounds, and through them all the phenomena of life on our planet. Chain molecules, with their elaborate structures, operate ultimately on the basis of atomic electric balances and imbalances in extremely complex patterns. It is well to keep this in mind when we read almost animistic descriptions of proteins and other substances "assisting" each other or "snipping" each other or creating "codes." The actual picture is rather like that of a moving jigsaw puzzle forming and re-forming in response to the negative-positive electric charges of its molecules with their various shapes and sizes. If at first it seems impossible that so simple an atomic mechanism could underlie all the varied forms of life, even though it has been demonstrated that it does, we might note that the most complex electric computers are based on the virtually infinite permutations and combinations of but two factors, a plus and a minus. We have also to consider the tininess and rapidity of action of molecules and atoms. Molecules (in our bodies for instance) may vibrate a million or more times a second, and as J. D. Bernal has pointed out, tracer elements have shown that "the atoms flow through them in an almost continuous stream." The picture is one of an intensity of interactivity not only beyond our experience but beyond the concepts of nineteenth-century science. [10]

When Engels wrote it was thought that there were many different kinds of atoms with different "atomic weights," but, as we have seen, these differences arise simply from different quantities and arrangements of the same constituent particles. Here, and elsewhere, however, not only quantitative factors but "arrangement" or, in Engels' phrase, "position," and the "pattern" which may follow from it, have to be stressed. Although Engels perceived something of the importance of this phenomenon, he did not stress it sufficiently or examine the relations of quantitative and arrangement factors. The capacity of carbon to bind, for instance, depends not just on the number of electrons in the carbon atom but on their orbital arrangement. We find the same phenomenon in regard to radiation (light). Whether radiation takes the form of visible light or X-rays depends not only on the number but the pattern (wave-length) of their constituent photons, which are themselves identical in all forms of radiation.

We have to note also that the concept of "opposites" or "contradiction" has to be employed with more flexibility than seems to be implied in Engels (or Hegel). Protons and electrons, with their opposite electric charges, are obvious opposites in the classic Hegelian sense, but protons and neutrons also act as opposites, and there are negatively charged protons and positively charged electrons. There are clearly different forms and degrees in the interactions of opposite phenomena. And things which are opposite in one process may be complementary in another. This is true also of the processes of living matter.

Living matter develops into life mainly by the interpenetrations of protein and nucleic acid molecules in the cell, which consists—rather like a plum or a peach—of an inner "nucleus," an outer area, the "cytoplasm," containing fluids and smaller bodies, and a surrounding membrane. Heredity depends primarily on the number and the patterns of the nucleic acid molecules in an intertwining "double helix" within the nucleus. Four types of nucleic acid act on twenty amino acids (in the cytoplasm). And here, again, a basically contradictory mechanism is involved. The possible combinations of these interactions if left to themselves would result in a virtually infinite number of protein molecule combinations, and life would be chaos. This does not happen because particular protein molecules, known as "repressors," limit the combinations. As each cell in a developing embryo has the potential of all the cells in the animal body, from nerves to bones, from liver to skin, there could be no specialization of cells if it were not for these "repressor" actions. Thus the new does not arise by direct "creation" but by a lengthy, mechanical action-reaction method of eliminating 99 or more percent of the molecular potential of each cell and allowing only one fragment to continue. In considering these and other molecular processes in living matter, we have, as with matter, to view "contradiction" not in a rigid way, seeing immutable "opposites" reacting to one another. A molecular formation can be an "opposite" to a number of other formations. Whenever molecules interpenetrate and produce change they act as opposites. Nor is this straining the meaning of the word, for living matter, like matter, is contradictory in its essence as a result of its basic atomic, positive-negative structure. Qualitative change does not arise, as one would gather from some accounts, by placid rearrangements but by active, electric interactions.[11]

Similar materialist-dialectical processes are beginning to appear also in evolution, which is now seen as resulting from genetic "mutations" that arise from new arrangements in the nucleic acid chain molecules in the cell nucleus and perhaps also in the cytoplasm. Some of these changes seem to come from chance "matching" errors inevitable in any complex process, some from external bombardment by photons and other particles, some, perhaps, from processes we do not yet understand. When nucleic acid molecules change, they in turn change the protein molecules whose patterns constitute the main metabolic basis for life forms, thus beginning a kind of biological chain reaction.

As most mutations hinder a life form's chance for survival and only a few are helpful, this is clearly a hit-or-miss process, without intent or direction. The process, a modern geneticist notes, exemplifies the operation of "the law of large numbers," a law implicit, as we noted, in Lucretius.

In other words, out of billions of interactions new qualities necessarily arise. The "selection" of those which are helpful to the survival of the species does, it is true, seem "purposeful," but like the production of mutations in the first place, this is also a "mechanism" which, as a modern biologist notes, "involves only chance events." To cite a standard example: before the industrial revolution with its smoke stacks, white moths flourished in the trees of Manchester; after it the few grey moths among the white became dominant—the white, now conspicuous on the smoke-grayed bark, eaten by birds. Although many problems have still to be solved—for instance, the processes involved in such complexly coordinated changes as the evolution of wings from limbs or the development of uprightness in the subhuman primate—it is apparent that evolution, like reproduction, is a basically material process involving the interpenetration of opposites, biological and physical. It is also being increasingly recognized that major qualitative changes take place in response to quantitative change and at a rapid rate—the theory of "punctuated equilibria" proposed by Stephen Jay Gould and others. Even scientists who perceive these things, however, usually do not acknowledge the essentially contradictory nature of the general process which underlies them. Evolutionary change did not arise simply by quantitative arrangements quietly re-forming and at times moving more rapidly. After all, the birds ate the moths. The forces of natural selection may now be seen as blind forces but they are still part of the Darwinian "struggle for life." What we now see is that this struggle has roots in other processes than those which were known to Darwin, in matter and in molecular interactions, but these are also, as we have seen, essentially contradictory. There is nothing placid about evolution, just as there is not about life processes in general.[12]

In recent decades science has begun to understand the functioning of the human brain. This has come about largely from neurological research, proceeding patiently upward from the basic entity involved, the brain cell (neuron). If Engels were alive today he would certainly include these findings in expositions of dialectical materialism and he and Marx would have welcomed them as further undermining that last bastion of idealist philosophy—"the mind."[13]

In the lowest forms of animal life, one-celled and simple multi-celled creatures, and in plants, there are no nerve cells; but they are vital to the functioning of all other forms of animal life, from crabs to mammals. Without them birds could not fly or fish swim. Without them we could not only not think, we could not lift a limb, for the same basic entity indifferently motors both functions.

Nerve cells consist of the same atoms and molecules as other cells, existing by virtue of proteins and nucleic acids, and are divided into nucleus, cytoplasm and membrane. However, they differ from other cells functionally in that they generate electricity, burning blood sugar as a slow generating source, and structurally in having long, weblike extensions running out at each end. When the electrons of the electric current reach the end of a web, they stimulate a group of molecules ("neurotransmitters") which then cross the space between the webs of two cells into another cell and set up another current. The current is either positively or negatively charged—by the interactions of potassium, sodium and chloride atoms. If it is positively charged, it "excites" action, such as the moving of a finger, if it is negatively charged it "inhibits" it. Thus complex though the total processes are, the underlying mechanism is, once more, rather simple and involves an interpenetration of negative-positive opposites. We might note, too, that nerve cells are the same in all the forms of life that possess them. The difference between the nervous sytems of lobsters and humans depends on the number and arrangements of the same basic material.

Although nerve cells exist throughout the animal body, they are concentrated in vertebrates in the spinal cord and the brain. If they end up in a muscle, they can move the muscle, if in a sense organ such as the eye, they record stimuli, if in other nerve cells in the brain, they can store a stimulus (memory), excite an emotion or an idea.

The key to understanding the human brain lies in the tinyness and immense number of its units—cells, molecules, atoms, particles. The brain contains some twenty billion nerve cells; as each of these is interconnected in intricate ways, sometimes with thousands of connections, the number of connections is virtually infinite, more, it has been calculated, than the total number of atoms in the universe. Most of these cells are contained in the forebrain, or cerebrum, which in humans is much larger than in animals and is the center for thought. In recent years neurosurgeons and others have discovered that the brain is extremely specialized in its parts. One small set of cells, for instance, "fires" in response to a vertical line, another set to a horizontal line, still another to a triangle—and this in the cat brain as well as in the human. Below the cell level certain molecules may have functions of their own, for instance, in memory, which may be stored segment by segment in the molecules of nucleic acid. Beneath the brain's complexity of function, then, there lies a specialized assembly of minute parts which must have been formed bit by bit in long evolutionary sequence.

Neurosurgeons and others have found that the human brain is also extremely specialized in intellectual function. One section of the brain contains spoken language, another "emotional" speech, still another written language. A second, learned, language is recorded in a different section of the brain to the original language. The content of the brain, then, is built up in each individual from infancy on little by little in response to various stimuli. If these stimuli are missing, the brain will not become functional, either in humans or higher animals. It has been shown also that brain development is not an even process but speeds up at various early stages of animal or human growth, including the embryonic. Recent investigations have also begun to shed light on how the brain reacts to stimuli. In essence, it converts all external stimuli—the molecules of odors, the vibrating atoms of sound, the photons of light—into electrons. It acts, that is to say, as a transformer of energy.[14]

In the fact that the nerve cells exist and interact in brain and body, we have the material connection between the two that Marx and other materialists posited. Marx's view that mind, senses and emotions were part of an interactive process has been given substance also by the discovery of the hormonal system. Hormones, complex molecular formations—some of them proteins—are produced by various "ductless" glands in the body and reach the brain not through the web of nerve cells but through the blood stream. The pituitary gland, located near the brain, governs the other ductless glands in a general way and releases hormones with opposite effects—stimulants and repressants. The epinephrine molecules released by the adrenal glands prepare the body for swift action—"flight or fight." A male animal injected with male sex hormones becomes sexually aggressive, a female animal injected with female sex hormones becomes sexually submissive.

Even if, it may be argued, the brain converts other forms of energy—particles, atoms, molecules—into electrons, still electrons are not thoughts, and so the basic problem of "cognition" is still unsolved. However, as in examining the higher nervous sytem itself, we have to proceed by degrees, mounting up the evolutionary scale, and not consider the human brain as an isolated phenomenon. Even animals as low on this scale as fish engage in elaborate rituals—mock-fighting or mating. The mechanism behind these rituals can be shown experimentally to be that of the transformation of photons, atoms, and molecules into the electric energies of the nerve cells. A chicken can be made to run or fluff its feathers by inserting electrodes into different areas of its brain. The electrons do not simply produce more electrons but psychological responses. So, too, with the photons, atoms, or molecules of the external world transformed by the chicken brain into electrons. They, too, produce not just more electrons but psychological responses, reflex actions in various patterns. That these reactions are nonconscious in birds and fish, even though in their complexity they sometimes appear conscious, is apparent from the fact that fish and birds have virtually no cerebrum—the source of consciousness.

If we move further up the evolutionary scale we might consider the case of Imo, "the monkey genius." Imo's troop lived in a jungle bordering a sandy beach. Naturalists observing the troop threw wheat on the sand. The monkeys found it difficult to eat wheat mixed with sand. Imo solved the problem by scooping up a handful of sand and wheat and throwing it into the water. The sand sank and she scooped up and ate the floating wheat. Possibly this was done at first by chance, perhaps in anger, but, regardless of this, the point remains that Imo immediately perceived the solution. [15]

In a classic experiment, a banana was tied to the top of an ape's cage well above reaching level, and three boxes of increasing size were scattered about the cage; the ape was able to place the boxes on top of each other in ascending order and climb up to seize the banana. We might note, too, that when the solution occurred to the ape, it did so suddenly, after experimentation mixed with periods of silent observation. Thus although the basic mechanism involved is still that of the transformation of photons, atoms and molecules into electrons, in higher animals the electrons stimulate not just complex reflex action but something clearly bordering on conscious reasoning.

Apes can be taught a rudimentary language by using hand signs and other means and they can use this language to combine various perceptions. For instance, on first seeing a duck, a trained ape signalled "water-bird." Again we are waveringly near the verge of conscious thought. (Yet we do not find idealist philosophers hailing the divine uniqueness of the ape "mind.") The development of consciousness, then, is a matter of further steps up the neurological evolutionary ladder, steps in which the new must again be the result of the increasingly complex combinations of the old. True, the apes are not in the direct line of human evolution but they are not far from it. Our direct ancestors now appear to have been small upright plains primates ("hominids") whose remains have been found in east Africa and whose brains were somewhat larger than those of chimpanzees. These creatures and their immediate descendents must have developed partly conscious reasoning; and the evolutionary path to consciousness was opened. [16]

As we survey modern science, then, from physics to neurology, it is apparent that process is based on matter—from the atoms of solids, liquids and gasses to the photons of radiation and the molecules of life. It is becoming apparent also that change takes place in response to the interpenetration of opposites of various kinds, that it takes the form of the new arising from combinations and arrangements of the old and that there are nodal points at which it takes place more rapidly. A star which has been building up for millions of years can collapse into another form within minutes. Mutation series in evolution appear to be concentrated in certain comparatively short periods. Reasoning in apes and humans alike suddenly speeds up into solutions. The essence, is indeed, as Engels contended, expressed in process. The apparently "dead" matter around us is in reality a swirling of atoms and particles; living matter is in a constant state of change, with interblending particles, atoms, molecules, and cells; the brain is constantly and electrically active—even in sleep.

On the other hand, the "negation of the negation" is clearly not the general developmental process that Hegel and Engels believed it was. The seed-plant-seeds process for example, is not a "negation" of a quality and its appearance on a "higher level" but simply a quantity-quality-quantity sequence. And so, too, with Hegel's and Engels's other examples. We might doubt also Engels' contention that motion is the essence of matter. Motion now appears to be the offshoot of the interaction of mass and energy, first on the particle and atomic levels and then on that of "clumped matter" (from planets to people).

Animal and Human Society

Development, as we have seen, takes place not only in nature in dialectical ways but in society also. The contradictory interpenetration of productive forces and relations provides the base for social evolution, and in exploitive class societies such change proceeds through the conflict of opposing classes. Quantitative change produces qualitative change but, as in nature, acting in conjunction with arrangement and pattern. It is not, for instance, just the growing number of people that makes a revolution but their arrangement—into effective revolutionary organizations. As in nature also, when a major social change is about to take place, the processes involved speed up. Nor is it only the major developmental processes of society that act in dialectical patterns. Secondary processes, observable in everyday life, also do so, for instance, in strikes, protest movements, or governmental decision making. Everywhere opposite forces interact and produce change in an oscillating, mounting wave pattern. So, too, in family life and personal relations, as well as in the thinking processes involved in these and other actions, including artistic creation.

Thus we have a succession not only from physical matter to biological matter to the higher nervous system, but to human society, of change and development following the same general patterns. Why should this be so? Marx and Engels do not seem to have specifically examined this problem and it seems strange that they did not because failure to do so leaves an obvious gap in their "outlook." There seems no reason on the face of it why society and matter should act in the same developmental patterns. The answer must lie in the fact that people are part of nature as well as of society, that they evolved from animal forms which ultimately arose from matter. This, however, is only a general answer. The specifics have still not yet been examined, although we are in a position today to make a beginning. We can now trace the facts of human biological evolution in more detail than was possible in the nineteenth century, and in recent decades a mass of information has been accumulated on animal societies that enables us to trace a progression from animal to prehuman to human society.

Although we can see humanlike behavior in apes and other animals in zoos, it is more marked in animal life in natural conditions, some of it fortunately recorded in motion pictures and scientifically observed. Animals play with each other and get obvious enjoyment from such play. Monkeys do somersaults, at which some are more expert than others, apparently "showing off." The elaborate rituals of the mating dances of ostriches and other birds are similar in general pattern to human rituals, personal, religious, or military. Animals also possess memory, dramatically revealed in fish or bird migrations. Some animals possess rudimentary language, sometimes of considerable, if mechanical, complexity, as in dolphins. And some show artistic patterns, as in the songs of the meadow lark (with fifty "types of sound") or the paintings of apes (in laboratory conditions). Some behavior patterns, as in amphibia, emerge automatically, others—mainly so in mammals—in interactions with learning processes, instigated mostly by the animal's parents. The indication is that in animals there are interactive inherited and learning patterns, the inherited patterns underlying the learning ones, forming as L. Tinbergen has suggested, a kind of "template."[17]

However, whether we are observing animals in zoos, labs, the home, or their natural habitats, we have to keep in mind that we are observing our evolutionary ancestors. Some of these, such as birds, are remote, others, such as the apes, are close. Unless this evolutionary base is recognized, the implication is that animal behavior is simply the humanlike actions of "clever" animals and, hence, irrelevant to human behavior. The situation is further complicated by the fact that investigations into animal societies have been distorted for reactionary—racist, sexist, imperialist—purposes by sociobiologists and others. Nevertheless the data on animal behavior has now become so massive that it has to be examined and evaluated.

Among the inherited patterns common to a number of animal societies we find a combination of strong cooperative patterns within groups and enmity towards outsiders, both clearly "survival" mechanisms. For instance, a new monkey in a cage is beaten by the group already there. Many animals establish hunting and mating areas for their exclusive use. Even in the lower evolutionary strata, amphibia (frogs) and birds establish such territories and keep others of their species out, thus cutting down on destructive combat. We find too that in many animal societies "pecking orders" exist and group leaders emerge. Along with common behavior patterns for both sexes, there are also specific behavior patterns for each sex. These are apparently connected with male and female hormonal differences, and must be inherited via the x and y chromosomes which contain the nucleic acids for sexual characteristics.

When sociobiologists and others take the characteristics of animal societies and apply them simply and directly to human society they come up with not only reactionary but absurd results. On the other hand the attacks on the sociobiologists and their biological determinist creed from the "left" have so far been simplistic, and a Marxist who accepts them can easily be driven into untenable positions that, in fact, degrade Marxism. It is time to recognize that we are dealing with a complex dialectical process in which biological and social factors interact, the social, in spite of its biological roots, being the basic social determinant. On the other hand the biological roots cannot be neglected. In fact when we examine them and put them in proper perspective we find that they throw considerable light on the nature of society. In short we have to make a distinction between the sociobiologists' data and their theories; the data are generally sound, the theories unsound.

In attempting to trace human behavioral roots in the evolutionary sequence we find at the outset that not only are there extraordinary and specific parallels between human and animal behavior, but a great many nonparallels also. Why some specific parallels occur with our remote evolutionary ancestors—such as birds—is a matter for investigation. But the number of nonparallels show that we cannot simply make sweeping comparisons between animal society—with its immense variety—and human but, if we really want to find our roots, should concentrate on our nearest evolutionary collatorals, the nonhuman primates. And here we are fortunate in having a number of good studies of ape and monkey societies, by Jane Goodall and others.

In ape societies we must be seeing behavior patterns similar to those of our direct evolutionary ancestors, the first subpeople ("hominids"). The variations must have at first been minimal, arising from the differences between a jungle and a plains primate. Gorilla groups—usually a dominant male, his several mates, their children, and younger males—hunt and live together much as did early food-gathering peoples (examined within recent decades among various "fringe" peoples). Gorilla groups have been observed having up to twenty-seven members. When groups meet they do not mingle—except for the very young apes, who play together. They live mostly on the ground, not in trees, and build nests but not shelters. In the social hierarchy there is a group leader, an older male; then the younger males; then the mature females; and finally the juveniles and infants. Apes communicate by gesture and stance but also have a rudimentary language. Chimpanzees hunt collectively, often in complex patterns, and use this "language" as well as gestures to coordinate their efforts. Apes have good memory for hunting grounds and the paths leading to them. They can show affection and pleasure in each other and sometimes after foraging males and females will greet each other with what one observer called "smiles and hugs." Some apes establish firm hunting territories and rally as a group if danger threatens; as do many other animals also—sometimes to a special "mobbing call."[18]

In 1977, scientists discovered two sets of footprints in East Africa which had been preserved in volcanic ash for three million or more years. If, one of the scientists wrote, we saw such prints on a beach today, we would immediately think that they had been left by people like us walking on the sand. The subhumans who made these prints were completely upright; and other discoveries—notably that of "Lucy"—showed that they were small, between three-and-a-half and five feet tall, but powerful, with arms slightly longer than humans, humanlike hands, teeth more apelike than human and brains about the size of those of chimpanzees. The footprints were made by two subpeople *(australopithecines)* walking side by side: one smaller, possibly female; the other, larger, possibly male. Their owners were perhaps attempting to escape a volcanic eruption. Skull remains of 1.7 million years ago reveal the existence of another group of subhumans *(homo habilis)* in East

Africa. They were somewhat larger, and whereas the earlier group had brain capacities in the 400–500 cubic centimeter range these were in the 600–800 range, and the forehead was higher, indicating cerebrum development. There is no evidence that the earlier group used weapons or tools—although they probably did—but the next group definitely did and they apparently also built stone structures. Remains of about one million years ago not only in Africa but in China and elsewhere show prehumans with brain capacities of 700 to 1,250 cubic centimeters, which overlaps with the human—1,000–1,800. These prehumans as, for instance, the extensive "Peking Man" remains show, had not only tools and shelter but fire, and they hunted large animals. This could only have been done by coordinated group hunting and implies some use of language. The first definitely human remains so far discovered are apparently about 200,000 years old.[19]

By integrating these bone, stone, and other remains from the past with observations of hunter-gathering societies existing into civilized times, we can reconstruct something of life in the earliest human societies, which can hardly have differed in certain basic respects from the various virtually human societies that preceded them. Subpeople, like the apes, doubtless lived in various kinds of family groups and united them to form larger groups. Like the apes also they presumably staked out hunter-gathering territories. There must have been—as in the early human societies at one end of the scale and ape societies at the other—cooperative endeavor within the group but enmity between groups, perhaps with fighting, or mock-fighting, to keep these territories. In the subhuman community, there were no doubt, again, as in human hunter-gathering societies, cohesion within the group, initial rejection of the alien, pecking orders, leaders, courtship, mating, family life, and, at some point, song and dance. In short, social life, on, or virtually on, a human scale, with families and the play and laughter of children, love and hate, joy and grief and fear, artistic creation and the struggle for existence, has been going on for about one million years, and, in a less conscious form, for three or more million. The primitive (and dehumanized) "cave man," with his club and his subdued mate, is of course, a myth, an extension back in time of the stereotyping of "primitive" people today and of male chauvinism. It is also a naive projection of psychological fantasies without relation to the social dynamics of family or community life—virtually none of which was associated with caves. There are, in fact, very few caves.

That, as subpeoples evolved, consciousness evolved is shown both in skull remains and in the bone and stone artifacts that indicate group-hunting of large animals. As Marx and Engels suggested, language and consciousness must have developed interactively: "Language is as old as consciousness, language *is* practical consciousness." Furthermore, language and consciousness must have emerged in interaction with non-conscious behavior patterns inherited from evolutionary predecessors.[20]

In the present century some Marxists have supported a virtual *tabula rasa* theory of human nature, arguing, in effect, that the human mind at birth is moldable into virtually any shape by social forces. Partly under the impact of the reactionary use of data on the genetic inheritance of underlying behavior patterns, they have either denied the existence of such patterns or given them so small a part in the human shaping process as to render them meaningless. This, however, in effect denies human evolution and implies human uniqueness, essentially a religious view. Furthermore, it is not based on Marx or Engels but on a mechanistic reading of Pavlov's "conditioned reflex" experiments (omitting the fact that Pavlov in time noted that his dogs showed inherited differences in psychological patterns). Marx and Engels accepted, as did nineteenth-century science in general, the existence of instinct in both animals and people, writing, for instance, in their early *The German Ideology,* of the origins of humanity:

> This beginning is as animal as social life itself at this stage. It is mere herd-consciousness, and at this point man is only distinguished from sheep by the fact that with him consciousness takes the place of instinct or that his instinct is a conscious one.

This, as we have seen, is not quite correct. It is not a matter of inherited behavior patterns becoming conscious but of their blending with conscious ones—through later-brain-early-brain interactions—with the inherited patterns forming a partial basis for the conscious ones. But the comment shows that Marx and Engels felt that humans as well as animals had instincts. And they obviously did not feel that this was at odds with their view that society developed basically in response to social forces.[21]

Once we become aware of inherited behavior patterns, we begin to see them all around us in personal life, mingled with conscious actions, for instance, in the introduction of the "alien" to a group, in the rituals of people greeting or leaving each other, the nonconscious essence of all of which we see in the apes (with whom, as Darwin long ago noted, we share facial expressions). However, although such personal behavior patterns as these have little historical effect, others, such as those of group coherence and enmity to the alien have considerable effect. Patriotism, for instance, is useful to an exploitive ruling class and is developed to forward its imperialist interests. But patriotism cannot be developed out of nothing. That its roots are those of group welfare, for which animals will sacrifice their lives, is indicated by its elemental nature. It is often also combined with the equally irrational exaltation of "the leader," which must have roots in animal society leader-following. Nor could the frenetic and obsessive group loyalties, ethnic and otherwise, seen at all levels of society and daily manipulated for reactionary ends, come into existence without such underlying patterns.

The other side of the same sociobiological coin is the rejection of the alien. This too, we see manifested not only in animal societies but among people as a conscious or partly conscious initial reaction. This can either be modified or it can lay a base for the prejudices and hatreds that are used to divide a working mass and, blending with patriotism, supply human fuel for war.

Whenever these hatreds and prejudices have been modified or eliminated as a social force, to some degree in capitalist nations through social struggles but on a large scale in socialist nations, it has been done—although this is not generally recognized—by making use of the same underlying general biopsychological patterns that produced them; for instance, by establishing new group loyalties that encompass the alien group. In capitalist societies we have seen such phenomena in, for instance, trade unions which have accepted Afro-Americans into membership and fought for their rights, as happened in the formative period of the C.I.O. in the United States. In socialist countries we have seen national minorities become part of the larger group—the working class or the "people." Without these new group formations and loyalties, education and propaganda would be acting in a social vacuum. So far, however, this work has been done on a pragmatic basis without understanding the role of the underlying inherited behavioral patterns, an understanding which would give a progressive movement greater depth and efficiency. Finally, it is clear that though these underlying patterns exist they are not immutable but represent potentials which can, within limits, be developed in different ways.

Although studies of human male and female psychological differences often turn out to be antifeminist, their findings cannot all be discounted any more than can the general facts established by animal research. Both questions are more complex than Marxists—or feminists—have acknowledged, involving an intricate interaction of social and biopsychological phenomena.

Scientific studies in recent years have revealed neurological differences in human male and female brain structures that in conjunction with hormonal factors might explain psychological and mental differences between the sexes. Psychological experiments indicate considerable differences between girl and boy babies. Girls are early more sensitive to sound and to the human face and are more adept at fine manual work, whereas boys are better at visual problems and solving mazes, differences which may be related to an apparent predominance in the human female of left cerebral hemisphere reactions and of the right in the male. Other experiments indicate that human females are better able to make connections between apparently unrelated phenomena (which is of the essence of artistic creation) but are less competent in mathematics and mathematiclike problems (indicated perhaps in the superiority of male to female chess players). Although some of these differences can be attributed to social factors, the indication is that there is also an inherited psychological "template" present. Some women scholars, reacting to these and other findings, have been asserting the particular intellectual qualities of women. Women, according to one such scholar, "are more conversational, more interested in collective thinking, more interested in building support than antagonism." According to another woman scholar, women tend more to "envision" things "as a functioning whole" than "to reduce them to their component parts." And to this we might add, more of a tendency in females to preserve and less to destroy than in males, a tendency perhaps with similar roots to childbearing, nursing, and nurturing. As these and other findings indicate, in all societies a balance of male and female qualities are needed in every field—including economic and political—for the society's most effective functioning. Nevertheless women in exploitive societies are virtually shut out from political and economic control and have been since at least the beginning of civilization. Exploitive classes are apparently willing to sacrifice greater efficiency in the interest of maintaining a suppressive order.[22]

What, however, of non-exploitive societies, specifically the socialist societies which have arisen in the present century? As we have seen women in these societies have made great advances but elements of female oppression still persist. In the German Democratic Republic, as Margrit Pittman noted, there are more men in the "top jobs" than women, and this is true in all socialist countries. Why is this? The answer given in these countries is that it is due to remnants from the past, particularly in male attitudes, and that it is being struggled against. This is certainly true but it is not the whole truth. The fact is that socialist countries as they exist today under imperialist political, economic and military pressures, which threaten to disintegrate their social structures—as in Poland—and destroy them, masculine qualities are more needed in some areas than feminine qualities. These nations are forced by these pressures to maintain a large military establishment and although feminine qualities are needed for the most effective running of that establishment—and for all others in all fields—the primary need is for masculine qualities. And this true also, although to a lesser degree, in parts of the economic and political systems. In a communist society presumably masculine and feminine in-put would be generally the same in all fields but in today's socialist societies certain distortions seem inevitable. Although this does not seem to be acknowledged in these societies it seems to be tacitly "understood," as least in some circles. The danger, of course, is that such "understanding" can be abused and used to retard the continuing advance of women in these societies. On the other hand it has to be recognized that this advance has limits at the present time.

Sometimes in reading both feminist and antifeminist writers, we get an impression not of two different sexes but of two different species. How-ever, the area of "identity" is clearly greater than the area of "difference." Men and women are both humans. Women may be more apt than men to fuse concepts and less apt to break things into their components but men can also fuse concepts and women can analyze components. The question is obviously one of degree. The humanity of women can be lost in the prevalent, but suggested rather than openly stated, view that because human females lack some of the psychological characteristics of the male—as the male does of the female—that they are somehow negative reflections of an essentially male humanity. Unless it is emphasised that the special psycho-logical characteristics of women are as positive and individualizing as those of men, the implication is antifeminist. Bourgeois theorists almost invariably consider society the product of the efforts of "Man," a term ostensibly including women but actually designating only men. So, too, in some Marxists studies (in socialist as well as in capitalist societies) whose "man," too, usually turns out to mean "men."

As we have seen, the "oppression of the female sex by the male" is greater in more exploitive and oppressive societies. The basic question, however, is why is there male oppression of the female in any society? The root cause must lie not in male aggression as such but in the fact that the sexes, both in human and animal societies, are almost classic examples of dialectical opposites, each dependent for its existence on the other in all areas of life. Hence, as Engels implied, "opposition" is built into the very nature of sexual difference. For instance, in animal mating behavior, we find a frantic, aggressive, and often undifferentiated male drive for copulation encountering female selectivity. And basically the same situation exists, although in conscious and more complex forms, in human society. Women's sexual power over men restricts the male area of power, a matter of special concern to the men of a ruling class, who aim at absolute power. One basic cause of male fear of and oppression of women, particularly again by men of the ruling class, must stem from women's opposition to war, which, as *Lysistrata* suffices to show, has been much greater than the historians indicate. And the fact that this opposition can assume the character of an elemental force—obviously so when women organize—indicates that it is based not only on a conscious desire to preserve the lives of, particularly, sons and mates but has underlying instinctive roots directed towards the preservation of offspring and perhaps of life as such. In general, also, women's penchant for "building support" rather than "antagonism" and for "collective thinking" in opposition to dictatorial decisionmaking must have been anathema to ruling class men throughout history. And ruling classes must have been aware of the revolutionary "feminine ferment" (which, Marx implies, is not quite the same as the "masculine ferment").

To remove all antagonisms between the sexes is impossible—as in any "contradictory" relationship—without destroying the differences that produce them, in this case sexual differences. In exploitive societies, however, sex-antagonism patterns can assume destructive, even violent, forms, and because of male dominance in these societies, they are converted into male oppression of the female, which blends with the ruling class exploitation and oppression of women. On the other hand the situation of women and the general relation between the sexes in socialist countries shows that male-female antagonisms can be greatly reduced, and indicates that they can be reduced still further in communist society—although an element of "opposition" must always remain so long as the sexes remain biologically what they are, which opposition is in its essence healthy and vital. Such a situation is possible because the underlying behavioral area of attraction between the sexes is greater than that of antagonism and is able to unfold further under favorable social conditions—as Engels anticipated.

As we observe sexual, racial, and other social phenomena, it becomes apparent that we face, on the one hand, neither a simple biological determinism, nor, on the other, none or inconsequential inherited psychological patterns. Researches in recent decades have certainly shown that such inheritance links people and nature, and through people, society and nature. However, society although linked to nature is obviously a unique entity with its own specific processes. What Marx and Engels believed these to be, we have already seen. What they did not know—except in a very general way—was how these social processes originated or how they blended with biological ones. When, some three million years ago, subhuman society inhabitants formed groups, chose leaders and excluded aliens, they must have done so because the underlying inherited behavior patterns which we observe in animal societies were responding to social necessity, essentially on a nonconscious level. They had no real control over their society—which shows no evidence of development—for they were bound within the confines of simple hunter-gathering social structures. And when prehuman hunter-gathering societies arose about one million years ago, they arose on the foundations of subhuman hunter-gathering societies and again followed patterns dictated in part by their biological inheritance and in part by their social inheritance and needs. The resulting society was, in spite of developing consciousness, still beyond any overall control. When consciousness developed fully (apparently some 40,000 years ago) and the first human societies arose, although it did not provide direct control over society, it did in time provide indirect control because it enabled the hunter-gatherers to create the new tools and weapons that increased the productive forces to the point of producing surplus goods. New production relations arose that included trade and the path to early-type farming society was opened.

When, apparently about 15,000 years ago, some hunter-gathering societies with auxiliary farming began to change into actual farming societies, not only the basic socioeconomic interaction of productive forces and relationships continued, but inherited behavior patterns did also. New groups formed in response to the new economic base but group formation with its structures and functions would again have been impossible without instinctive behavioral roots. No doubt the people in these societies believed that they were forming such groups entirely consciously and deliberately, being, as were later people also, unaware of either the instinctive or the objective social forces directing their actions (and so on into later societies, from feudal to capitalist). When the feudal barons formed alliances and the bourgeoisie formed businesses or parliaments, they were unaware that they did so in response to underlying biopsychological as well as to social forces. In socialist societies people are aware of determinant socioeconomic forces and can make conscious use of them but they seem generally uninformed about the instinctive patterns which blend with these forces and with their own behavior in all aspects of life.

The genetic, neurological, and animal society researches of recent decades have begun to help to fill in the links between nature and society, a major aspect of the materialist world-outlook. It became clear in the nineteenth century that biologically people were part of nature, demonstrated in particular, as Engels noted, by the discovery of the biological cell, which indicated the oneness of all life, including human, and the theory of evolution, which revealed the evolution of people from earlier animal forms. The general dependence of society upon nature for its economic life was noted by Marx and Engels, but the actual biological and psychological links between nature and society were then perceivable only in a general way. We can now begin to see how heredity works—in the interactions of nucleic acids and proteins—and in part at least how evolution works: through mutations of the nucleic acids. We understand something of the nature of nerve cells and can see that (like other cells) they inherit a structure and function which in the higher nervous system result in instinctive behavior patterns that will either perish from nonuse or develop in "practice". We can link prehuman and early human social evolution with the fact that nerve cells in their growth and combinations can produce, in evolutionary sequence, nonconscious, partly conscious, and conscious psychological life.

We can also begin to visualize our own direct evolutionary ancestors more clearly, the small but swift and strong plains primates of east Africa. Finally, we have begun to realize that human society is not the only society on earth; that animals also live in societies and that ours grew out of theirs. Without animal society, no subhuman society; without subhuman society, no prehuman or human society. And with all this, the nature-background to the human drama has been coming into focus, the earth, once regarded as "dead" matter, now shown to be constantly active, almost like a breathing animal, and the universe beyond, once thought to be cold and serene, revealed as massively and violently active, its fires, in muted form, alive within us.

We can see, too, that in the ascent of matter from the atomic to the human mind, the processes at each step are materialistic and dialectical. The reactions of opposite particles within and between atoms produced molecules. The combinations of interpenetrating molecules produced the chain molecules of living matter. The chain molecules of living matter and the electrons of atomic matter in combination formed nerve cells, and nerve cell combinations formed nerve webs which resulted, in interactions with other biological cells, in the development of the higher nervous system of spinal cord and brain. Everywhere in nature development arises from the interpenetration of opposite elements and takes the form of the new arising from the combinations of the old. This is as true of living matter as of physical matter, of animal forms as of living matter, of animal societies as of animal forms. Animals are in a constant struggle for food and mates. Animal groups react to the conflicting (and nonconscious) forces of group coherence and enmity to the alien. The new—offspring—arises from the (genetic) combinations of the old.

Society, with such roots as these, biological and social, could hardly act in any but dialectical processes. As with the levels of matter, however, although the general processes are the same, the specific ones are unique. We might make a general parallel with the relation of life to matter. The basic functional unit of living matter is the cell and it is the cell that primarily determines the functioning of an organism. Although the cell's molecules have evolutionary roots in atomic matter, the functionings of the animal body are not atomic but biological, even though atomic reactions are still present within it. Thus although the general patterns of development—the conflict of opposites leading through quantitative-arrangement changes to the new—are the same, the specific forms of the interactions of atomic particles or atoms are not the same as those of nucleic acid or protein chain molecules. So, too, with society. The interactions of social forces, although again following general dialectical patterns, clearly have their own identity and their own specific patterns. So, too, also with human behavior. Psychological patterns have their specific units and forms. And these are not the same as those of society (or of nature). The fact that psychological patterns exist within social structures no more makes the evolutionary processes of society psychological and not social than the presence of atoms within the cell makes the functioning of living matter atomic and not biological.

The nature of people obviously determines the way in which people act to effect social change, and these ways are influenced by inherited behavioral patterns to a greater degree than was previously realized. The form of such basic social structures as the productive relationships and classes is ultimately a result of the nature of people. Nevertheless, although the general form of social structures is determined by the nature of people, the structures themselves and the social dynamics that arise from them provide the basic historical determinant. Although people create the underlying structures of society, these structures once created acquire their own dynamic—as does the biological cell—and people can only bring about major historical change when, by social action, they change these structures.

Marx's and Engels' view of the relationship of people to nature does not, as they realized, differ basically from that of natural science, and its philosophical implications, as we have noted, are essentially the same as those of materialism in general, of Lucretius or Diderot. There are no supernatural forces, no God, no immortality. Life has to be accepted for what it is; death is part of life. Without death, life could not exist. The choice which nature presents us is either life with death, or no life.

That religious beliefs are not necessary for meaningful living, as Churchmen and others claim, has been demonstrated in the present century in the socialist world, primarily in the U.S.S.R. Even with the limited social controls of socialism religion has there shrunk to a minor status and clearly will disappear in communist society. That nonreligious people are any less able to face death and its implications, has been disproved by the courageous resilience of the Soviet people in the face of twenty million war dead.

Psychological and animal society research indicates that our reactions to death are not primarily a matter of conscious thought, but of unconscious psychological patterns which are partly inherited. Grief and fear—both found in animals—arise from such patterns and are only slightly modified by the fact of consciousness, so that much of what has been considered a fear of death is actually a reaction to general fear-producing stimuli, which we then associate consciously with death. The fact is that we have no adequate reaction to death but are limited by these deeper psychological patterns, patterns which we cannot transcend but which can be mitigated or aggravated by social forces.

Modern scientific research has made materialism more real and more deeply believable than at any time in the past, for it has begun to show the exact mechanisms by which nature works and the intimacy of our connection with it. We now know the facts of biological life in sufficient detail to make them a real part of our daily living. As, for instance, we now watch a child grow from infancy we can see the intricacy of growing neuron formation, and the marvel of the human brain is visible as never before. We also see more clearly how we arose from the long chain of evolution with its fluid intertwinings of nucleic acid and proteins. The endless complexities of the processes that have gone into the creation of each human being indeed "teases us out of thought." But when we grasp these realities we see with greater vividness the horrors of the reckless destruction of human life with which exploitive classes have since their beginning bloodied our planet. Each of the tens of millions killed or maimed in imperialist war had been borne for nine months in a woman's body, tendered through babyhood, nurtured into adolescence, the intricacies of brain and body slowly unfolding to display the vistas of four billion years of ascending life. And when individual life ends all ends. Small wonder that the bourgeoisie works to hide these truths in a narcotic mist of superstition and lies. But the reality has to be faced, and facing it in itself acts as a revolutionary catalyst.

"The philosophers have only interpreted the world in various ways; the point is to change it." When Marx wrote these words he was thinking primarily, if not exclusively, of social change. Modern science, however, has opened vistas of natural change, and these could have profound effects, unforeseen by Marx and Engels, in communist society. Neither the scope nor the limitations of such change can at present be properly envisaged but they will certainly include biological change. General predictions of the future, based on these possibilities alone and failing to take into account the actual forces of social evolution, however, are misleading. And current speculations, even some emanating from socialist countries, about "intelligent beings" and "civilizations" on other planets are simply fantasy. It is virtually certain that conscious life exists on Earth alone, because, as we have seen, it arose from a series of chance events so complex that their duplication elsewhere—or here—is almostly infinitely improbable. It is apparent also that speculations on travel beyond the solar system are not based on reality for the time and space elements involved are too great to allow it. The fact is that we are almost certainly alone in the universe. And this knowledge gives us all the more motive to thwart the efforts of those who would destroy us. Finally, if the perspective of many millions of years of future human society—in a communist world—seems hard to grasp, it seems less so when we remember that we have a million years of human or virtually human living already behind us.[23]

If we put together all these various facts on nature, society and people, it becomes apparent that we now in a position to begin to understand everything. But it is also apparent that this understanding can come about only if we integrate these facts with Marxism and dialectical materialism. Only dialectical materialism enables us to apply a consistently materialist interpretation to the findings of natural science. Only Marxism allows us to see what society is and how it works. If, then, we take the total "world outlook" of Marx and Engels we can see also that there is no set barrier between nature and society, but that, on the contrary all is one. The processes of nature and society are essentially the same and blend one into the other. Furthermore, these processes in spite of their surface complexities are basically simple. We can now begin to see how we came about, what we are, and where we are going.

Notes

Chapter One

[1]There was, of course, no Communist Party in 1848. As Engels noted in 1884: "On the outbreak of the February Revolution, the German Communist Party, as we called it, consisted only of a small core, the Communist League, which was organised as a secret propaganda society." ("Marx and the *Neue Rheinische Zeitung* [1848–1849]", Karl Marx and Frederick Engels, *Selected Works*, Moscow, 1973, III, 164.) Marx and Engels, then, were using the word "party" not to designate an actual political party but a general social or political grouping, as in Marx's comment: "The petty-bourgeois democratic party in Germany is very powerful. . . ." (*Address to the Central Committee of the Communist League*, 1850, ibid., I, 177.) Jenny Marx, "Short Sketch of an Eventful Life," 1865, *Reminiscences of Marx and Engels* (Moscow, n.d.), pp. 223–224. For Marx's version of his arrest (in a letter written at the time) see Boris Nicolaievsky and Otto Maenchen-Helfen, *Karl Marx, Man and Fighter* (London, 1936), pp. 144–145. Philippe Gigot, a librarian, was a leading Belgium communist. Marx tells us that Gigot accompanied Jenny Marx to the police station (in Brussels) and was there arrested and imprisoned.

The *Holy Family*, containing a section by Engels, was an attack on the followers of Hegel, *The Poverty of Philosophy* an attack on the bourgeois "socialism" of Pierre Joseph Proudhon.

[2]Frederick Engels, *The Condition of the Working Class in England, from Personal Observation and Authentic Sources*, 1845 (Moscow, 1973), pp. 333–334; *Inaugural Address of the Workingmen's International Association*, 1864, *Selected Works*, II, 17: *The Civil War in France, Address of the General Council of the International Workingmen's Association*, 1871, ibid., p. 241.

194

³Erasmus Darwin, *The Temple of Nature* (London, 1803), Additional Notes, p. 45; William Godwin, *Enquiry Concerning Political Justice,* ed. F.E.L. Priestley (Toronto, 1946), I, 384, II, 463–464; Jean Antoine Nicolas Condorcet, *Outlines of an Historical View of the Progress of the Human Mind,* (London, 1795), pp. 4, 316; *Political Justice,* II, 475; Engels to Marx, March 17, 1845, *Letters of the Young Engels,* 1838–1845 (Moscow, 1976), p. 227.

⁴Quoted in Lucio Colletti, *Marxism and Hegel* (London, 1973), p. 251; Marx to Joseph Weydemeyer, March 5, 1852, Karl Marx and Friedrich Engels, *Correspondence, 1846–1895* (London, 1934), p. 57; James Madison, *The Federalist,* No. 10; William Godwin, "Of Avarice and Profusion," *The Enquirer* (London, 1797), pp. 177–178; P.B. Shelley, Preface to *Hellas,* 1821; Shelley, *The Masque of Anarchy,* 1819, stanzas 38, 91; Robert Owen, *Report to the County of Lanark,* 1821 (London, 1927), pp. 247–248; Hodgkins, quoted in E.P. Thompson, *The Making of the English Working Class* (New York, 1966), p. 778. Many of the ideas in his *Report* Owen had expressed at public meetings in 1816 and 1817.

⁵Engels, *On the History of the Communist League,* 1885, *Selected Works,* III, 177–178, 175. Engels did not, of course, mean that there would not be equality in communist society. He was objecting to the view that equality could come on "demand," a view that ignored not only historical evolution but the need to develop tactics to suit each stage of advance.

⁶Ibid., p. 177; Frederick Engels, *The Condition of the Working-Class in England,* 1845 (Moscow, 1973), pp. 264–265; Karl Marx, Frederick Engels, *Collected Works* (New York, 1976), V, 566; *Condition of the Working-Class,* p. 333; George Julian Harney, *On Engels,* 1897, *Reminiscences of Marx and Engels,* p. 192. For more on Engels's relations with the Chartists and Owenites see: *Frederick Engels: A Biography* (Moscow, 1976), pp. 38–41.

⁷Franz Mehring, *Karl Marx, The Story of his Life* (New York, 1935), p. 112; Hal Draper, *Karl Marx's Theory of Revolution* (New York, 1977), I, 174–177; "On the History of the Communist League," *Selected Works,* III, 178; *Karl Marx, A Biography* (Moscow, 1973), pp. 88–90. Marx wrote of his early collaboration with Engels as follows:

> Frederick Engels, with whom, since the appearance of his brilliant sketch on the criticism of the economic categories (in the *Deutsch-Franzosische Jahrbucher*), I maintained a constant exchange of ideas by correspondence, had by another road (compare his *The Condition of the Working-Class in England*) arrived at the same result as I, and when in the spring of 1845 he also settled in Brussels, we resolved to work out in common the opposition of our view to the ideological view of German philosophy, in fact, to settle accounts with our erstwhile philosophical conscience. The resolve was carried out in the form of a criticism of post-Hegelian philosophy.

(*Preface to a Contribution to the Critique of Political Economy*, 1859, *Selected Works*, I, 504–505.) Engels' "brilliant sketch" of capitalist economics is reprinted in Karl Marx, *The Economic and Philosophic Manuscripts of 1844*, ed. Dirk J. Struik (New York, 1973), Appendix. The manuscript Marx refers to has been published in part under the title *The German Ideology* (New York, 1938) and in full in *Collected Works*, V. It was begun, as Marx states, in the spring of 1845 but it was not completed until the summer of 1846. Engels also comments on his and Marx's relative share in formulating their views in a footnote to his *Ludwig Feuerbach and the End of German Classical Philosophy*, 1886:

> What I contributed—at any rate with the exception of my work in a few special fields—Marx could very well have done without me. What Marx accomplished I would not have achieved. Marx stood higher, saw further, and took a wider and quicker view than all the rest of us. Marx was a genius; we others were at best talented. Without him the theory would not be by far what it is today. It therefore rightly bears his name. (*Selected Works*, III, 361)

Although Engels' statement is doubtless correct in essence it requires modification. Engels, who had never attended a university, seems to have been overwhelmed by Marx's wide knowledge and catalytic insights in their 1844 meetings and tended to underestimate his own contribution. We must also take into account Engels's typical modesty: the "few special fields" include the examination of society before the rise of civilization and the development of dialectical materialism, especially in its relation to science. On the other hand Engels later hinted that he felt that he had not received "the recognition one thinks one deserves." (Engels to Franz Mehring, July 14, 1893, Marx, Engels, *Selected Correspondence*, Moscow, 1975, p. 433.)

It cannot be, however, that the differences between Marx and Engels arose primarily if at all from innate intellectual differences, that Marx had "genius" and Engels only talent. Marx as the editor of a radical publication had been more in the swirl of the class struggles than had Engels, and had suffered oppression and imprisonment. Marx had a kind of unrelenting class-struggle fierceness that Engels lacked—as may be seen in contrasting their writings on the Paris Commune.

One other question arises out of the relation of Marx and Engels. As dialectical materialism was almost entirely developed by Engels, it cannot, as we have noted, rightly be embraced under "Marxism." Historical materialism, on the other hand, and the specific economic analysis of capitalism—which is a subdivision of historical materialism—were primarily the work of Marx although Engels made major contributions to them. We can thus speak of Marxism and dialectical materialism when we wish to encompass the world-view originating in Marx and Engels, but there is no single term which embraces it. Perhaps it should simply be called "communism," using the word not in the sense of a system of society but of a body of thought.

[8]Friedrich Lessner, *Before 1848 and After*, 1898, *Reminiscences of Marx and Engels*, pp. 150, 153; *Communist Manifesto, Selected Works*, I, 118; Engels, *On the History of the Communist League*, ibid., III, 178. On Weitling and Marx, see *Karl Marx, A Biography*, pp. 110–112, Saul K. Padover, Karl Marx, *An Intimate Biography* (New York, 1980), pp. 116–121, *Frederick Engels: A Biography*, pp. 79–81, and Carl Wittke, *The Utopian Communist, A Biography of Wilhelm Weitling, Nineteenth Century Reformer* (Louisiana State University Press, 1950), pp. 105–123.

[9]*The Early Chartists*, ed., Dorothy Thompson (London, 1971), p. 57; Alfred Plummer, *Bronterre* (London, 1971), pp. 197, 118; *The Early Chartists*, pp. 99, 186; *Bronterre*, p. 87; O'Brien, quoted in E.P. Thompson, *English Working Class*, p. 803; *Bronterre*, pp. 42, 18, 122; G.D.H. Cole, *Chartist Portraits* (London, 1965), pp. 274, 276.

Engels met the Chartists in the early 1840s, during his first stay in England, and Marx in the summer of 1845. In November 1847, Marx and Engels spoke at a Chartist meeting in commemoration of the 1830 revolutions, speaking on the same platform as Harney and Ernest Jones, one of the left Chartist leaders. Marx noted that "Of all countries, England is the one where the conflict between proletariat and bourgeoisie is most developed." (Padover, p. 127.) In 1847 or 1848, Harney and Jones joined the Communist League. (*Frederick Engels*, pp. 119–120.) In 1850 Harney published the *Communist Manifesto* in his paper, *The Red Republican*, giving—for the first time—the authors' names. (Ibid., p. 162.) In 1852 Marx wrote: "Harney published our *Communist Manifesto* in English in his *Red Republican* with a note saying that it was "the most revolutionary document ever given to the world." (Marx to Joseph Weydemeyer, March 5, 1852, Karl Marx and Friedrich Engels, *Correspondence, 1846–1895*, London, 1934, p. 55.) And later in the century Marx told the English reformist socialist, H.M. Hyndman, that his view "of the social economic forces of the time, working themselves out quite unconsciously and uncontrolled into monopoly and socialism, beneath the anarchist competitions and antagonisms of the Capitalist system, first arose in a coordinated shape from his perusal of the works of the early English Economists, Socialists and Chartists." (*Bronterre*, p. 250.) Among the Chartists whom Marx read was Bronterre O'Brien, who was, along with Harney, their most advanced theorist, and was described by Marx—in contrasting him to other Chartists who had compromised their beliefs—as "an irrepressible Chartist at any price." (Marx to Engels, Jan. 14, 1858, *Correspondence*, p. 102.) In April 1856, Marx spoke at a Chartist meeting "to celebrate the anniversary of the *People's Paper*. (Marx to Engels, April 16, 1856, *Correspondence*, p. 86.) The speech was published in the *People's Paper*, April 19, 1856 (ibid., pp. 90–91). "During his stay in London," Mrs. Marx remembered, "Karl was always in close contact with the Chartists, and contributed to Ernest Jones' Journal *The People's Paper*." (Jenny Marx, "A Short Sketch of an Eventful life," in *The Unknown*

Karl Marx, ed. Robert Payne, New York University Press, 1971, p. 128.) Engels contributed regularly to Chartist papers and helped them financially. (*Frederick Engels,* p. 163.) Engels told Harney of his and Marx's attempts in 1846 to put their theories into book form—which Harney jocularly referred to as the "manufacturing of revolution." (Karl Marx, *A Biography,* p. 94.) Marx and Engels also early read widely in the works of Robert Owen and his early "socialist" followers, and received many important ideas from them—for instance on labor and value—even as they rejected their "Utopian" view that what Owen called a "new moral order" could be accomplished by propaganda. (*Marx, A Biography,* pp. 91–92.) Engels met Owenite leaders as early as 1843 in Manchester and attended their meetings. (*Engels, A Biography,* p. 38.) He discussed Owen's views in some detail in *Anti-Dühring.* It seems strange that the Soviet authors of the above-noted scholarly biographies of Marx and Engels, although noting their connections with the Chartists and other British working class radicals do not take the next step and conclude that the basic roots of Marxism lay—and had to lie—in the British proletariat. Marx and Engels also were acquainted with the—basically mass-oriented and powerfully agitational—writings of William Cobbett. (Engels to Marx, Oct. 25–26, 1847, Karl Marx, Frederick Engels, *Collected Works,* XXXVIII, New York, 1982, p. 140; *Karl Marx, A Biography,* p. 553; Draper, *Theory of Revolution,* I, 305.)

Chapter Two

[1]H.G. Wells, *The Outline of History* (New York, 1949), p. 1062; Arnold Toynbee, *Civilization on Trial* (New York, 1957), pp. 20–21, 25.

[2]*Communist Manifesto, Selected Works,* I, 108–109, 108 fn.; Frederick Engels, *Herr Eugen Dühring's Revolution in Science (Anti-Dühring),* (New York, 1939), p. 24.

[3]Marx, *The Class Struggles in France, Selected Works,* I, 206, 224.

[4]Engels, 1885, Preface to Marx, *Eighteenth Brumaire, Selected Works,* I, 396–397.

[5]Marx, Preface to *A Contribution to the Critique of Political Economy, Selected Works,* I, 503, and *A Handbook of Marxism,* ed. Emile Burns (New York, 1935), pp. 543, 544. I prefer the *Handbook* translation—quoted in Lenin, *The Teachings of Karl Marx*—but the opening section of the passage is not included in it; hence, for it, I use the *Selected Works* version.

[6]Marx to P.V. Annenkov, Dec. 28, 1846, Karl Marx and Frederick Engels, *Correspondence, 1846–1895* (London, 1934), p. 7.

[7]P.B. Shelley, *Prometheus Unbound,* III, iv, 195.

[8]Engels to J. Bloch, Sept. 21, 1890, *Correspondence,* pp. 475–476.

[9]Marx, *The Civil War in France, Selected Works,* II, 218; Marx, *The Eighteenth Brumaire of Louis Napoleon,* ibid., I, 421. There is a problem with the word "social." It has both a specific and general connotation. In the former it means that aspect of society—from family life to trade unionism—not covered by its economic or political aspects. In its general sense it includes all the functions of society. The difference is usually indicated only by the context.

[10]G.V. Plekhanov, *Fundamental Problems of Marxism,* 1908 (Moscow, 1974), p. 70; Nikolai Bukharin, *Historical Materialism, A System of Sociology* (New York, 1925), p. 156; Joseph Stalin, *Marxism and Linguistics* (New York, 1951), p. 9; Raymond Williams, *Marxism and Literature* (Oxford, 1977), pp. 75–82, which has philosophically anarchistic implications. See also my article, "The Fallacy of 'The Superstructure,' " *Monthly Review* XXXI (Jan. 1980), 27–36. In addition to the sources I there cite as examples of the "fallacy" we might note Maurice Cornforth, *Historical Materialism* (New York, 1954), pp. 97–118, a book still in print, and a recent Soviet Publication, V.G. Afanasyev, *Marxist Philosophy* (Moscow, 1978), pp. 201–205, for example (p. 202): "The basis is important because it serves as the *real foundation* upon which the *superstructure* arises, i.e., political, legal, philosophical, moral, artistic and religious views and their corresponding relations, institutions and organizations." This, of course, is straight from Stalin; although this is not noted, and it is presented as though it was Marx's view. It seems strange that recent Soviet scholars have failed to return if not to an analysis of Marx's passage in relation to Stalin at least to Lenin, whose views are the same as Marx's and contain no hint of a "category" known as "the superstructure." On the other hand, we must note that in such a Soviet work of actual (and insightful) historical analysis as *A Short History of the World,* Moscow, 1974, in two volumes, there is no talk of "the basis" and "the superstructure" but generally a class analysis of each civilization and its culture.

This difference, we might note, is typical of Marxist writing in the U.S.S.R. and other socialist countries. In discussions of Marxist general theory in such semiofficial works as *The Fundamentals of Marxist-Leninist Philosophy,* Moscow, 1974, the approach to Marxist general theory is semidogmatic—a method also inherited from Stalin, and the reverse of Lenin's scientific approach. On the other hand, Soviet analysis of current history is Marxist and factual. The reason for the dogmatic approach to general theory seems to be a fear that a basic examination and testing of the various views of Marx, Engels, and Lenin might lead to a flood of revisionism. And for this fear there was certainly justification in the past—as the Khrushchev "thaw" or, in China, the "hundred-flowers bloom" period demonstrated—but the time would seem to be ripe for a more enquiring method, one based on the established fact of Marxism's general scientific validity. The situation is similar in respect to dialectical materialism. In the *Fundamentals,* dialectical materialism is not only presented dogmatically but largely in terms of Kant-like "categories," an approach which is closer to idealism than materialism and obscures the central role of the interpenetration of opposites in nature and society. Yet in such a work as *Lenin and Modern Natural Science,* Moscow, 1978, the essays, by individual scientists, generally use dialectical materialism nondogmatically and sometimes creatively.

We have to recognize, however, that the matter of a general approach to Marxism is not an easy one. Let us take, for instance, that of E.P. Thompson in his *The Poverty of Theory and Other Essays,* New York, 1978. Thompson argues that the "concepts" of Marxism "are found to be more true" than others and (p. 44) "stand up better to the test of historical logic." We can either see Marxism as "closure and tradition," in which case it is viewed as a "theology," or (p. 188) we assume the position of "open investigation and critique." This sounds reasonable enough at a first reading but when we examine it more closely, questions arise. Why, for instance, "historical logic" as the test of Marxism? Why not historical fact? Are there other "concepts" of social evolution which are perhaps "almost as true" as Marxism? Is Marxism, then, just one among various views, all of which have virtues but not so many as Marxism? Does Thompson's "theology" category include those who hold that Marxism is the science of society? How far does "open investigation" go? Does it include a possible rejection of some of the basic premises of Marxism? Thompson also, we might note, does not examine Marx's view of objective processes underlying historical evolution but seems to assume that it is basically the result of human collective action.

[11]*The Left Academy: Marxist Scholarship on American Campuses*, ed., Bertell Ollman and Edward Vernoff (New York, 1982), p. 217, 212. Ibid., p. 208. Hal Draper, *Karl Marx's Theory of Revolution* (New York, 1977), II, 481, 459; Stanley Aronowitz, *The Crisis in Historical Materialism: Class, Politics and Culture in Marxist Theory* (New York, 1982), p. 113.

Draper quotes some passages from Engels (I, 336–338) to suggest that Engels believed in the autonomized State. In 1886, when Bismark was combining aristocratic and bourgeois elements in the German State, Engels wrote to Marx that it seemed to him that "the bourgeoisie has not the stuff in it to rule directly." (*Selected Correspondence*, p. 166. See also *Correspondence*, pp. 205–206.) And he made a parallel also with Britain, in whose State feudal and bourgeois elements were also combined. In 1892 in his Introduction to *Socialism: Utopian and Scientific* (*Selected Works*, III, 110–111) Engels argued that the bourgeoisie did not have the direct one-class control of the State that the feudal landowners did in feudal times. This was primarily the result of two factors: the still continuing influence of the feudal interests and the rise of the proletariat: "the working people are already knocking on the door." None of this, however, supports the view that the State is autonomized. When Engels argues that the bourgeoisie does not rule "directly"—as the feudal lords did—he is not saying that they do not rule, only that they rule indirectly through parliament and other bodies, sometimes making use of an existing bureaucracy with feudal ties. (Actually this was an advantage to them because it helped to disguise their domination.) And when Engels notes that feudal forces, at one end, and proletarian, at the other, push into the realm of nineteenth-century bourgeois power he is again not endorsing a doctrine of an autonomized State but only pointing out that the bourgeois State is subject to a variety of class pressures.

[12]Marx and Engels, *Preface to the German Edition of 1872* (of the *Communist Manifesto*), *Selected Works*, I, 99.

[13]*Origin of the Family* (New York, 1942), p. 5.

¹⁴On Reich see, for instance, Bertell Ollman, *Social and Sexual Revolution: Essays on Marx and Reich* (Boston, 1979), pp. 159–203. See also Herbert Marcuse, *Eros and Civilization,* Boston, 1955 and *One-Dimensional Man,* Boston, 1964. The Freud-Marx analogies (and confusion) began in Germany following World War I in the so-called Frankfort School and later spread to the United States with the immigration of some of its followers. Such recent critics of Marxism as Stanley Aronowitz (*The Crisis in Historical Materialism,* pp. 127, 239–246, 291–292 and *passim*) still take Reich—and Marcuse—seriously.

Chapter Three

¹Engels, *Speech at the Graveside of Karl Marx,* March 17, 1883, *Selected Works,* III, 162; Chapter I, above, n. 7; Preface to *A Contribution to the Critique of Political Economy, A Handbook of Marxism* (ed. Emile Burns, New York, 1935; retranslated), p. 372.

²*Origin of the Family, Private Property and the State* (New York, 1942), p. 160. *See also The German Ideology, Selected Works,* I, 21–22 and *The Communist Manifesto, ibid,* p. 109. The slavery-feudalism-capitalist historical succession has unfortunately become a general tenet of Marxism.

³The nature of Engels' relation to Morgan is clear from Morgan's Table of Contents. He divides his book into four parts: Growth of Intelligence Through Inventions and Discoveries; Growth of the Idea of Government; Growth of the Idea of the Family; Growth of the Idea of Property. Morgan, then, in spite of his careful research and deduction from fact, has a largely idealist approach; and behind this is a religious teleology: "Their [our ancestors' in early societies] labor, their trials and their successes were part of the Supreme Intelligence to develop a barbarian out of a savage, and a civilized man out of this barbarian." (Lewis, H. Morgan, *Ancient Society,* Chicago, n.d., p. 563.) Morgan was a member of the New York State Legislature and although a strong supporter of Indian land claims and opposed to the power of the railroads, was far from being a socialist. (David Oberweiser, "A Note on Lewis Henry Morgan," *Science and Society,* XLII [fall, 1978], 344–46) Marx also made a study of Morgan, and Engels made use of his notes. (*Karl Marx: A Biography,* pp. 549–551.)

⁴Morgan, p. 9; *Origin of the Family,* pp. 19, 20, 144. The fish stage idea also came from Morgan (pp. 10, 21).

⁵*Origin of the Family,* pp. 21, 145, 9, 147.

⁶Ibid., pp. 149, 150, 154, 155. See also p. 158. Engels, we might note, does not use the technocratic terms, "stone age," "bronze age," "iron age," which serve only to obscure the social reality.

⁷Morgan, p. 9; Carleton S. Coon, *The Story of Man,* (New York, 1955), p. 176.

⁸Julius Caesar, *The Conquest of Gaul* (Penguin Books, 1953), I. 2; *Tacitus on*

Britain and Germany (Penguin Books, 1954), pp. 109–110; George Thomson, *Studies in Ancient Greek Society: The Prehistoric Aegean* (New York, 1949), p. 328; G.C. Vaillant, *The Aztecs of Mexico* (Penguin Books, 1951), p. 128.

[9]*Origin of the Family,* pp. 156–157.

[10]Dylan Thomas, *The Hand that Signed the Paper Felled a City;* Henri Frankfort, *The Birth of Civilization in the Near East* (New York, 1956), pp. 104–105.

[11]Kenneth Neill Cameron, *Humanity and Society: A World History* (Indiana University Press, 1973; New York, 1977), p. 54.

[12]Cameron, *Humanity and Society,* pp. 87, 88, 93, 94.

[13]Herrlee Glessner Creel, *The Birth of China* (New York, 1961), pp. 310, 316.

[14]On Cato, see F.R. Cowell, *Cicero and the Roman Republic* (Penguin Books, 1956), p. 106.

[15]Cicero, *De lege Manilia,* vii, 18–19, quoted in: Will Durant, *Caesar and Christ* (New York, 1944), *The Story of Civilization,* III, 140.

[16]V. Gordon Childe, *What Happened in History* (Penguin Books, 1948), p. 275; Durant, *Caesar and Christ,* p. 642; *Cambridge Economic History of Europe* (Cambridge, 1952), I, 239.

[17]Tacitus, *On Britain and Germany* (Penguin Classics, 1954), p. 80; *The German Ideology, Selected Works,* I, 22.

[18]Cameron, *Humanity and Society,* pp. 248–49.

[19]June 2, 8, 1853, Karl Marx and Friedrich Engels, *Correspondence, 1846–1895* (London, 1934), pp. 66–67.

[20]Frederick Engels, *Herr Eugen Dühring's Revolution in Science (Anti-Dühring),* (New York, 1939), p. 200: Marx to Engels, June 14, 1953, *Correspondence,* p. 70.

[21]*Origin of the Family,* p. 160; *Anti-Dühring,* p. 201.

[22]*Anti-Dühring,* p. 200.

[23]*Cambridge Economic History of Europe,* pp. 103–104.

[24]Ibid., pp. 119–120

[25]Wolfram Eberhard, *A History of China* (London, 1950), p. 181; *Encyclopedia Britannica,* 14th ed., *Japan.*

[26]Engels to Marx, July 17, 1951, *Correspondence,* p. 40, fn.: *Communist Manifesto, Selected Works,* I, 111.

[27]*Anti-Dühring,* pp. 293, 295, 296; Karl Marx, *Capital* (Chicago, 1912), I, 835.

[28]*Cambridge Economic History,* p. 386; Henri Pirenne, *Economic and Social History of Medieval Europe* (New York, n.d.), p. 202.

[29]*Capital,* I, 823.

[30]Julius Caesar, *The Conquest of Gaul* (Penguin Books, 1953), p. 36; Samuel Noah Kramer, *History Begins at Sumer* (Anchor Books, 1958), p. 134.

[31]*Communist Manifesto, Selected Works,* I, 108–109; Hal Draper, *Karl Marx's Theory of Revolution,* II, 466.

Chapter Four

¹Frederick Engels, *The Condition of the Working Class in England* (Moscow, 1973), pp. 63, 118–19, 285. Engels wrote the book between September 1844 and March, 1845. (*Frederick Engels: A Biography,* Moscow, 1974, pp. 57–58. See also Gustav Mayer, *Frederick Engels, A Biography,* New York, 1936, p. 57.) Engels spent ten days with Marx in Paris in the late summer of 1844 (Mayer, p. 48) but does not seem to have discussed the projected book with him in any detail. (Engels to Marx, Nov. 19, 1844. Karl Marx and Frederick Engels, *Collected Works,* New York, 1982, 38, 210–11). In preparation for writing the book, Engels visited the working class districts in Manchester and Bradford and got to know the workers at first hand—as he tells us in his introductory note "To the Working-classes of Great Britain." See also *Frederick Engels,* pp. 37–38. Engels went to England to work in the management of Ermen and Engels, a spinnery in which his father was a partner. He hated the work from the beginning. (Engels to Marx, ca. Jan. 20, 1845, Marx and Engels, *Collected Works,* 30, 19–20.)

²*Condition of the Working Class,* pp. 197, 323, 181.

³Ibid., pp. 239–40, 143, 317–18.

⁴Ibid., pp. 264–65; *Anti-Dühring,* p. 287; Mayer, p. 40, 44–45. On Engels and Shelley, see Mayer, p. 415, *Letters of the Young Engels, 1838–1845* (Moscow, 1976), pp. 10–11, 137–140, 220, Ernest Rose, *Journal of English and Germanic Philology,* XXVI (1927), 141, and Yvonne Kapp, *Eleanor Marx,* II (New York, 1976), 250: "Only a few months ago, I [Eleanor Marx] heard Harney and Engels talking of the Chartist times, and of the Byron and especially Shelley-worship of the Chartists; and on Sunday last Engels said: 'Oh, we all knew Shelley by heart then.'" In addition to *Queen Mab,* Engels also translated Shelley's *The Sensitive Plant.* (*Letters,* p. 141.) On *Queen Mab,* Owen and other radicals see Kenneth Neill Cameron, *The Young Shelley: Genesis of a Radical* (New York, 1950), pp. 273–274, 387; Kenneth Neill Cameron, *Shelley: The Golden Years* (Harvard University Press, 1974), pp. 118, 596. On Marx's interest in Shelley see Edward Aveling and Eleanor Marx, *Shelley and Socialism,* 1888 (London, 1974), p. 5. See also Kenneth Neill Cameron, "Shelley and Marx," *The Wordsworth Circle,* X (Spring, 1979), 234–39.

⁵*Condition of the Working Class,* pp. 331, 332. On Engels's early economic views, see also his 1844 essay "Outlines of a Critique of Political Economy" in Karl Marx, *The Economic and Philosophic Manuscripts of 1844* (New York, 1973), pp. 197–226; see also *Frederick Engels,* pp. 41–46.

⁶When he first received from Marx the proof sheets of *Capital,* Engels replied:

The second sheet [a printer's sheet containing many pages] especially bears rather strong marks of the carbuncles, but that cannot be altered now and I do not think you should do any more about it in the additions, for, after all, the philistine is not accustomed to this sort of abstract thought, and will certainly not bother himself with it for the sake of the form of value. At most the points here established dialectically might be demonstrated historically at rather greater length, the test to be made from history, so to speak, although what is most necessary in these respects has already been said. In these more abstract developments you have committed the great mistake of not making the sequence of thought clear by a larger number of small sections and separate headings. (June 16, 1867, *Correspondence*, p. 220)

Although there is no question of Engels's acceptance of Marx's arguments in *Capital* (the following year he published an enthusiastic review: *Selected Works*, II, 146–152), there is clearly an element of disappointment in his reply. (Evidently Marx had—surprisingly enough—not previously shown Engels any extensive parts of the work.) Engels apparently had expected a more factual and historical treatment and fears that Marx's dialectical abstractions will make for difficult reading. Marx had been complaining about his "carbuncles" (large boil-like infections), and Engels is divertingly attributing the deficiencies in treatment he hints at to this physical cause. Although Marx was pleased with Engels' general "satisfaction" with the work (Marx to Engels, June 22, 1867, *Correspondence*, p. 221) Engel's reply is not the unreservedly enthusiastic one which we might expect on his receiving a work which he had looked forward to for years as Marx's masterpiece. As a result of Engels' criticism, Marx added an appendix in which he described "the same thing as simply and as pedagogically as possible" and "divided each successive proposition into paragraphs, etc., with separate headings." (Ibid., p. 222.)

[7]Karl Marx, *Wages, Price and Profit, Selected Works*, II, 45. Marx left his manuscript untitled; it was given the title "Value, Price and Profit" by Edward Aveling; this the editors of *Selected Works* (II, 439) changed to "Wages, Price and Profit" but the work is still generally known by its old title. It was read by Marx at meetings of the General Council of The International Working Men's Association on June 20 and 27, 1865, in answer to arguments by an Owenite worker, John Weston. (Marx to Engels, May 20, 1865, *Correspondence*, p. 202.) Karl Marx, *Capital*, (Chicago, 1912), III, 209–210; *Selected Works*, II, 48.

[8]*Selected Works*, II, 49. (I omit the underlinings and capitals of Marx's original text, which he perhaps added to suggest emphasis as he read.)

[9]*Selected Works*, II, 49.

[10]Marx to Engels, April 2, 1858, *Correspondence*, p. 107; *Selected Works*, II, 55, 56, 58; *Anti-Dühring*, p. 226.

[11]*Selected Works*, II, 59–60. Although in *Capital* and other works Marx speaks of capitalism as a closed system, he was aware that it had colonial extensions and that it derived profits from the exploitation of colonial labor:

In India serious complications, if not a general outbreak, is in store for the British government. What the English take from them annually in the form of rent, dividends for railways useless to the Hindus; pensions for military and civil service men, for Afghanistan and other wars, etc. etc.—what they take from them without any equivalent and quite apart from what they appropriate to themselves annually within India, speaking only of the value of the commodities the Indians have gratuitously and annually to send over to England—it amounts to more than the total sum of income of the sixty millions of agricultural and industrial labourers of India! This is a bleeding process, with a vengeance!

Marx, however, did not discuss this influx of capital from colonial exploitation as a world economic phenomenon or speculate on its general historical effects. (Marx to N.F. Danielson, Feb. 19, 1881, *Correspondence*, pp. 385–386.)

[12]Engels, *Outline of a Critique of Political Economy*, in Karl Marx, *The Economic and Philosophic Manuscripts of 1844*, ed. Dirk J. Struik (New York, 1973), p. 214; *Selected Works*, I, 113–114.

[13]*Capital*, III, 304, 303; Engels, *Socialism: Utopian and Scientific, Selected Works*, III, 141–42.

[14]*Selected Works*, III, 138; *Capital* (New York, 1967), III, 814.

[15]*Selected Works*, I, 113; Engels to August Bebel, Jan. 20–23, 1886, *Correspondence*, p. 445; *Selected Works*, II, 144; *Capital* (New York, 1967), III, 242; *Anti-Dühring*, p. 299.

[16]*Capital*, III, 279; *Capital* (New York, 1967), III, 247.

[17]*Capital*, I, 836.

[18]Preface, *Condition of the Working class*, p. 35.

[19]*Monthly Review*, XXXI (Dec. 1979), 2.

[20]Ibid. (March, 1980), p. 7

[21]Paul M. Sweezy, *Theory of Capitalist Development* (New York, 1968), p. 106. See also Bertell Ollman and Edward Vernoff, eds., *The Left Academy: Marxist Scholarship on American Campuses* (New York, 1982), pp. 72–73.

Chapter Five

[1]*Capital*, I, 836–837. This "polarization" concept had, as we have seen, been partly anticipated by Engels in *Condition of the Working Class* (p. 331).

[2]*Selected Works*, III, 448. Engels, as I note, is using "abstraction" to mean that the "privileged minority" of the workers form a separate elite. "Abstraction" was used in the sense of "separation" by John Stuart Mill and others in the nineteenth century.

[3]Marx to the Communist League, Sept. 15, 1850, quoted in *Correspondence*, p. 92; ibid., pp. 456–57. Engels' comments appeared in a *Preface* he wrote in 1887 for a pamphlet by his and Marx's German friend, Sigismund Borkheim, *Zur Erinnerung fur die deutschen Mordspatrioten 1806–1807*. See *Frederick Engels*, p. 412 and Franz Mehring, *Karl Marx, The Story of his Life* (New York, 1935), index. Engels repeated his views on the coming war in a letter to Friedrich Sorge, Jan. 7, 1888.

(*Correspondence*, pp. 455–56.) The British Museum Catalogue lists Borkheim's pamphlet as published in 1871. Perhaps the 1887 edition was a second edition.

[4]Engels to Karl Kautsky, Sept. 12, 1882, *Correspondence*, p. 399.

[5]Mayer, *Engels*, p. 233; *Critique of the Gotha Program*, p. 27; *Selected Works*, III, 13; *Critique*, pp. 44–45, 29, 30, 31, 27, 28. See also: *Frederick Engels*, pp. 291–294 and Yvonne Kapp, *Eleanor Marx* (New York, 1976), II, 449–453.

[6]Marx to Georg Weydemeyer, March 5, 1852, *Correspondence*, p. 57; ibid., p. 92.

[7]Engels' Introduction to Marx's *The Civil War in France, Selected Works*, II, 189; Marx, ibid., pp. 220–21, 225.

[8]R.N. Postgate, *Revolution from 1789 to 1906* (London, 1920), p. 299; Frank Jellinek, *The Paris Commune of 1871* (London, 1937), p. 402; Postgate, pp. 300–302; Jellinek, p. 370.

[9]*Selected Works*, II, 186–87.

[10]Marx, *The Hague Congress*, ibid., p. 293; Kapp, *Eleanor Marx*, II, 450; *Instruction for the Delegates of the Provisional General Council, Selected Works*, II, 83.

[11]Jellinek, p. 172; *Selected Works*, II, 186, Engels, *On Authority*, ibid., p. 379; ibid. p. 187; Preface to the German edition of *The Communist Manifesto*, 1872, *Selected Works*, I, 99 (quoting Marx, *The Civil War in France*).

[12]Engels, *Principles of Communism*, 1847, *Selected Works*, I, 92; *Anti-Dühring*, pp. 306–307; Engels, *On Authority, Selected Works*, p. 378.

[13]*Anti-Dühring*, pp. 221, 320, 323–24; Engels, *Principles of Communism, Selected Works*, I, 94. The concept that "the great towns will perish" in communist society Engels had found in Owen. *Frederick Engels*, p. 55. The concept was later challenged by Stalin: *Economic Problems of the U.S.S.R.* (New York, 1952), p. 23. Some writers on Marxism have stated that Marx and Engels left their view of a future communist society indefinitely vague. That this is not true is clear from the works I have cited and is demonstrated also by Bertell Ollman in his *Social and Sexual Revolution: Essays on Marx and Reich* (Boston, 1979), pp. 42–98. Those putting forward these views seem in the main to be intent on denying that the USSR and other socialist states are in fact socialist and on presenting their own abstract versions of socialism and communism. A somewhat different approach is that of Paul Sweezy: "Marxism calls it communism, and implicitly recognizes that it can only be approached, never attained." This clearly is not so. Both Marx and Engels did expect communism to be attained. In fact part of the reason for their attack on the Gotha program was that its authors did not recognize this fact. Paul Sweezy, *Marxism and Revolution 100 Years After Marx's Death, Monthly Review* XXXIV (April, 1883) 11.

[14]Frederick Engels, *Ludwig Feuerbach and the Outcome of Classical German Philosophy* (New York, 1941), p. 12.

[15]Engels to Vera Zazulich, April 23, 1885, *Correspondence*, p. 437; Michael T. Florinsky, *Russia: A History and an Interpretation* (New York, 1953), II, 1418; James H. Bunyan and H.H. Fisher, *The Bolshevik Revolution, 1917–1918, Documents and*

Materials (Stanford University Press, 1934), p. 13; Florinsky, pp. 1419, 1390; Bunyan and Fisher, p. 11; *Materials for the Study of the Soviet System*, ed. James H. Meisel, Edward S. Kozera (Ann Arbor, Michigan), p. 50.

[16]Meisel and Kozera, pp. 13, 28, 36; James Bunyan, *Intervention, Civil War, and Communism in Russia: April-December 1918, Documents and Materials* (The Johns Hopkins Press, 1936), p. 400; Meisel and Kozera, p. 27; V. I. Lenin, *"Left-wing" Communism, An Infantile Disorder*, Lenin, *Selected Works*, X, (New York, 1938), 88–89; Meisel and Kozera, p. 88; *The Woman Question, Selections from the Writings of Karl Marx, Frederick Engels, V.I. Lenin, Joseph Stalin* (New York, 1951), pp. 52, 61.

[17]*"Left-wing" Childishness and Petty-bourgeois Mentality*, Lenin, *Selected Works*, VII, 374. For a discussion of incomes in the U.S.S.R. see Victor and Ellen Perlo, *Dynamic Stability: The Soviet Economy Today* (New York, 1980), pp. 171–181.

[18]Ollman, *Social and Sexual Revolution* p. 4; Paul Sweezy, *Marxism and Revolution 100 Years After Marx, Monthly Review* XXXIV (March, 1983), 4, 6, 8, 9; Ollman, pp. 24, 173, 192.

[19]Engels, *Principles of Communism, Selected Works*, I, 91–92; Engels, *Introduction to Marx, Class Struggles in France*, p. 19. In 1915, Lenin argued that "the victory of socialism is possible, first in a few or even in one single capitalist country." (*The United States of Europe Slogan*, Lenin, *Selected Works*, V, 141.)

[20]*The Hague Congress, Selected Works*, II, 293; ibid., p. 217; Saul Padover, *Karl Marx: An Intimate Portrait* (New York, 1978), pp. 258, 257, *Confidential Communication, Selected Works*, II, 176.

[21]Engels, *A Critique of the Draft Social-Democratic Programme of 1891, Selected Works*, III, 434; Engels, Introduction to Marx, *Class Struggles in France*, p. 21; ibid., pp. 24–25. Engels to Friedrich Sorge, Jan. 6, 1892, *Letters to Americans* (New York, 1953), p. 239.

[22]P.B. Shelley, *Prometheus Unbound*, III, i, 80 (the cry of Jupiter as he fell before the power of Demogorgon—Necessity); Engels, *Anti-Dühring*, p. 183.

Chapter Six

[1]Godwin and Wollstonecraft as quoted in Kenneth Neill Cameron, *The Young Shelley: Genesis of a Radical* (New York, 1950), pp. 267, 268; Percy Bysshe Shelley, *On Marriage, Complete Works* VII, 149, *Laon and Cythna*, 1.1045; Edward Aveling and Eleanor Marx Aveling, *Shelley's Socialism*, 1888, (London, 1975), p. 13.

[2]Samuel Bamford, quoted in E.P. Thompson, *The Making of the English Working Class* (New York, 1966), pp. 415–416; Samuel Bamford, *Passages in the Life of a Radical*, ed. Henry Dunckley (London, 1893), II, 150–157 (on Peterloo); Flora Tristan quoted in Sheila Rowbotham, *Women, Resistance and Revolution* (New York, 1974), p. 55.

[3]*Communist Manifesto, Selected Works*, I, 123, 124; Engels, *Origin of the Family,*

Private Property and the State (New York, 1942), p. 66. (See also Engels, *Socialism: Utopian and Scientific, Selected Works,* III, 118.)

⁴Marx to Ludwig Kugelmann, Dec. 12, 1868, *Correspondence,* p. 255; Marx, *Capital,* I, quoted in *The Woman Question* (New York, 1951), p. 27. For vivid examples of the way "the feminine ferment" works in the general revolutionary ferment see: Arlene Eisen Bergmen, *Women of Viet Nam.* San Francisco, 1974.

⁵Engels, *Origin of the Family,* pp. 8, 10, 58, 63–67, 126, 142. The translation in the edition cited, seems to be clearer and more natural than that in *Selected Works,* III.

⁶*Origin of the Family,* p. 73; Nov. 1, 1891, *Correspondence,* p. 495. Marx and Engels, we might note in view of Lenin's usage, now common in Marxist circles, used "opposition," "antagonism," and "contradiction" more or less interchangeably.

⁷See Cameron, *Humanity and Society,* index, "women." G. G. Coulton, *Medieval Panorama* (New York, 1957), p. 118.

⁸*The Good Old Cause: The English Revolution of 1640–60,* ed. Christopher Hill, Edmund Dell (London, 1949), p. 287 (quoting Samuel Butler's *Hudibras*); Rowbotham, *Women, Resistance and Revolution,* p. 15; Leon Trotsky, *The Russian Revolution* (New York, 1959), p. 105.

⁹On mass rape in war, see Susan Brownmiller, *Against Our Will: Men, Women and Rape* (New York, 1975), pp. 31–34 and *passim.* Engels's argument (p. 125, above) that "male supremacy" is based on "property" is only partly true. It has, as we shall see, biological roots, and these can be distorted into male chauvinism by exploitive–class infusions into the proletariat.

¹⁰Marx, *Confidential Communication,* 1870, *Selected Works,* II, 176.

¹¹Engels also writes of extramarital relations for a woman being considered "a crime, entailing grave legal and social consequences, but not for a man". (*Origin of the Family,* pp. 66, 68.)

¹²Margrit Pittman, *Encounters in Democracy: A U.S. Journalist's View of the GDR* (New York, 1981), pp. 136–141. See also William M. Mandel, *Soviet Women,* New York, 1975.

Chapter Seven

¹Engels to Franz Mehring, July 14, 1893, *Correspondence,* pp. 510–512; A.W. Palmer, *A Dictionary of Modern History, 1789–1945* (Penguin Books, 1976), p. 21.

²*Selected Works,* I, 125, 126.

³Confucius, Aristotle and Locke as quoted in Cameron, *Humanity and Society,* pp. 120, 217, 329. In surveying the history of ideas in civilized societies, we have to recognize that we are not, as bourgeois historians believe, dealing with an infinite variety of free-floating phenomena but a few only and all of them anchored in specific social structures. Since the beginnings of civilization, there have until recently only been two main forms of society, feudal and capitalist, with slave-

commercial societies being (historically speaking) a temporary aberration and mainly confined to the Mediterranean area. On Plato, see Alban Dewes Winspear, *The Genesis of Plato's Thought*, New York, 1940.

[4]P.B. Shelley, *Oedipus Tyrannus or Swellfoot the Tyrant*, II, ii, 11–14.

[5]William Domroff, *The Higher Circles: The Governing Class in America* (New York, 1970), pp. 34–35, 87, 105.

[6]"When Adam delved . . ." was part of a revolutionary speech by John Ball during the English Peasants' Revolt of 1381. See John Richard Green, *A Short History of the English People* (New York, 1916), 250–251.

[7]Debate on the Frame-work Bill, House of Lords, Feb. 27, 1812, *The Works of Lord Byron, Letters and Journals* (London, 1898), II, 429; *Childe Harold's Pilgrimage*, IV, stanzas 167–170; *A Philosophical View of Reform*, Shelley, *Complete Works*, VII, 53. (Shelley continues: "The right of insurrection is derived from the employment of armed force to counteract the will of the nation.")

[8]Engels to Heinz Starkenburg, Jan. 25, 1894, quoted in Karl Marx and Frederick Engels: *Literature and Art: Selections from their Writings* (New York, 1947), p. 9. Referred to hereafter as *Selections*. See *Selected Correspondence*, p. 441, where the recipient is identified as W. Borgius. Marx, Introduction to the *Critique of Political Economy*, quoted in *Karl Marx, Frederick Engels: On Literature and Art*, ed., Lee Baxandall and Stefan Morawski (New York, 1974), p. 136. Referred to hereafter as *Marx-Engels*.

[9]Marx, quoted in *Marx-Engels*, pp. 51–54; Engels, from *The Part Played by Labor in the Transition from Ape to Man* (1876), ibid., p. 54.

[10]Percy Bysshe Shelley, *A Defence of Poetry, Complete Works* (New York, 1930), VII, 111.

[11]Marx, Introduction to the *Critique of Political Economy* (1859), quoted in *Marx-Engels*, p. 36. On *Prometheus Unbound*, see Kenneth Neill Cameron, *Shelley: The Golden Years* (Harvard University Press, 1974), pp. 475–564.

[12]Samuel Noah Kramer, *History Begins at Sumer* (New York, 1959), pp. 213, 123; Cameron, *Humanity and Society*, p. 77 (William Ellery Leonard's translation of *Gilgamesh*).

[13]Engels, Preface to the Italian edition of *The Communist Manifesto* (1892), *Marx-Engels*, p. 93.

[14]*Selections*, pp. 72–73; Shelley, Preface to *Prometheus Unbound*.

[15]Lafargue, *Reminiscences of Marx* (1890), *Marx-Engels*, p. 152; Eleanor Marx, *Recollections of Mohr* (1895), ibid., p. 149. " 'Mohr' was the regular, almost official name, by which Marx was called, not only by us, but by all the more intimate friends." (Eleanor Marx, *Karl Marx: A Few Stray Notes, Reminiscences of Marx and Engels* [Moscow, n.d.] p. 251. "Mohr" is German for "moor." The nickname was given to Marx because of his dark complexion. Marx probably had some negroid ancestry. See Herbert W. Vilakazi, "Was Karl Marx a Black Man?" in *Monthly Review*, XXXII (June, 1980), 42–58.

[16]Engels to Margaret Harkness, April 1888, *Marx-Engels,* pp. 116–117. "Margaret Harkness" was a pseudonym for John Law, an English radical writer. *(Selected Correspondence,* p. 521.)

[17]Edward Aveling and Eleanor Marx, *Shelley's Socialism,* (London, 1888), *Selections,* p. 132. See Yvonne Kapp, *Eleanor Marx* (New York, 1976), II, 250–251.

[18]Engels, *George Weerth,* 1883, *Marx-Engels,* pp. 126–129; Engels to Hermann Schluter, May 15, 1885, ibid., pp. 129–130; Marx to Ferdinand Lassalle, April 19, 1859, *Marx-Engels,* pp. 107–108. In *Correspondence* (p. 110) "fistic right" is rendered as "club-law."

[19]Engels to Minna Kautsky, Nov. 26, 1885, *Marx-Engels,* p. 114; Engels to Margaret Harkness (see note 16 above), April, 1888, ibid., pp. 115–116.

Chapter Eight

[1]Engels, *Foreword to the 1888 Edition* of *Feuerbach, Selected Works,* III, 336; Engels, *Speech at the Graveside of Karl Marx,* March 17, 1883, ibid., pp. 162–163. The term "dialectical materialism" was first used in G.V. Plekhanov, Appendix (1892), *Fundamental Problems of Marxism* (Moscow, 1974), p. 89: "The philosophy of Marx and Engels is not only a *materialist philosophy;* it is *dialectical materialism.*" It was subsequently used by Lenin. The chapter heading "Dialectical Materialism" to part four of Engels's *Feuerbach* in the International Publishers' edition (New York, 1941) was silently added by the editors. Engels designated the four sections of the work only by numbers.

[2]Engels, *Feuerbach, Selected Works,* III, 346, 347.

[3]On Lucretius, Holbach and Diderot, see Cameron *Humanity and Society,* pp. 213–215, 343–345. Lucretius was apparently part of an intellectual circle around Cicero who was recognized as a commercially based political leader opposing the landed aristocracy. Diderot and Holbach represented the anti-great-landowner opposition which led up to the French Revolution and which had economic roots in a rising commercial capitalism. Earlier Indian materialism, that of the Jains, had roots in the city merchants and artisans, and earlier Greek materialism seems to have been similarly based. Materialism before Marx and Engels, that is to say, arose out of the commercial struggle against great landowner economic domination, including its church. Marx and Engels, like all radicals of the time, were well-read in Lucretius, Holbach and Diderot. For Marx on Diderot, see *Selections* p. 79.

[4]Marx, *A Criticism of the Hegelian Philosophy of Law,* quoted in: J.D. Bernal, *Marx and Science* (New York, 1952), p. 12; Engels, *Anti-Dühring,* p. 42. Marx's "opium" comment came before he was fully aware of the role of classes in society. He fails to note the use of religion by the ruling classes but thinks of it as a needed narcotic. Nor would he later have seen religion as providing "the soul" for a "heartless world." Rather he would have seen dialectical materialism and Marxism as providing the "soul" for the proletariat.

[5]Engels, *Feuerbach, Selected Works,* III, 349; Engels, *Socialism: Utopian and*

Scientific, ibid., p. 131; Marx, *Theses on Feuerbach,* ibid., I, 13–15. For more on the "old materialism," see Engels, *Feuerbach,* ibid., III, 366–367. Ludwig Feuerbach (1804–1872) began as a disciple of Hegel but moved into a kind of naturalist as well as humanist position. Although he attacked some aspects of Christian theology he remained religious: "God is the essence of man, seen as the highest truth." His most influential book, *The Essence of Christianity* (translated into English by George Eliot), was read by Marx shortly after its appearance in 1841, when Marx was finishing his thesis. *Karl Marx: A Biography* (Moscow, 1973), pp. 31–32 and *passim.*

⁶Engels, *Anti-Dühring,* p. 68; Engels, *Dialectics of Nature* (London, 1940), p. 327; Stephen Jay Gould, *Ever Since Darwin* (New York, 1977), pp. 25–26.

⁷Engels, *Feuerbach, Selected Works,* III, 362; Hegel, quoted in David Guest, *A Textbook of Dialectical Materialism* (New York, 1939), p. 48; Hegel, quoted in Engels, *Dialectics of Nature* (London, 1940), p. 30; *Anti-Dühring,* pp. 132, 148–152.

⁸Marx, *Afterword to the Second German Edition of the First Volume of Capital,* Jan. 24, 1872, *Selected Works,* II, 98; Marx to P.V. Annenkov, Dec. 28, 1846, ibid., I, 519; to J.B. Schweitzer, Jan. 24, 1865, ibid., II, 30; Engels, *Dialectics of Nature,* pp. 27–29; Plekhanov, *Fundamental Problems of Marxism,* pp. 35–36; *Anti-Dühring,* pp. 146–149. It had been discovered that such elements as carbon or phosphorus could exist in more than one form; these were called "allotropic."

Actually Dühring was not wrong in his specific denial of a "negation of the negation" being present, as Marx claimed, in the movement from feudalism to capitalism to communism. Marx, as we saw, believed that capitalism grew by acquiring the private property of small independent producers, especially in cottage industry—a "negation" of this property—and that capitalist private property would in turn be "negated" by communism. There were, however, few such small owners. The cottage industry workers, in fact, as we noted, owned nothing. Capitalism grew not by taking their property but by long centuries of internal growth within commercial-feudal society—aided by colonial exploitation—until by the eighteenth century it was well established. As it did not in fact grow by "negating" small individual private property, the destruction of capitalist private property in communist society would not be a "negation of the negation."

⁹Engels, *Feuerbach* pp. 66–67. On modern physics and astrophysics, see Gerald Feinberg, *What is the World Made of? Atoms, Leptons, Quarks and other Tantalizing Particles,* New York, 1978; Nigel Calder, *The Key to the Universe,* Penguin Books, 1978; *Lenin and Modern Natural Science,* ed., M.E. Omelyanovsky, Moscow, 1978; Steven Weinberg, *The First Three Minutes: A Modern View of the Origin of the Universe,* New York, 1977. Einstein quoted in *ABC of Dialectical and Historical Materialism* (Moscow, 1976), p. 94.

¹⁰Stephen Jay Gould, *The Panda's Thumb: More Reflections in Natural History* (New York, 1982), pp. 179–185. Gould's theory of "punctuated equilibrium" is derived from Engels. J.D. Bernal, *The Natural Sciences in our Time, Science in History,* III (Cambridge, Mass., 1965), 902.

[11]On these and related biological matters, see Mahlon B. Hoagland, *The Roots of Life*, New York, 1977 and S.E. Luria, *Life, The Unfinished Experiment*, New York, 1973.

[12]Hoagland, *The Roots of Life*, pp. 90, 80–81, 87–88; Luria, *Life, The Unfinished Experiment*, pp. 21, 120. See also George Gaylord Simpson, *The Meaning of Evolution*, New York, 1951, which is still one of the best general studies of evolution. For some of the problems being debated, see also Stephen Jay Gould, *The Panda's Thumb*.

[13]On modern discoveries on the brain and nervous system, see, for instance, William H. Calvin, *Inside the Brain*, New York, 1980; Richard M. Restak, *The Brain: The Last Frontier*, New York, 1979; Carl Sagan, *The Dragons of Eden: Speculations on the Evolution of Intelligence*, New York, 1977; Isaac Asimov, *The Human Brain, Its Capacities and Functions*, New York, 1963.

[14]See, for instance, M.C. Wittrock, ed., *The Human Brain*, (Englewood Cliffs, New Jersey, 1977), p. 9.

[15]Edward O. Wilson, *Sociobiology, The Abridged Edition* (Harvard University Press, 1980), p. 88.

[16]Sagan, *Dragons of Eden*, pp. 116–117.

[17]Lewis Thomas, *The Lives of a Cell: Notes of a Biology Watcher* (New York, 1979), p. 25; Restak, *The Brain*, p. 117. For a general survey of the evidence gathered on animal societies in recent decades, see Edward O. Wilson, *Sociobiology, The Abridged Edition*. Wilson's extensions of these findings to human society are simplistic and often reactionary in implication but the findings themselves on animal societies are well presented. For good brief summaries of the evidence on this and other relevant matters, see Alvin Silverstein, *The Biological Sciences*, San Francisco, 1974. See also *The Sociobiology Debate*, ed., Arthur L. Caplan, New York, 1978.

[18]C.R. Carpenter, noted in William Howells, *Back of History* (Garden City, N.Y. 1954), p. 40. On gorilla societies, see George B. Schaller, *The Year of the Gorilla*, Chicago, 1964. On chimpanzees, see Jane Van Lawick-Goodall, *In the Shadow of Man* (1971) and other books.

[19]Donald Johanson, Maitland Edey, *Lucy: The Beginnings of Humankind* (New York, 1981), pp. 274–275, 246–247, 100–103; Sagan, *Dragons of Eden*, pp. 93–95; *New York Times*, Dec. 16, 1982.

[20]*The German Ideology, Selected Works*, I, 32.

[21]*Selected Works*, I, 33. See also, Engels, *The Part Played by Labor in the Transition from Ape to Man*, ibid., pp. 73–74, on animal behavior.

[22]Restak, *The Brain*, pp. 222–229; Calvin, *Inside the Brain*, p. 71; *The New York Times*, Nov. 23, 1981.

[23]John Keats, *Ode on a Grecian Urn;* Marx, *Theses on Feuerbach, Selected Works*, I, 15.

Index

Address to the Communist League (Marx), 93
Aesthetic sense, 151–52
Africa: ancestors in, 178, 182–83, 190; capitalism and, 60; early societies in, 43, 47; feudalism in, 51, 136; oppression of women in, 136
Agriculture, 2, 61–62, 65, 110, 113. *See also* Farming societies; Feudalism
Aliens, in groups, 181, 184–85, 191
America: discovery of gold in, 60; farming societies in, 40, 42; feudalism in, 51, 136; ideas in, 138; proletarian revolution in, 95–96. *See also* names of specific countries
Ancient Society (Morgan), 37
Animal life, 5, 37–40, 124, 175–93
Anti-Dühring (Engels), 18, 53, 70, 82, 120, 198n
Apes, 178, 180, 182–83
Arabia, 57, 129, 134
Aristocrats: and class struggle, 7, 15, 23, 63, 118; coherence of, 147; of labor, 84, 115; and literary figures, 156–57; as ruling class, 2, 140; women, 130. *See also* Landowners
Aristotle, 7, 31, 140–41, 146, 153, 164
Armament production, 87
Army: in feudalism, 46, 53; as landowner, 44, 54; officer caste in, 45–46; standing, 101; State, 43
Aronowitz, Stanley, 30
Art: creation of, 139, 180, 183, 186; in early societies, 61, 153; nature of,

149–53; and social consciousness, 28, 33, 159–60
Asia: ideology in, 146; oppression of women in, 132, 136; social systems in, 36, 38–39; war in, 86–87. *See also* Feudalism, in Asia; names of specific countries
Athens. *See* Greece
Atoms, functioning of, 164, 166, 170–73, 176–79
Australia, 42, 73, 95
Aztecs, 40–41, 51

Bacon, Francis, 146, 155
Balzac, Honoré de, 156
Banks and bankers, 19, 65, 71, 104, 109, 142
Belgium, 2–3. *See also* Brussels
Bismarck, Otto von, 118
Bolsheviks, 29, 108–9
Bourgeoisie: and art and literature, 154–57; Chartist attack on, 10; in class struggle, 19–20, 22, 29, 68, 94, 108, 120; in communism, 111; and ideology, 140–41, 143–47, 187, 208n; French, 2; intellectuals of, 139–40, 146; and marriage, 124–25; monopoly, 30; new, 110–11; rule of, 57–58, 66–68, 77, 118, 120, 200n
Brain, functioning of, 170, 175–79, 184, 190, 192
Britain: bourgeoisie in, 2, 117, 140, 197n; economy in, 150; feudalism in, 51–52,

Britain *(Continued)*
54–56, 64; guilds in, 130; industrial capitalism in, 66–69, 86, 88, 115, 118; literature in, 155–57, 159; peasant ideology in, 147; proletariat in, 1, 4, 13, 16, 66–69, 117–19, 167, 197n–198n; revolutions in, 22, 63, 131, 155
British Reform Act (1832), 2
British Revolution, 63, 155
Brussels, 2–3, 12–13, 18, 59, 162, 194n–195n
Bukharin, Nikolai, 27
Byron, Lord, 23, 146–47, 157, 159–60

Caesar, Julius, 31, 41, 62–63, 148
Capital, 78, 80–83, 86, 91
Capital, Das (Marx), 60, 66, 70, 95, 114, 151, 162, 203n–204n
Capitalism: and Chartist movement, 15; in class struggle, 15, 22–23; on Continent, 11, 16, 22, 59–60; cyclical crises of, 9, 70, 77–82, 84, 86–88, 94, 110; decline of, 85–88, 94; early stages of, 59–60, 64–65, 154, 211n; industrial, 66–82; intellectuals in, 139; international aspect of, 83, 92; marriage in, 125–27; nature of, 57–59, 140, 142; social conditions under, 67–68, 85, 92; in social evolution, 24, 56. *See also* Monopolies and monopoly capitalism; Women, in capitalism; names of specific countries
Capitalist class, 2, 19, 30, 64, 91, 118
Cato, 49, 76, 131
Cell, biological, 169, 174, 179, 190–91. *See also* Nerve cells
Centralization, 90–91
Chartist movement: class struggle and, 18; poems in, 157; proletariat in, 3, 5, 31, 68–69, 138, 144, 198n; roots of Marxism in, 10–16, 197n; women in, 123
China: commerce in, 56–57, communism in, 114–15, 120; feudalism in, 46–47,

51, 53–54, 91; ideology in, 146; prehumans in, 183; revolutions in, 96, 131, 144; women in, 129, 131, 135–36
Church(es): exploitation by, 58; as landowner, 44–45, 51, 54, 101; and social revolution, 23, 167; and women, 130, 132
Cicero, 49, 146
Civil War in France (Marx), 117
Class antagonism, 18, 138–39, 156. *See also* Class struggle
Classless society, 23, 105
Class struggle: concepts of, 8, 18–20, 28, 91, 179; on Continent, 22–23, 59; and culture, 150; in development of communism, 94, 99, 120, 135; in 18th century, 7; in England, 4, 12, 14, 70; in history, 31, 42, 62–65, 91; in Russia, 108
Class Struggles in France, The (Marx), 26
Cobbett, William, 9, 14, 198n
Cold War, 86
Colonialism, 83–84, 204n–205n
Colonies, revolution in, 95–96
Commerce: in early societies, 39, 49, 61, 73; in feudal society, 44, 47, 50, 53, 56, 65
Commune(s): ancient Asian, 53–54; of Fourier, 9; Paris, 4–5, 43, 94, 100–4, 116–17, 131, 145, 196n; workers, 5
Communism: development of, 14, 90–100; as dictatorship, 99–100, 102–3; first phase of, 97–99, 104, 110, 136; material basis for, 105; and revolution, 117–21; Russian, 108–13; as social system, 97–99, 106–7; in Third World, 115. *See also* Women, in communism
Communist League, 3, 10, 13–14, 57, 157, 194n
Communist Manifesto, The (Marx and Engels), 3, 13, 18, 20, 32, 77, 81, 104, 116, 123, 138, 197n
Competition, 79–80, 84, 94

Condition of the Working Class in England, The (Engels), 3–4, 12, 66, 81, 92, 116, 123, 133
Condorcet, Antoine Nicolas, 6, 15, 17–18
Confucius, 31, 140, 146
Conglomerates, 83–84
Consciousness: class, 58, 138; determinants of, 21–22, 32, 60–61, 138, 149; and emotion, 192; evolution of, 183–84; false, 137; social, 28, 31, 33; source of, 178
Contradictions, in processes, 167–69, 173–74
Contributions to a Critique of Political Economy, A (Marx), 20–21
Corporations, 83–86
Corporations, 83–86
Cottage industry, 2, 11, 58, 76, 92, 144, 211n
Council of People's Commissaries, 109
Crisis in Historical Materialism, The (Aronowitz), 30
Cuba, 114, 135
Culture, foundations of, 150–51, 159–60
Czechoslovakia, 96, 113, 115

Darwin, Charles, 5, 35, 164, 167, 175, 184
Dialectic, Hegelian, 7
Dialectical materialism. *See* Materialism, dialectical
Dialectics of Nature (Engels), 154, 169
Dictatorship of the proletariat. *See* Proletariat, dictatorship of
Diderot, Denis, 163–66, 192, 210n
Diseases, of workers, 67–68
Draper, Hal, 29–30
Dühring, Eugen, 94, 120, 169, 211n
Dürer, Albrecht, 155

Economic determinism, 25, 36
Economic factors. *See* Production, means of

Economic processes. *See* Process(es), economic
Egypt: feudalism in, 43–48, 51–52, 54, 62, 64–65, 128; financial structure in, 73; ideology in, 145; revolution in, 95; women in, 128
Electricity, 166, 168, 171–72, 176
Electrons, 170–71, 173, 176–78
Elements, 171–72
Energy, transformation of, 169, 171, 177
Engels, Friedrich: and Chartists, 10–14, 16, 69, 197n–198n; and class struggle, 18–19, 63–65, 93–96, 110; collaboration with Marx, 195n–196n, 198n, 203n–204n; and development of communism, 96–97, 100, 102–8, 113–14, 116, 118–20, 195n, 206n; and ideas and ideology, 137–39, 142, 144–45, 148–50; and industrial capitalism, 66, 68–70, 74–75, 78–81, 83–85, 88, 92; as intellectual, 5, 7; and literature, 149–61; and Marx's concept of history, 25–26, 29, 31, 35; and nature, 143; and philosophy, 162–63, 165–69; and science, 169–73, 179, 183–84, 190; and State, 42–43, 200n; and status of women, 125–27, 132, 134–35, 188; and theories of family, 30–32, 123–29, 133; and theories of feudalism, 36, 50, 52–55, 57–60; and theories of society, 12, 26, 35–37, 40–42, 48; writings of, 3, 7. *See also* Materialism, dialectical
England. *See* Britain
Europe, 95–96, 132, 135. *See also* Feudalism, in Europe; names of specific countries
Evolution, 5–6, 151, 165, 169, 174–75, 178–81, 183–84, 190, 192. *See also* History, evolution of; Social evolution
Exchange, 71–73, 84
Exchange-value. *See* Value, theories of

Family: and art, 152; in capitalism, 67, 123; in history, 33–34, 37–38, 41,

Family *(Continued)*
128; in Marxist theory, 32–34, 123–27. *See also* Engels, Friedrich, theories of family
Farming societies: evolution of, 36–42, 47–48, 60–63, 189; exchange in, 73; ideas in, 148; marriage in, 128; women in, 127
Feminist movement, 123–24, 127, 135–36, 185. *See also* Women
Feudalism: in Asia, 42–48, 50–54, 62, 64–65, 83, 91, 146; and class struggle, 22–23, 43–44; end of, 5; in Europe, 1–2, 22, 43–44, 48–52, 56, 62, 65, 91, 113, 132, 146, 159; ideology in, 146, 148, 159; labor value in, 75–78, 84; and social evolution, 52–65, 91. *See also* Women, in feudalism; names of specific countries
Feuerbach (Engels), 162
Feuerbach, Ludwig, 16, 166, 211n
Fourier, Charles, 9
France: capitalism in, 31, 86, 115, 118; feudal regime in, 140; guilds in, 130; history of, 55; population in 1789, 1–2; Renaissance, 154; working class in, 4. *See also* Commune(s), Paris; Revolution(s), French
Franco-Prussian War, 4, 100
Frankfort School, 116, 201n
Franz von Sickingen (Lassalle), 157–58

General Workingmen's Association of London, 10
German Ideology, The (Marx and Engels), 184
German Social Democratic Party, 97, 118
Germany: capitalism in, 66, 86, 96, 115; fascist, 30, 142; feudalism in, 51, 55–57; invasion of U.S.S.R. in, 114; Renaissance, 154; revolution in, 2, 115, 131, 144; socialism in, 97, 116, 118, 194n; tribal society in, 41–42, 62, 148; women in, 135, 186; workers in, 4

God, 7, 140, 163–64
Godwin, William, 6–8, 15, 17–18, 23, 122–23
Gotha socialists' program, 97, 99–100, 103, 106, 111–12, 136, 206n
Gould, Stephen Jay, 170, 175
Great Depression, 86, 88, 149
Greece: culture and art in, 150, 152–53, 159; early society in, 41, 48–50, 54–55; ideology in, 138, 146; slavery in, 36, 43, 49, 52, 54–55, 57, 64–65, 73, 140; struggle against Turkey of, 8, 147; women in, 129
Group behavior, 182–85, 189, 191
Guarantees of Harmony and Liberty (Weitling), 13
Guild system, 59, 63, 130

Harney, George Julian, 11, 13–16, 145, 197n
Hegel, Georg Wilhelm Friedrich, 1, 7, 16, 23, 107, 146, 163, 167–69, 179
Hellas (Shelley), 8
Hellenism, 55, 57
History: conflict in, 91; evolution of, 6–7, 15, 17, 23, 31, 34–35, 55; socioeconomic foundation of, 20–26, 33; theories of, 17–18, 165. *See also* Marx, Karl, historical theories of
Hodgkins, Thomas, 9
Holbach, Paul, 163–66, 210n
Holy Family, The (Marx), 3
Homer, 40, 54, 153, 161
Hunter-gathering societies: art in, 159; family in, 33; ideas in, 148; nature of, 39, 182–83; stages of, 37, 42, 60–61, 63, 189; women in, 127–28

Idealism, 7, 163, 166–69, 175, 178, 199n
Ideas. *See* Ideology
Ideology, 24, 27–28, 32, 36, 61–62, 137–43, 145–46, 150–52, 159–60

Imperialism: of capitalism, 83, 86–88, 140, 142; English, 17; German, 112–13

Imperialism (Lenin), 83, 96

India: colonial, 204n–205n; feudalism in, 44–45, 47, 51, 53; ideology in, 146; in nineteenth century, 36; revolution in, 95; trade in, 73; women in, 129

Industrial Revolution, 1, 8–10, 16, 21, 23, 60, 64, 175

Indus Valley, 44–45, 52, 54

Inferno (Dante), 154, 159

Inflation, 85–87

Intellectuals: in communism, 98, 111; and ideology, 137, 139; liberal, 139; and social revolution, 23

International Workingmen's Association, 4–5, 13, 101, 117, 138, 162

Iran. *See* Persia

Italy: capitalism in, 86, 115; fascist, 142; feudalism in, 54–55; Renaissance, 154; unification of, 2; workers in, 4. *See also* Rome

Japan: capitalism in, 65, 86, 115; commerce in, 47, 56–57; feudalism in, 54; invasion of China by, 114

Kant, Immanuel, 5, 163, 165, 168

Karl Marx's Theory of Revolution (Draper), 29

Kautsky, Karl, 95–96, 136, 158

Kautsky, Minna, 158

Korea, 114–15

Krushchev, Nikita, 111

Labor: division of, 38, 40; in early societies, 38, 40–42; instruments of, 58; manufacturing, 59; Marx's theories of, 72, 74–77; as source of wealth, 8, 74–75, 77, 80

Lafargue, Paul, 155

Landowners, 2, 41, 43–45. *See also* Feudalism; Property

Language: animal, 178, 180, 182; beginning of, 37, 183–84; in brain, 177

Laon and Cyntha (Shelley), 123

Laos, 87, 114

Lassalle, Ferdinand, 157–58, 161

Lenin, V.I.: and capitalism, 83; and Marxist theory, 28–29, 167, 199n; in Russian revolution, 108–10

Lessner, Friedrich, 13

Literature, 28, 149–61

London, 10, 57, 76, 92, 156

Lucretius, 146, 159–60, 163–64, 166, 174, 192, 210n

Lysistrata, 152–53, 188

Machine(s): atom as, 172; in capitalism, 9, 60, 76, 78, 80, 82, 88. *See also* Production, means of

Madison, James, 7, 14, 146

Male chauvinism, 133, 135, 183, 208n

Manchester, 2, 10, 12, 66, 70, 77, 123

Manchester Massacre, 123

Manufacturing: in capitalism, 69; in Europe, 2, 76; under feudalism, 53, 56, 65, 73; under slavery, 49

Marcuse, Herbert, 34, 116

Marriage, 69, 107–8, 122, 124–26, 128, 132–34

Marx, Eleanor, 123, 155–57

Marx, Jenny, 3, 194n

Marx, Karl: in Brussels, 3–4, 18, 162, 194n; and capitalism, 70–85, 88, 90–92, 211n; and Chartists, 13, 197n; and class struggle, 63–65; collaboration with Engels, 195n–196n; and communism, 97–100, 103–7, 111–12, 114–17, 120, 136, 206n, 211n; critics of, 28–32; description of, 13; historical theories of, 12, 18, 20–31, 48, 50, 53, 60, 93, 196n; and ideas and ideology, 32, 137–39, 142, 144–45, 148–50; as intellectual, 5, 7; and the International, 4–5, 35,

Marx, Karl *(Continued)*
101, 162; and literature, 149–61; materialist theory of, 12, 20–26, 36, 162–70; and nature, 190; and philosophy, 162, 175, 177, 183–84, 191, 193; and proletariat, 19, 109–10, 134; and revolution of 1848, 19; as revolutionist, 35, 93–95, 118–19; theories of family, 32–34, 123; theories of feudalism, 57–58, 60, 62–63; and weavers' revolt, 11; and women's oppression, 124, 135; writings of, 3

Marxism: beginnings of, 1–5, 14, 16, 167; and class ideology, 148–49; philosophy of, 170, 181, 193, 199n–200n; in Soviet Union, 199n; writers and artists of, 160

Masque of Anarchy, The (Shelley), 8–9, 157

Materialism: dialectical, 162–70, 175, 190, 193, 196n, 199n, 210n; French, 163–67; Greek, 163, 210n; scientific 155, 170–79, 192–93; of working class, 145

Materialism and Empirio-Criticism (Lenin), 167

Matriarchy, 124, 127

Matter, nature of, 164–67, 170–74, 190–91

Mayans, 40, 47, 51

Mechanization, 82, 88

Mediterranean area, 43–44, 48–50, 52, 54–56, 64

Megasthenes, 45–46

Mehring, Franz, 137

Mensheviks, 108

Merchants, in feudal system, 44–45, 47, 52, 62, 150

Mesopotamia, 40, 43, 45, 54, 65

Mind, nature of, 7, 164–68, 175, 178, 184. *See also* Brain; Consciousness

Mines and mining, 44–45, 52, 67

Molecules, 169, 172–74, 176–79, 190–91

Monetary system, 85–86

Money, 71, 73–74, 79, 126

Monogamy. *See* Marriage

Monopolies and monopoly capitalism, 30, 81, 83–90, 107, 141–42

Morgan, Lewis Henry, 37, 39, 128, 201n

Motion, nature of, 164, 166, 179

Murasaki, Lady, 129, 131, 154

Mutation. *See* Evolution

Mythology, Greek, 153

Napoleon Bonaparte, 31

Napoleonic wars, 8–9

National Assembly, French, 19–20

Nationalization, 15–16, 109

Natural selection, 164, 169, 175

Nature: materialism of, 164–65; relation to society, 23, 162, 165, 179, 188, 190–93, 199n; science and, 24, 169–79

"Negation of the negation," 7, 169

Nerve cells, 174, 176–77, 190

Neutrons, 170–71

Nietzsche, Friedrich, 97

Nucleic acids, 172, 174, 176, 181, 190, 192

O'Brien, Bronterre, 14–16, 144–45, 197n

Ollman, Bertell, 114–15, 206n

Origin of the Family, Private Property and the State (Engels), 32–33, 37, 124

Owen, Robert, 9, 14–16, 69, 158, 198n

Owenite movement, 123

Paris, 2, 4–5, 19, 102. *See also* Commune(s), Paris

Particle matter, 170–72, 174, 177, 179

Patriotism, 184–85

Peasants. *See* Feudalism; Revolution(s), peasant

Peasant Revolt, English, 144

Persia, 46–47, 52

Philosophical Notebooks (Lenin), 167

Photons, 171–74, 177–79

Physics. *See* Science(s)

Pittman, Margrit, 135, 186

Planned economy, 80, 110, 113

Plato, 140, 146, 153, 163, 166

Plekhanov, G.V., 27, 169
Poetry. *See* Literature
Poland, 113–14, 187
Pope, Alexander, 23, 155
Poverty of Philosophy, The (Marx), 3
Prehistoric societies, 182–84, 190
Prices, Marx's theories of, 71, 73, 75, 79
Primitive peoples. *See* Hunter-gatherer societies; Tribal society
Process(es): economic, 20, 22–23, 27, 29, 48, 70–71; historical, 21, 24–25, 32, 62, 91, 93; intellectual, 23, 137, 144, 166, 168, 180; Marxism as, 149; in nature, 143, 167, 174–76, 192–93; social, 29, 32, 48, 142, 144–45, 191, 193
Production, means of: in capitalism, 31, 60, 69, 77–81, 84, 88, 90–92, 94, 106; in class struggle, 20; in communism, 105, 110, 113; in feudalism, 31, 58; in historical evolution, 20, 60–62, 64, 125, 189; and reproduction, 30–32; in social revolution, 21–22, 24, 29–31, 35–36
Productive forces. *See* Production, means of
Profit, in capitalism, 22, 69, 74–84, 88, 90
Proletariat: in capitalism, 9, 14–16, 64–68, 74–75, 84, 92; deficiencies of, 115–16; in development of communism, 91, 93–96, 99–100; dictatorship of, 90–100, 103–4, 107, 109–10, 121; ideology of, 144–45, 147, 149; literature of, 157–58; Marx as champion of, 5, 11, 13–14; Marx's theories of, 72; in Paris, 19; rise of, 1–2; in Third World, 114–15. *See also* Britain, proletariat in; Chartist movement, proletariat in; Class Struggle; International Workingmen's Association
Prometheus Unbound (Shelley), 152–53, 157, 161
Property: abolition of, 107; distribution of, 7; institutional, 41; preservation of, 140; private, 38, 41, 53, 58, 62, 69, 81, 90, 128; State, 128; women as, 122, 129. *See also* Feudalism
Property relationships, 22–23
Property rights, of women, 128–30
Prostitution, 46, 68, 123–27, 129–30, 132, 134
Proteins, 172, 174, 176–77, 190, 192
Protons, 170–71, 173
Proudhon, Pierre Joseph, 102–4, 169, 194n

Queen Mab (Shelley), 69

Radiation, 171, 173, 179
Reason and reasoning, 166, 169, 178–79
Recession, 86–88
Reich, Wilhelm, 34, 116
Religion, 69, 148, 164, 167, 192, 210n
Renaissance, 131, 154–55
Reproduction, 30–32
Revolution(s): bourgeois, 141; in development of communism, 90–96, 104, 113–15, 117–20, 136, 145; in Europe, 1848, 2–3, 9, 19, 21–22, 29, 32, 119, 142, 147; French, 1–2, 22–23, 63–64, 102, 119, 210n; peasant, 31, 43, 53, 64, 91, 131, 140, 144; personal, 152; in Russia, 29, 108–11, 119–20, 145; social, 21–23, 137, 157–58, 161; workers, 11, 16, 70, 94. *See also* Class struggle
Rheinische Zeitung, 3
Ricardo, David, 23, 70
Rituals, animal, 177, 180
Rome: capitalism in, 99; classes in, 63; decline of, 49–51; ideology in, 146; literature in, 159; slavery in, 36, 43, 49–50, 52, 55–57, 64–65, 73, 91; women in, 129–31
Ruling classes, 15, 31, 42–44, 47, 57, 120, 132, 134, 138–47, 188
Rumania, 113–14
Russia: communes in, 53; development of socialism in, 96, 108–12, 115, 206n; feminist movement in, 135; feudalism

Russia *(Continued)*
   in, 56, 65. *See also* Revolution(s), in
   Russia
Russian Social Democratic Party, 108

St. Simon, Henri, 9, 158
Sartre, Jean-Paul, 116
Science(s), 28, 139, 165, 167, 169–79
Sexual differences, 185–88
Sexual relations, 125–27, 134–35, 152,
   188. *See also* Marriage; Prostitution
Sexual repression, 116
Shakespeare, William, 131, 150, 155–56,
   159
Shang, 46, 52
Shelley, Percy B., 8–9, 23, 69, 122–23,
   146–47, 155–57, 159–60
Slavery: ideology and, 146; labor value in,
   75–76; in past societies, 36, 38,
   41–50, 52, 56–57, 63, 134; women
   in, 129–30. *See also* names of specific
   countries
Smith, Adam, 23, 137
Social and Sexual Revolution (Ollman) 114,
   206n
Social behavior. *See* Society
Social evolution: concept of, 6–7, 9, 24,
   138, 179–80, 191, 193; in early societies, 42, 48, 182–83, 189; Marx's
   theories of, 20–26, 48
Socialism: and Chartists, 15–16; development of, 57, 95–96, 110–11, 113–14,
   116–20; and writers, 157–58; and
   women, 135–36. *See also* Communism
Society, 179–93
Song to the Men of England (Shelley), 147,
   157
Soviets, 108–9
Space, nature of, 167, 170
Spartacus, 43, 64, 131
Stalin, Josef, 27–28, 30, 112, 199n
State: beginning of, 39, 42; disappearance
   of, 105–6; as instrument of repression, 43, 45, 68, 106; as landowner,
   41, 44, 46, 51, 53; in Russia, 109;

and social classes, 20, 29–30, 34, 42,
   144; workers, 103
Strikes, 16, 59, 68, 108
Sumer: commerce in, 73; feudalism in,
   43–45, 54, 62, 64, 128; ideology in,
   145–46; literature in, 153, 159;
   women in, 128
Superstructure of society, 21–23, 26–30,
   57, 142, 199n
Supply and demand, 71
Surplus value, 70, 75–76, 79–81, 84. *See
   also* Value, theories of
Sweezy, Paul M., 85, 114, 206n

Tacitus, 41–42, 50, 148
Tale of Genji, The (Murasaki), 129, 154
Tax(es), 41, 43–47, 51–52, 99
Third World, 114–15
Time, nature of, 167, 170
Tolstoy, Leo, 159
Tools, 58, 60–61, 189
Trade unionism. *See* Unions
Trading. *See* Commerce
Tribal society, 38, 62. *See also* Hunter-
   gathering society
Tristan, Flora, 123
Turkey, 8, 46, 52, 147

Unemployment, 82, 86–88, 110
Unions: British, 4, 9, 16, 68–69; in capitalism, 76; in communism, 14; in
   Germany, 135; in Marxist theory, 92,
   103; in Paris, 102; in Russia, 108–9;
   in United States, 185; women in,
   123–24, 130, 135
United States: capitalism in, 83, 85,
   87–88, 115, 118, 142; invasion of
   Vietnam, 114; Marx's views of,
   116–17; political structure of, 119;
   southern slavery in, 134; women in,
   136
Use value, 72–73
Utopians, 15

Value, Price, and Profit (Marx), 70
Value, theories of, 70–77, 79, 84
Vietnam, 86, 114–15, 120, 132, 136
Vindication of the Rights of Women (Wollstonecraft), 122
Voltaire, François-Marie, 140, 164
Voting rights, 2, 10–11, 15, 118, 123

Wages, Marx's theories of, 71, 74, 99, 103, 111
War: in capitalism, 85–89, 93–94, 142; in early farming societies, 40–41; in feudalism, 44; ideology in, 143; nuclear, 120–21; Roman, 49–50; women's opposition to, 188
Weerth, George, 157
Weitling, Wilhelm, 13–14

Wollstonecraft, Mary, 23, 122–23, 127
Women: and art, 159; in capitalism, 67, 130, 132–33, 136; in communism, 109–10, 114, 135-36, 186–88; cultural contributions of, 131; in farming society, 40, 127–28; in feudalism, 45, 47, 128–32, 134–36; oppression of, 122, 124–36, 186–87; in revolutions in France, 102, 131; in slave societies, 129–30; in tribal society, 38, 127; working class, 123–24, 127, 130. *See also* Family; Marriage; Prostitution; Sexual differences
Working class. *See* Proletariat
World War I, 112
World War II, 83, 113
Writers and artists, Marxist, 160. *See also* Literature
Yugoslavia, 113–14

About the Author

Kenneth Neill Cameron was born in England but early moved to Canada where he attended McGill University in Montreal. In 1931 he went to Oxford as a Rhodes Scholar. In the summer of 1934 he went on a trip to the U.S.S.R. From 1934–35 he was Executive Secretary of the Canadian League Against War and Fascism in Toronto. In 1939 he received his Ph.D. from the University of Wisconsin. From 1939 to 1952 he taught English at Indiana University. His first book, *The Young Shelley: Genesis of a Radical* (New York, 1950, London, 1951) was awarded the Macmillan-Modern Language Association of America Prize for the best work of scholarship in 1950. In 1952 he came to New York to work at the Carl H. Pforzheimer Library and published four volumes of the library's Shelley collection manuscripts—*Shelley and his Circle,* 1961 and 1970 (Harvard and Oxford). In 1961 he made a second trip to the U.S.S.R., this time with his wife and daughter, and met with Soviet scholars in his field. In 1973—paperback, 1977—he published a Marxist history of the world—*Humanity and Society: A World History;* and in 1974, *Shelley: The Golden Years* (Harvard), a study of Shelley's later works in prose and poetry. In 1976 he published *Marx and Engels Today: A Modern Dialogue on Philosophy and History.* In 1977 he brought out a volume of poetry, *Poems for Lovers and Rebels* (privately printed). In 1963 he became Professor of English at New York University and is now Professor Emeritus. In 1967 he was awarded a Guggenheim Fellowship. In 1971 he received an honorary D.Litt. from McGill University. In 1978 a "festschrift" volume of essays honoring his work—*The Evidence of the Imagination: Studies of Interactions Between Life and Art in English Romantic Literature*—was published by his fellow scholars and former students. In 1982 he was presented the Distinguished Scholar Award of the Keats-Shelley Association of America at the convention of the Modern Language Association of America. He lives in New York with his wife, Mary Owen Cameron, a sociologist and author of *The Booster and the Snitch: Department Store Shoplifting.* They have a summer house at Gay Head, Marthas Vineyard.

Related Books from Bergin & Garvey

Marx Beyond Marx
Lessons on the *Grundrisse*
Antonio Negri

The Politics of Education
Culture, Power, and Liberation
Paulo Freire
Introduction by Henry Giroux

Development and Decline
The Evolution of Sociopolitical
  Organizations
*Henri J.M. Claessen, M. Estellie Smith,
  Pieter van de Velde*

The Crisis in Historical Materialism
Class, Politics, & Culture in Marxist
  Theory
Stanley Aronowitz

Education Under Siege
The Conservative, Liberal, & Radical
  Debate over Schooling
Stanley Aronowitz and Henry Giroux

The Yugoslav Search for Man
Marxist Humanism in Contemporary
  Yugoslavia
Oskar Gruenwald

**Community & Organization in the
  New Left 1962–68**
The Great Refusal
Wini Breines

The Struggle for Rural Mexico
Gustavo Esteva

Longshoremen
Community and Informal Resistance
  on the Brooklyn Waterfront
William DiFazio
Introduction by Stanley Aronowitz

Steelworkers Rank-and-File
The Political Economy of the Union
  Reform Movement
Philip W. Nyden

**Transnationals and the Third
  World**
The Struggle for Culture
Armand Mattelart

Language as Work and Trade
A Semiotic Homology for Linguistics
  and Economics
Ferruccio Rossi-Landi

Passion & Rebellion
The Expressionist Heritage
Stephen E. Bronner and Douglas Kellner

**The Trials & Tribulations of Little
  Red Riding Hood**
Versions of the Tale in Sociocultural
  Context
Jack Zipes

Bergin & Garvey Publishers, Inc.
670 Amherst Road
South Hadley, Massachusetts 01075

DATE DUE

APR 1 2 2012	
FEB 21 2015	